Ber̩ \ ̩nald's writings have appeared in *The Times* and various
UK̩ ̩el magazines. He is also the author of guidebooks for
Fo̩ **03** ̩ Handbooks and co-wrote *The Book of Cities*
(P̩a̩ ̩ Now a born-again Germanophile he still has no facial
ha̩ ̩ while possessed with incurable wanderlust and
dr̩e̩ ̩g ̩o̩f owning a Schloss in Saxony, he lives with his wife
an̩ ̩ ̩ildren in west London where, in his spare time, he
als̩ ̩ ̩ ̩for BBC Worldwide.

Springtime for Germany

BEN DONALD

Little, Brown

LITTLE, BROWN

First published in Great Britain in 2007 by Little, Brown

Copyright © 2007 Ben Donald

Lyric credits appear on page 307.

A CIP catalogue record for this book
is available from the British Library.

ISBN 978-0-316-73247-5

Typeset in Sabon by M Rules
Printed and bound in Great Britain by
Clays Ltd, St Ives plc

Little, Brown
An imprint of
Little, Brown Book Group
Brettenham House
Lancaster Place
London WC2E 7EN

A Member of the Hachette Livre Group of Companies

www.littlebrown.co.uk

For Meringue, Boobie and little Gigi

Contents

Acknowledgements

The ambition of turning Germany into a travel destination was always going to be difficult, and one that could not be realised alone. I am indebted to many people who, despite their better judgement, urged me to persist in the dream.

To my agent, Patrick Walsh, for initially picking up the project and also convincing me that no one would ever buy a straight travel narrative on Germany; to Tim Whiting for the original commission and subsequently to Stephen Guise for guiding me through the editorial process and, notably, stopping the book turning into a dense Germanic doorstop; to two German ambassadors, Thomas Matussek and Wolfgang Ischinger, for their hospitality and support for the book and also to their head of protocol, Sybille Fürchtenicht (meaning 'fear not'!); to Linda Borchert and Udo Grebe at the German National Tourist office for their constant availability and help in providing useful contacts for my visits to Germany; to the tourist offices, particularly of Lübeck, Munich and Heidelberg; to Henning Wehn for making me laugh – twice; to Siegfried Helm; to Ray Furlong for his insights as BBC correspondent in Berlin; Elisabeth Sandmann for her contacts and advice on background reading; to Matthias Mueller for his knowledge and analysis of modern German pop music and its malaise; to Oliver Dienhoff for his hospitality during the World Cup; to Andrea Wulf for her advice, her biography of Beate Uhse and, in particular, for showing me the nightlights of Hamburg; to Claudia Amhor-Croft at the Goethe-Institut; to Sebastian Payne and Marcel Orford-Williams at the Wine Society for that midday glass of Riesling and overview of German wine in the rolling concrete of Stevenage; to Adrian Bridge at the *Daily Telegraph*. On top of this I am indebted to the many Germans, strangers who, along the way, unwittingly contributed to my newfound love and understanding of their country.

And now to friends and family: to Nina Heisel for her endless supply of insights and updates on modern German life, her ironic take on her homeland and for her company in the Baltic and in Heidelberg (the exhaustive wedding mentioned in chapter four was hers); to Claudia Zell for her recommendations on Germany comedy and for introducing me to the Towel Club; to Marco and Svetlana for their company through the Oktoberfest and After-Wiesn parties; to Hans von Trotha for his insight into his beloved Berlin and for his expert history of German philosophy over a memorable dinner in a Prenzlauer Berg restaurant; to Charlie 'Jürgen' Bailey and his wife Sarah for their company in Baden-Baden and for braving the mixed naked spas with me; to Robin for his encouragement and editorial critiques; to Gordon for his one-liners and editing of early drafts; to all my German teachers at school and the wonderful writers they taught; to Mum and Dad for always having exposed me to travel, encouraged me and, looking back on it, particularly for that year in Sandhausen where it probably all began, and to my brother Ed for helping piece together memories from that time; to my wonderful wife Merida who not only became a German convert – and now wants to send our children to a German school – but accompanied me to the Baltic and the Christmas markets and then, back at home, fed and watered me through many lonely nights while I sat Goethe-like in my garret wrestling with words. But most of all my thanks must go to one man who probably won't thank me for naming him, and thus shall go by the name of Fritz, without whose total grasp of the editorial process, company throughout the project, editing and design talent and, not least, understanding of Germans, what I was trying to say about them, and how instead it needed to be said I would have been lost. In fact I feel this book is as much his as mine, though such is his modesty or fine judgement – or like a Frenchman – he will probably deny any complicity.

Praia da Luz by way of Kensal Green

1

Weltschmerz

nm, *world-weariness*

(Welt (nf) *world; Schmerz* (nm) *pain)*

'What about you, Ben? Been anywhere cool lately? Where *did* you get that tan?'

Imagine the scene. A dinner party. The Sancerre's been flowing. We've had the Parma ham and balsamic vinegar salad with focaccia on the side, followed by the Atkins-friendly grilled tuna steak. Then, over tiramisu and coffee, the conversation turns to travel. The atmosphere becomes politely competitive as everyone secretly compares the kudos of their respective destinations. It's like a game of Condé Nast travel poker. The stakes are fairly tame as the host opens with a classic, like Paris – we'll always have Paris; or the villa in Tuscany or Provence. Not exactly new or original, but even after all these years probably enough to command a place at the table. Then, having waxed lavender and distilled their experience into a few extra-virgin platitudes, up pops a long weekend in Prague. Ah, the anointed Paris of Middle Europe, once hidden from tourism and all-importantly 'undiscovered'. But, now so 'last season', it might as well be Prada, its social currency diluted by the beer of so many stag weekends. Try Riga or Montenegro, darling! At this point, depending on the company you keep, someone might throw in their recent trip to China. Respect, awe and a few ruffled feathers all round. A Ming royal flush. But for how long? Will the world and his wife soon be Shanghai-ed?

How are you feeling now? Confident that where you've been is cool and hip enough to keep you in the Condé Nast club? Or slightly defensive that you thought you had a good time in some less fashionable clime? Are you looking at a pair of twos?. . .

I am at one such dinner party. I've sat through one person's trek across Patagonia and another's encounters with gorillas and obscure tribesmen somewhere in Africa. Then, over coffee, the spotlight falls on me.

'Germany,' I say perkily.

My fellow guests look repelled by the idea and exchange curled lips and raised eyebrows of amazement.

'Oh, of course, the World Cup. What games did you see?'

'No. Not for the football,' I shake my head. 'I just went to Germany.'

'On holiday? To Germany? Are you mad?'

'Actually I've been there quite a few times recently.'

Then, one by one, it starts:

'What, to a holiday camp?'

'. . . lots of leather and thigh-slapping, I bet.'

'Fighting them on the beaches, over a few sun-loungers?'

'. . . or going native and marching around in the buff saying "*Ich habe einen grossen Pimmel*"!'

'. . . hence the attempt at growing a moustache, eh?'

Then a pause. Am I bluffing? Perhaps they think I should fold. But I have an ace up my sleeve.

'Well, that's what I thought,' I interrupt, 'until I met Manny, my travel therapist.'

I had met Manny – where else? – at the airport. The lounge teemed like a busy high street. Brands shouted out from brightly lit duty-free stores while lists of destinations all over the globe glowed blandly on monochrome departure monitors. Advertising hoardings touted the local credentials of multinational corporations. While, slightly muffled by the low ceiling and synthetic carpet, a constant babel of badly pronounced translations of flight announcements was whispered through loudspeakers.

I used to enjoy travel so much, but where was the magic in this? And what were all these other people doing here? With their guidebooks and annoying, clicking rucksacks. Tourists! Chavellers! They could keep Thailand and Australia. For I was a trailblazer, a true traveller! But if that was so, why wasn't I happy to speak to any stranger? Why had I shut myself off and sat as far away from everyone as possible. Did I have some kind of traveller's block? Never mind. Surely once I arrived at my destination I would talk to locals and strangers, and seek new experiences. But not here among these lemmings . . .

Then, all of sudden, this American came and invaded my space.

'Mind if I sit here?'

He already was.

'Manny,' he beamed, thrusting his hand forward. He was gangly, late-forty-something, with salt-and-pepper beard, chiselled features and short, spiky, silver hair. He was dressed blandly in Business Class Casual but had the mysterious Ivy League air of one of those quiet Americans who pop up in odd places.

'So, where are you off to?' he said in a warm, 'howdy' way, after I had coldly ignored his outstretched hand but conceded to mumble my name at him.

I told him.

'First time?'

It wasn't. I don't remember where, but it was somewhere suitably unique and competitive; a place I felt I owned. I had, after all, had the wit to visit it before the distasteful hordes 'discovered' it.

'Nice. Never been myself,' he exclaimed. And I felt duly flattered.

It was clear I wasn't going to be able to escape conversation.

'I hope you won't mind me saying this, but for a traveller about to embark on a journey you don't exactly look happy.'

'I'm sorry . . .?' I tried to sound offended. Just because I didn't have a permanent Burger King smile, that didn't make me unhappy. But Manny was strangely disarming and I didn't quite manage to pull if off. Besides, he was right.

'And for a traveller you're not exactly sociable . . .'

'Whereas you clearly like accosting strangers,' I ventured with a smile.

'You could say that,' he grinned. 'As a matter of fact I'm doing some research. I've been watching you and your whole attitude. You are disappointed with this whole experience,' he said, wafting his hand at the crowds, the shops, the advertising hoardings, 'but you don't want to be. And this is depressing you all the more.'

He was reading my mind. Well, at least my face.

'Maybe I can help you. I am a travel therapist.'

A what? I'd heard of life coaches and reading tea leaves. Did we now need some Trinny and Susannah to tell us how and where to go on holiday? 'Where you go can change your life?'

'You may laugh. But you have all the classic symptoms.'

'Symptoms?'

'Of Heimway Syndrome.'

'Never heard of it.'

'You won't have done. Even though it's an increasingly prevalent malaise that's affecting all of Western society and causing widespread depression and cultural disconnection.'

A Californian, Manny had the laid-back drawl and slightly baffling turn of phrase to match.

'I identified it and named it a number of years ago, after myself, Manny Heimway.'

Ah, a new berth on the American psychobabble bandwagon! Shrinks were like naturalists constantly naming new species after themselves. I was leaving.

Mercifully I was saved by the tannoy and got up to leave Manny to his private syndrome.

'Take this just in case.' With a priestly smile he gave me his card. 'I'll be happy to cure you. Meanwhile, you know what they say?'

I didn't. But 'Have a nice day?' was as good a guess as any.

'The journey is the destination.'

And with those words in my ear I walked to my gate, a combination of dazed, rumbled and affronted.

Home and garden makeovers, fair enough. But travel makeovers! Come off it, one half of me said. What on earth could this Manny know about travel? Most Americans don't even have a passport. But another voice told me to take note. Why be so negative? If I really considered myself a traveller I should have an open mind, be curious. After all Manny had seen through my gloomy demeanour. It troubled me that I hadn't been able to resolve or articulate why I felt this way. I looked around at the teeming lounge and was paralysed by more misanthropic inertia. I felt quite ill. Was this Heimway Syndrome? No matter how much I disliked the notion, maybe I did need help. Manny seemed harmless enough, and seemed to have my best interests at heart.

The offices of Infinity were in a Harley Street basement: a soothing synaesthesia of low-lit, yellow-tinted glass, trickling fountains and, unusually, the musky smell of cinnamon. The descending piano scale of Beethoven's 'Emperor' Concerto rose above the water feature as I sank into a plush red and black chair with the pretzel and coffee that Renate, the receptionist, had given me, served in finest, contemporary Villeroy & Boch porcelain. If I hadn't known otherwise I would have asked for a massage. But no. Leaflets on the table told me this was the jumping-off point for 'Insperience – the temporary abandonment of "experience" and the need of the outside world'. 'Leave your troubles outside!' exhorted a huge sign on the wall behind reception.

And more travel aphorisms in various languages, together with various oil paintings, greeted me on the walls of Manny's inner sanctum.

'Ben! Hi! Come on in. I had a feeling we'd meet again.'

There was Manny, seemingly unchanged in billowing slacks, black polo neck and sneakers.

'Now sit yourself down and tell me what's on your mind.'

I pinched myself and sank back into the patient's sofa. On the ceiling the words 'Travel Makes you Free', credited to 'Anon', greeted me.

'The thing is, I regard myself as pretty well travelled,' I embarked. 'I'm by no means an adventurer or an explorer. But I've been lucky enough to see quite a bit of the world. And "travel", the thought of seeing far-off places, especially those not undiscovered but little visited, and of meeting new people, has always been one of my driving passions. There are still plenty of places I have not been, and even more people I have not met . . .'

'You're a lucky man,' said Manny. 'But let me guess: all this cannot take away from the growing sense of pointlessness you are having of it all, driven by an increasing elitist distaste for the whole mass-tourism circus of which you are not wanting to admit you are part?'

I thought I was supposed to be doing the talking! But Manny was spot on, if still a little wayward with his present participles. I nodded uncomfortably.

'Ever more often it is seeming to you that the world's cultural sites have become mere Little Chefs on the global motorway, their essence distilled into ersatz craftware and overrun by kitsch.' I had visions of those faux-Peruvian bands who are playing 'Hey Jude' on panpipes at the restaurant beneath Machu Picchu! He was spot on. 'You are despairing at not being able to look on mighty works like the Pyramids without the intrusion of thousands of multicoloured be-backpacked tourists, before whom you selfishly presume these wonders are but pearls before tourist swine! And sometimes you are becoming jealous that people can now go in their masses to places you always regarded as your own, the key to your very soul and which you alone thought you had some special bond with!'

Manny was in full swing now, like a breathless Kelsey Grammer complete with enraged sense of injustice but strangely perturbed grammar.

'I expect you have wished you were Hiram Bingham or Giovanni Belzoni discovering Machu Picchu or Abu Simbel for the first time? I bet you have even pined for the return of Communism so that places you regard as private conquests might still lie beyond the reach of all but the most dedicated adventurer, and certainly beyond the reach of stag weekends and the orange-bespattered cheer of no-frills, no-class airlines.'

It was a soliloquy. Manny had clearly rehearsed the diagnosis of 'his' syndrome.

'In this age of mass displacement and shopping lists of city-breaks you have sometimes asked yourself "What is the word 'travel' meaning any more?" You cannot bear to pick up the weekend travel supplements, with their weekly superimposition of the latest "Unforgettable Places to See Before You Die" for fear of what dreams of yours might be in them, written by self-appointed "travel experts", that will now be invaded by hordes of the unwashed people. Now you couldn't possibly go there. It would be like two women at a wedding in the same outfit!'

Had Manny been to too many dinner parties, too? Now he paused to catch his breath.

'Do you rage at the rape of a world you think was only made for you to bestride?'

I felt exposed, humbled, if not a little dirty.

'I wouldn't go that far. But sometimes I feel so . . . disenchanted I'd almost rather stay at home. It's like I'm sated and jaded, or something.'

'Ah, enchantment! We'll come on to that. But what about everyone else?' prodded Manny. 'Are they not entitled to think like you about the world, and places dear to them? To dismiss you in the same way you dismiss them? What makes you so unique?'

'That's the worst thing,' I replied. 'There are probably thousands out there who think the same as me . . . But I just can't stand the crowds, and all this, this . . . globalisation!'

'Ah yes,' said Manny, 'this is the "not so lonely planet" we are living on. "Travel". The holy grail, the opium of urbanites, the first word under "Interests" on every young man's CV, dream of gap year students and cure for the midlife crisis. All this rubbish about "finding yourself" through travel. You've got to find yourself before you leave. Or preferably leave yourself behind!'

'So what can you do about it, Manny? Cure me. Help me regain my love of the exotic.'

'As I suspected when we first met, you have a totally normal case of Heimway Syndrome, or what the Germans would call *Weltschmerz* – world-weariness . . . pain of and for the world.'

Now not only a self-named malaise, but the Freudian lingo to go with it.

'You need an idea, a place that is reawakening your sense of wonder and exciting those travel antennae you once held proud and symbolic of your very interested being; of a person open-minded to all things, people and places and able to embrace the world as new every day.'

'Sure. But where can I go?'

'You mean, now that every corner of the earth has been explored?

Manny composed himself for the big reveal.

'Well, contrary to what you and your like believe, there *is* a new frontier; a lost, or rather overlooked horizon; a place that is remaining undiscovered, cloaked in poisonous myth and all but unvisited, as we speak, for over sixty years, since it became obscured from the minds of most of the world. It is a place people find so hard to visit, so little known and so inaccessible is it to their minds. Where is this far-off place, you ask? Well, in fact it is not far off. It is a European Shangri-La: a romantic, wooded place, a country of rivers, vineyards, forests, castles, poetry and music . . .'

Manny now seemed transported as, quivering, he continued, '. . . of fast cars, *schöne Ladies* – "ver ze girls are bioodiful". A country preserved by neglect; ripe and waiting to be revealed again.'

Dramatic pause.

'I am talking about Germany!' said Manny, a triumphant, almost post-coital relief in his voice.

Even more silence as I tried not to splutter into my coffee.

Germany, a Shangri-La? Germany, a panacea for the world and cure for depression? It hardly had a good track record.

Manny stood up and wandered around the edifice of the pre-posterous idea he had just cast into the room. He was smiling now and began humming a faintly recognisable ditty to himself, as if I wasn't there.

> *'I know what you're thinking!*
> *You wonder why I chose her.*
> *Out of all the countries in the world.'*

What was that tune?

'As with all kinds of mental illness, self-awareness is the first step to recovery. The Germans call it *Selbstwahrnehmung*,' Manny continued, clearly finding my incredulity distastefully predictable. 'What do you know of Germany?'

Well, the tabloids, *'Allo 'Allo* and Basil Fawlty had taught me everything I'd ever wanted to know. But Noël Coward had once implored 'Don't Let's Be Beastly to the Germans'. Was it time to cut them a bit of slack?

My only contact with Germany had been on short business trips in a parallel universe of hotels, offices and Mercedes taxis. I'd been to places like Frankfurt and Munich for meetings that could easily be conducted in English because almost all Germans seemed to be Überlinguists. Germany was important, but only as a market; a victim of its own economic success. Otherwise my only experience of Germans was limited to racing them for Spanish sun-loungers at dawn, wrestling for *Lebensraum* on the beach in Italy or clashing elbows in the queue for the ski lift. I'd certainly never had any desire to go to Germany on holiday. And the sheer number of them on the beaches of the Med was a clear indication that not even the Germans were to be found in their own country!

Manny now changed to business consultant mode.

'You see, in this day and age nations are brands.'

Oh no! I thought, Please, not one of those management-training-course-style theories! Why hadn't I simply self-diagnosed with a two-week meditation course in Kerala?

'Travel is the new high street and, just as some brands are in and some are out, so every country, region, city or island has a stock that is rising and falling according to fashion.'

I thought about the dinner parties that had propelled me towards Manny where guests dealt in destinations like stocks and shares. He was right.

'And just as people are refusing to wear certain brands, like C&A, which incidentally is also German' – and by the looks of it Manny's tailor of choice! – 'so there are some places people are refusing to go on holiday.'

Yes, and Germany was right up there with Taiwan and North Korea.

'But a brand is like a stereotype – you might say it is all some people get to know about a country's culture. As such it is a prejudice and has to be exploded.'

Fine. But surely it was precisely too much past branding, of the wrong sort, that was Germany's problem now!

'Did you know, an average of just 1.6 million Britons visited Germany each year recently, compared to the eleven or so million that went to France and fourteen million that descended on Spain?'

Manny was strangely well informed on the statistics.

'What's wrong with Germany?' he ventured.

Immediately I could hear a chorus around a dinner table giving me lists of German failings.

But Manny was clearly serious.

'Why not try it for your summer holiday?'

I baulked.

'Sun – banal as it may seem, isn't that the first commandment of travel, even for real travellers like you say you are? Well, you can relax and get a tan in Germany too, you know.'

I thought of Keats's desire for 'a beaker of the warm South . . . tasting of Flora and the country green/Dance, and Provencal song and sunburnt mirth'. That didn't sound much like Germany to me.

'If you agree to follow my cure I can send you to a beautiful, sunny side of Germany you scarcely thought existed.'

'But even if it is sunny,' I countered, 'how is Germany going to cure my . . . my, whatever you called it?'

'Your *Weltschmerz*? Never mind. That will come. This is an easy first step. And if you stick with my course of treatments you will see. For you are about to embark on a series of extraordinary, entertaining and unexpected journeys into a country and people you maybe thought you knew. Together we will revive and enrich your soul and release the German inside you. You will discover the art of being German!'

2

Freikörperkultur

nf, *nudism*

(lit. free body culture)

When I announced to my wife that we were going to spend our summer holiday in Germany she politely declined and said she'd rather go to Wales. Not that Wales is a fate worse than Germany. She has family there. And besides, even if good weather can't be guaranteed, at least there's a beach.

'But there's plenty of beach in Germany,' I protested, having just found out for myself.

I had been busily studying a map Manny had given me as part of a little therapy pack of cultural background notes and discovered Germany had a coast – two in fact. On some level I was sure I had always known Germany had a coastline. But in terms of sun, sea and sand Germany might as well have been landlocked, so far was it off my seaside-holiday radar.

As a fan of the Radio 4 shipping forecast I knew modern Germany owned a whole mouthful of the Nordsee, or North Sea, between Holland and Denmark called German Bight. But now I discovered Germany also owns a section of coastline to the east of Denmark that used to stretch a lot farther but now finishes at the Polish border. Hence the Germans call this the

Ostsee, or East Sea. We call it the Baltic, which has an altogether different and colder ring. Not an obvious place to think of
bathing, but somehow resonant and mysterious; two adjectives
not normally used to describe the ideal bucket-and-spade holiday.

I got out the copy of the unlikely-sounding *Charming Hotels
Germany* that Manny had given me – it was a 2003 edition and
hadn't been updated recently – and with a few rusty phrases was
soon pretty sure I'd booked us a *Zimmer* with a view in a resort
called Kühlungsborn on the Baltic 'Riviera'.

Now I was going to see Germans, a race that one usually
only encounters in other people's countries, on holiday in their
own for a change. What to pack? A towel, certainly. Maybe
two each in case we needed extra ammunition for the annexation of sun-loungers. Swimming costume? Maybe not. I had
grown up assuming that if you saw a group of tourists wandering around in their birthday suits on any European beach they
were most likely to be German. So maybe they didn't wear costumes in their own country either. Hearing of our plans to go to
the German seaside, a friend of mine had quipped, 'Germans
hate wearing clothes unless it's a uniform,' and recounted the
story of a girlfriend of his who had met her German husband on
a nudist beach in Spain.

Now, now! That was enough prejudices. Like a German and
his clothes, Manny had said I must divest myself of these. But
he'd also said I had to get into character and release the German
in me. So I'd gone and got myself some Birkenstocks. They were
very comfortable, their shape born of scrupulous orthopaedic
experimentation. But also clunky and quite ugly. It was surely an
accident that these solid pieces of pragmatic cork and leather
should have suddenly become so fashionable. I was pleased I
would be bestriding German soil in German shoes. But I drew
the line at wearing them with white socks, particularly as I had
neither mullet nor facial hair. Yet . . .

We finished sorting out our clothes and began packing them into that other essential German invention, a *Rucksack*. And now we were all set. All that was missing was the VW Westfalia camper van. Lufthansa would have to do instead.

The gateway to the Baltic was Lübeck, in the state of Schleswig-Holstein, a beautifully preserved, moated medieval port city of seven dreaming, light-green corroded copper spires and tall, thin and gabled gingerbread buildings that reminded me of Amsterdam. With pronounced white pointing, built on many low floors and with tiny windows, they were like some miniature fairytale world I was now seeing through a looking glass. The medieval gate, the Holstein Tor, stood with its thick, cylindrical towers and slate-grey pointed sorcerer's hats like two wizards petrified in the night.

A proud maritime city, I now read, Lübeck was once Queen of the Hanseatic League. Nothing to do with anyone called Hans, the word 'Hansa' is German for 'guild' – as in 'Lufthansa', the aviation guild (a loose political, economic and military union of trading cities which in the fifteenth century established a virtual north German nation and a powerful monopoly on trade in the whole North Sea and Baltic basin). As much through Hansa power as anything else Germany's coastline once stretched as far east as what is now Kaliningrad, an island of Russia wedged between Lithuania and Poland, formerly known as Königsberg and capital of East Prussia. I hadn't fully appreciated how big the German Second Reich (the first, I clarified for myself, had been under Charlemagne) had been on the eve of the First World War. If only they'd left it at that . . .

A university city, bone-shaker bicycles lay everywhere up against walls or organised in phalanxes of cycle racks. In the Altstadt, the old town, shadowy porticoed squares were connected to narrow, cobbled and car-less streets whose briny, dewy surface gleamed in the coppery streetlights. The city was by and large deserted but I could see cosy student life as I peeked in through the misted windows of its discreet pubs and bars. Silhouetted against the moonlit sky, Lübeck's pointed spires seemed more like Transylvania than north Germany.

The countryside east of Lübeck, in the catchily named state of Mecklenburg-Vorpommern, became surprisingly lush and the country roads like avenues lined by lime and beech trees with beyond them a child's idea of green meadows speckled with daisies and buttercups and full of fat, grazing cows. It was almost too perfect, like something out of a Lurpak advert. With its unending canvas of sparsely populated arable land the region is known as 'Germany's granary', but driving through these vast, untouched acreages of field bisected by straight, raised roads lined on either side by metronomic rows of trees felt very much like being in France. If we'd been driving a 2CV and the trees had been planes I'd have thought we'd been transported to Provence. It was a pristine and motionless countryside, a quiet corner of Europe left to nature. Rivers, tributaries and lakes extended like capillaries all over the province and as far as Berlin to the south. It was a landscape every bit as beautiful as Britain's Lake District with the bonus that you didn't have to go via Carlisle.

Kühlungsborn, just like Eastbourne and other '-bournes' along the English coast, turned out to be one long seafront. Except this was Germany and if you looked from the coast you'd almost not know it was there. Instead of the front being despoiled by cars, crazy golf, tawdry amusement arcades, the litter of chip shops and the peeling paintwork of Victorian hotels and lace-curtained B&Bs, Kühlungsborn was almost entirely hidden from sight by a thick band of fragrant pines. A car got you nowhere near the beach. In fact cars were kept hidden from view and their polluting potential reduced by an infernal one-way system set well back from the sea. Access was by foot or bicycle only; whole armies of bikes were supplied free of charge by all hotels and equipped with dynamo lights.

The Residenz Waldkrone lay at the western extremity of the town in a cul-de-sac of trimmed lawns demarcated by low chain fences and off-road parking. Clean, orderly and white, it seemed like the toytown set from *The Truman Show*. The Waldkrone was a pristine building with understated Jugendstil curves. But not so the buildings nearby: the Hotel Schloss am Meer (Castle on the Sea) right on the beach was a thickset Bavarian mock-Tudor villa with turrets and excrescent follies and all striped in heavy red sandstone as if to resemble from afar a medieval half-timbered house. Opposite the Waldkrone were the Residenz Tannhäuser and the Residenz Rheingold, named after two Wagner operas, the second with a house-high fresco covering the whole of one wall. It depicted wild mountains, brooding forests and a torrential rocky river with the hero Siegfried at its centre. Pagan deities like Aphrodite were all right, if cheesy, in places like Greece. But this didn't exactly say sun, sandcastles and relaxation. Indeed Siegfried would have made a formidable sun-lounger opponent.

Just as Kühlungsborn was no Torquay, so the Residenz Waldkrone was no Fawlty Towers. There was no Sibyl and sadly no Polly. Instead an air of polished, ordered calm. The formal, square-faced gentleman trussed up like a porter in a five-star London hotel turned out to be the owner. These Towers were more '*in Ordnung*' than 'faulty'.

With that endearing trait of Germans to be unable to pronounce their English w's or v's, he said that as English visitors we were 'wery velcome'. He also announced that we were in luck: our arrival had coincided with a hot spell and the forecast for tomorrow and the next few days was very good. I had taken a quick look at the Baltic on our way in and as it reflected the scudding, dark-grey clouds above it had been hard to believe it could ever be warm here. But if it was suddenly going to be hot I didn't want to miss out on a sun-lounger the next day, and so went to bed early, setting my alarm for a running start . . . Tomorrow would belong to me!

Dawn. A cock crows, a chorus of cuckoo clocks go off, sending fat and hairy German sun-worshippers into pandemonium as they gather their towels and rush downstairs to claim the best loungers while the rest of the hotel sleeps. Or so they think. As they emerge into the swimming-pool area a Union Jack towel sails through the air ahead of them, then bounces twice on the pool before landing on the best sun-lounger and rolling open to reveal a can of chilled beer. The Germans look up in shock and horror to whence the bouncing towel came, to see a smooth British hunk saunter lazily on to his sixth-floor balcony, open a can of lager and smugly greet them with the words, 'Turned out nice again.'

That was the Carling Black Label advert in the early 1990s. My movement was not quite so slick. But I did get up at seven and, if not run, then hasten down to the beach in search of my ideal spot for the rest of the day. Towel in hand and full, not of lager but expectation, I reached the beach anticipating a quilt of towels already laid out. Or at least some other people.

Not a sausage. Not even the slightest *Wurst*.

For a start Germans don't actually have sun-loungers. Not for Germans something so slight and temporary. That would leave too much to chance. No, the Germans clearly need a more solid and permanent structure whose ownership can be guaranteed. And so they have invented the *Strandkorb*, or beach basket. But 'basket' doesn't come close to doing justice to what is really a hefty piece of permanent beach furniture. Imagine a two-seater sofa on a wooden frame, with brightly coloured cushions, all clad in a wicker shell and with a wicker canopy shaped like the soft top of a vintage car so that the entire object stands a metre and a half high. There are footrests that pull out from underneath the seats so you can put your feet up or stretch fully out, and two wooden lockable cupboards for storing clothes, a picnic – or lager.

A cross between a beach hut and a Punch & Judy booth,

Strandkörber line the beach all year round in regimented rows, usually three or four deep and a designated four or five metres apart: white and blue stripes, green and white check, red and yellow stripes, all grouped together according to the company that rents them out. Their weight makes them virtually impossible to shift around and at night, when boarded up with padlocked panelling, they are like sentinels, creating an eerie, alien atmosphere, and make a moonlit beach look like a cemetery.

The first *Strandkorb* was invented in 1882 by Wilhelm Bartelsmann, a basket-maker from nearby Rostock. It was tailor-made for a lady holidaymaker with rheumatism who wanted to be able to sit comfortably on the beach. The imaginative Bartelsmann converted a linen basket he had lying around and the prototype was born. His wife turned his idea into a rental business and now some ten thousand beach baskets are made every year and cover the coasts of Germany from the East Friesian islands in the west to Rügen island in the east. They look positively Victorian and as an Englishman I felt unusually outplayed for eccentricity. Among Germans *Strandkörber* have taken on a cult image and are now used in the home, in the garden and even on the terraces of alpine restaurants as retro fashion curios. I quite fancied one for my London garden. Some Germans even have them tailor-made, with stereos, chintz upholstery, underseat heating and lights, as if they were high-performance cars. *Vorsprung durch Strandkorbtechnik.*

Strandkörber can be hired for about seven euros a day and are usually booked by holidaying Germans by the week and often months if not years in advance. Many Germans like not just to have their own *Stammstrandkorb*, or regular beach basket, but like to know who their neighbours, and ideally also regulars, are going to be. They used to build walls around them to define their private *Lebensraum* or living space, and even though this is not allowed any more there can be no doubt that a German's

Strandkorb is his *Schloss* and that the Teutonic love of castles begins at the beach.

So no battle to be done with the sun-loungers. I felt deflated; the thunder of malicious enjoyment stolen, and the chance to pit traditional English beachmanship with Germanic beachcraft denied. A German lawyer once actually researched the legality of treating beach towels as freehold contracts. His conclusion: 'a British tourist would be quite within their legal rights to ignore the reservation implied'. Perish the thought of something so dishonourable! But maybe this was really just an Anglo-German thing, as much to do with British self-perception as phlegmatic purveyors of fair play. If anything, it highlighted our similarity to the Germans and the search for *Lebensraum* when on holiday in someone else's country. If an Italian came along and saw a towel on a sun-lounger he liked with no one sitting there, he'd probably just remove it without a thought, and still less write whole ad campaigns around it. I consulted our host on the matter. He nodded, misunderstanding my question: 'Yes, I have heard that the English are liking to reserve their sun-loungers.' How rich was that!

It was time for a swim.

The Baltic seemed as tideless and waveless as the Med. Two well-insulated German ladies of a certain age had joined me and were already wading fearlessly out for their morning constitutional. 'Turned out nice again,' I greeted them under my breath and, not wanting to be outdone, ventured in up to my waist. Not too cold. And I was just about to take the plunge when something in the water caught my eye. *Qualle!* Jellyfish! And not just one but, multiplying before my eyes, everywhere small, pink or white billowing mushrooms of translucent gelatin. Surely jellyfish share with mosquitoes the award for 'most useless species on the planet'. But these couldn't be too bad as the two portly *Frauen* seemed to be brushing them aside nonchalantly. It turned out the jellyfish just formed a thin band in the shallows after which the

Baltic could be enjoyed without fear of stingers. Talking to the two ladies on the beach after we'd all enjoyed a paddle together, I understood that jellyfish are a feature of the sea in these parts. The white ones are harmless but the pink ones give a nasty sting and German kids apparently grow up throwing them at one another for fun. There are so many different ways of growing up . . .

I was still itching for some Anglo-German competition but even over the toaster at the breakfast buffet back at the hotel this did not materialise. It was only when we went to the hotel's bike store that we found that someone had taken the keys to a selection of the best bikes the previous evening. I had found one I liked and was just trying it out and adjusting the saddle when a German lady appeared, smugly holding the key to the integral lock. I'd just seen it had a puncture and so gracefully gave way.

As in many northern European countries the bicycle, or *das Fahrrad* in Germany, is king. But in Germany it is a peculiarly unfashionable type of bicycle. Not for earnest Germans the lithe lines and frilly accessories of trendy mountain bikes or racers, these were sturdy, honest, 1930s sit-up-and-beg bikes, the Birkenstock of bicycles, and would make anyone riding them look German.

Half the road through Kühlungsborn was given over to a cycle lane in both directions, but there was also a separate cycle lane between the road and the pedestrian lane, and here too cycling was permitted. It was as if the whole population, like in some Flann O'Brien nightmare, had grown bicycles. Everywhere were man-bicycles: young couples, families and pensioners all embarking on wholesome outings, complete with the latest in practical equipment – sidecars containing picnics, trailers containing children, aqualungs of extra water, rucksacks, panniers – you name it. Every group seemed an epitome of nature-loving exploration and self-sufficiency. And I was struck by the average age of our fellow cyclists. Kühlungsborn, it was clear, was as much a destination for the elderly as Eastbourne. But unlike the south coast of England this was not a case of stooping room only and soulful gazes from tearooms out over the horizon of their past. No, this was Protestant *carpe diem*: here and now, life begins at seventy.

It was nice to be in a place where there were no English people. Certainly one clear advantage of Germany as a potential cure for *Weltschmerz* or Heimway Syndrome was the sheer lack of other people visiting it. What's more, German was being spoken all around me and for once that was OK! Usually I would bristle or my heart would sink at the sound of competitive Germans on holiday and the ubiquitous sight of signs saying '*Zimmer frei*'. In fact it was noticeable that Germany, or at least this part of it, was not advertising itself to anyone in any other language than German. According to Manny, Mecklenburg-Vorpommern was supposed to have overtaken Bavaria and the Black Forest as Germany's number-one holiday region for Germans. But, refreshingly, they were making no attempt to let the secret travel beyond the country's borders.

It was odd, though, for some reason, to see the German flag flying everywhere on masts and hotel roofs. It is not a flag you see very often and indeed Germans have hardly allowed themselves to fly it since 1945. Maybe it was the contrast of the frivolity of the sunny seaside with the associations of the strong black, red and yellow colours. No doubt part of the baggage that Manny was asking me to shed. I was used to seeing other nations' colours used in travel adverts, on billboards and the like. But you don't see many German flags draped across five-by-ten-metre billboards in London. People would probably think the Third World War had started.

Yet, in my mind, yellow was somehow the colour of Germany: Lufthansa, the post office, the phone boxes and any amount of public signage. Even the border guards, the first Germans we'd seen, wore mustard shirts (with brown ties and muddy-green hats – not an easy look for a pasty northern people to carry off). Yellow was a very difficult colour, both to wear and to have around the place in large amounts. Slightly sickly, bare, honest and without mystery. And hardly sexy. The yellow (technically gold) was in fact Austrian, from the Habsburg 'Black and Gold Monarchy'. The original German colours were really red, black and white, a merging of the black and white of Prussia with the red and white of the Hanseatic League. Hitler apparently hated the yellow, referring to it as 'chicken shit'. And for once he might have been right.

After a gentle half-hour ride along well-tended cycle paths through fragrant woodland and with glimpses now and again of the sea, we emerged from the woods and into the splendid isolation of Heiligendamm.

It is strange to think there was a time when people avoided the sea, considering it to be dirty, dangerous, unhealthy . . . and full of jellyfish. It was the English who, some time in the late eighteenth century, invented the idea of swimming in the sea as a mass leisure activity. The Prince Regent had already eloped to Brighton and invented the dirty weekend, and the future jet-set had already headed off to Nice, ensuring the seafront Promenade there would be named after 'les Anglais', before the idea caught on in Germany. At the time, around 1793, the Duchy of Mecklenburg was ruled from the elegant lakeside seat of Schwerin, some hundred kilometres inland. Here Duke Friedrich Franz I had a beautiful white-and-gold Louis IV-style chateau and gardens. But he also had an illness and is said, on doctor's orders, to have taken the plunge into the sea, the first German ever to do so, here in Heiligendamm, which means 'holy (or healing) pier'. There's not much of a pier in the Brighton sense, but what Friedrich Franz founded was Germany's first *Seebad*: 'sea bath' or seaside resort. The *Seebad* would captivate the German imagination and unleash a whole array of health concepts that have become central to the German psyche and lifestyle.

While in England the seaside remained merely a place of leisure, with a vague notion that the sea air did one good, in Germany there were designated health resorts, or what the Germans call a *Kurort* (place of cure), where the word *Kur* covers all notions of care, health and cure. Central to the *Kurort* was the *Kurhaus*, which was not, as I thought, some form of spa but the town hall and municipal tourist service for the resort all rolled into one. In Kühlungsborn and here in Heiligendamm, as in all the resorts and *Kaiserbäde* (Imperial resorts) that were built in the later nineteenth century all along the coast, the *Kurhaus* was always the grandest building and a focal point of activity.

The seaside resort for the German is not a place of informal, take-it-or-leave it leisure. It is like entering a healing zone with its own autonomous administration paid for through a *Kurtax*, a health tax for all visitors. All hotel rooms in the area charge *Kurtax* as an automatic supplement to their room rates and now I understood the two funny vouchers our hotelier had given me and told me to carry at all times. I had now contributed to the maintenance of the litter-free beach, to the cycle tracks and to the general pristine nature of the resort's hedges, lawns and municipal services. The vouchers were proof that I was a paid-up health tourist and this granted me access to the beach, free use of beach toilets, free access to local concerts and events, free use of the municipal library and access to and discounts on various *Kur* facilities and services. Day visitors who just wanted to lie and sunbathe on the beach for a while didn't get away without paying either. All along the promenade there were ticket machines like parking meters where for €1.20 you could get your all-day sunbathing ticket. If your Protestant sense of responsibility was not enough and you were thinking of evading the fare, there were signs galore saying '*Bitte Kurtaxschein lösen*' – 'Please pay your

Kurtax' – to make you feel guilty. I'm not sure how stringent the controls are and certainly never saw a 'beach conductor' – not that I would have known what he would be wearing. Maybe a blue uniform, or plain clothes, or maybe even no clothes at all.

In the beginning Heiligendamm was very much an aristos' hang-out. Writers, artists and royals such as Proust, Mendelssohn and the Romanovs followed Friedrich Franz's lead and you could easily imagine Thomas Mann being inspired here for his story about that other famous lido, 'Death in Venice'. The Duke had to commission worthy buildings to put his mates up in and, inspired by Regency Brighton, these were the fine buildings that now formed the St Petersburgesque 'White City' by the sea, all reachable, if not by bicycle, then by the stylish narrow-gauge steam railway – still kept in pristine working order – that Friedrich commissioned to convey him and his friends to the coast in playful comfort.

As the fashion for bathing in the sea spread like towels along the German coastline, so the newly comfortable middle-class Germans, or *Biedermeier*, came to the coast and left their mark in bombastic and twirly architecture that I found totally unsuited to the seaside.

The Schloss am Meer and the Rheingold in Kühlungsborn were two good examples but the whole seafront was bedecked with would-be medieval castles that made it look as if Rio Ferdinand and not Friedrich Franz, together with some of his Premiership team-mates, had recently moved into the area and invested a few weeks' salary and about the same amount of taste in a squad of holiday homes.

I was used to the Mediterranean, where the soft colour of locally hewn stone merges gently with the landscape and the irregularity of the stonework, and the odd weed and Latin decay, make it look natural and lived-in. But here many of the houses wore none of the ravages of time and their strong lines, heavy colours and fake timber stood out violently against the gentle colouring of the coastline. They looked as if they were superimposed or imported from another culture and reminded me of the colonial German architecture I had seen in Namibia.

Germany was very slow to the sun-loungers of colonialism, particularly in Africa. At the end of the nineteenth century it was too busy finding and founding itself. But it did get a few chunks of the world, notably Namibia (formerly Südwestafrika), just next door to South Africa. The town of Lüderitz, named after Namibia's founder, Adolf Lüderitz, is about as German looking as they come and even has shops run by German-speaking '*Südwester*' that serve Black Forest gateau. Set against the sandy backdrop of the Namib desert in one direction and huge Atlantic rollers in the other, the Teutonic half-timbered architecture with the odd turret thrown in is an unexpected and incongruous sight. But I suppose no more than seeing a facsimile of Victorian St Pancras in the middle of Delhi.

The German diaspora is, however, quite significant, particularly in the Americas. Think Donald Rumsfeld, Norman Schwarzkopf and Kevin Costner. I had always thought that those who ended up in South America were all Germans who fled arrest after 1945. But according to Manny's notes – he was clearly anxious to show Germany's rightful place in European colonial heritage – they have been there for several centuries. Brazil imported its royal family from Germany (having given us ours and the Russians theirs via Catherine the Great – the Germans are good at rent-a-royal) and more Germans were imported into the south of the country to roll back the agricultural boundaries with their already established hard work ethic and mastery of technology. There were places in Brazil, I learnt, called Blumenau and Novo Hamburgo, full of ethnic Germans, where the architecture looked more like that of the Bavarian Alps and the men wore *Lederhosen* and the women those lace-frilled tablecloths. Blumenau apparently hosts the world's biggest Oktoberfest after Munich. And there is even an Argentinian newspaper, its title written in 1930s neo-Gothic script, called *Argentinisches Tageblatt*, of which the 'World News' section seemingly covers only the German-speaking world.

The bizarre thing about any beach on a north-facing coast (as almost all of Germany's coast is) is that since the sun for most of the day shines from the south, sunbathers, who generally like to face the sun, are obliged to lie with their feet up the beach, facing not the sea but inland. If you think about it, there are very few parts of the world where this is possible and in northern Europe you'd have to sunbathe either at the top of Scotland near John O'Groats or at the top of Sweden. This might not seem odd at first but it was striking to emerge from amid the bushes that separated the cycle track from the beach to see hundreds of Germans lined up facing you like the audience at some alfresco beach theatre as they sat or reclined in their canopied *Strandkörber*. And it was even more striking when the beach we emerged on to turned out to be a nudist beach and we were confronted by a full-frontal of the collected genitalia of tens of naked Germans.

Silly me. I had forgotten to read the signpost which quite clearly stated that for one kilometre from where we stood the beach was now an *FKK Strand*. Always assuming I knew what *FKK* meant; to me it sounded like a sister branch of the Ku Klux Klan. But no. FKK, pronounced 'eff-kar-kar', apparently stood for 'Freikörperkultur', meaning 'free body culture'. Free body culture? What on earth did that mean? Well, in words of just one syllable, basically, 'get your kit off'. Only the Germans could treat nudity as a philosophical concept and talk about the human body in business-consultant-speak.

'You British are so prudish and uncomfortable with nudity,' came Manny's response; he from the land of *Baywatch*. 'Even in your own bedroom! But this is such a superficial attitude. It only goes skin deep. The German approach goes deeper, beyond the surface and all its inevitable imperfections. It is more liberating. Your mind will be set free by German attitudes to bathing and the human body . . .'

The idea of *Körperkultur*, or 'body culture', was developed in Germany at the end of the nineteenth century to encourage cosy, urban middle-class Germans to get out more as well as to loosen their collars. Early bathing costumes covered pretty much everything and this was obviously too constricting. But here we were now in Prussia and weren't Prussians famously fond of uniform? It was curious that they had suddenly been keen to shed it. Well, it seems they were originally more tolerant and forward-looking than the rest of Germany.

Suddenly, at the dawn of the twentieth century, Germans started to develop a national urge to get naked. A German sociologist named Heinrich Pudor wrote a best-selling (in Germany) book called *The Cult of the Nude* and became the Germans' father of nudism. Then followed a manifesto called *Die Nacktheit* (Nudity), by a guy called Heinrich Ungewitter, which set out a utopian life of total nudity. In nearby Hamburg in 1903 Paul Zimmerman founded the world's first *Freilichtpark* (nudist park) and in 1920 on the North Friesian island of Sylt the world's first nudist beach opened its gates – or should that be legs? At the same time a bunch of evangelists who went by the name of *die Kinder des Lichts*, 'the Children of the Light' went about proclaiming that nothing should come between the sun, our life force, and our skin. Germans were undoubtedly the inventors of organised mass nudity.

Not content with sexing up their own beaches, the flow of German immigrants to the USA in 1929 brought with them the new German gospel of nudity under the leadership of Kurt Barthel and his American League for Physical Culture and a movement called American Social Nudism. I wondered if Manny was a member? Hitler banned FKK. Who knows what complexes he might have been hiding? But with the advent of mass tourism and the 1960s 'make love not war' movement, and in particular the 1968 student revolution, FKK got a new rush of blood and stood proud once more. Other countries, like Croatia, welcomed rich German tourists who wanted to get naked. While in Germany cities like Hamburg, Munich and Cologne students let it all hang out in protest against Vietnam and against a return to the traditionalism and conservatism they blamed for the horrors of the Third Reich. And here in former Communist East Germany, where there was once no freedom of movement or speech, going naked was one of the few possible expressions of freedom.

That's right, blame it on the DDR (Deutsche Demokratische Republik) as if it were something only weird commies or old people did now. This was patently not true. Before me, in the early twenty-first century, lay prostrate naked young German couples, while young families, sons of the new united Germany, frolicked around them in their birthday suits.

In Germany, I learnt, there are dozens of high-profile organisations and associations for nudists offering tips on where to go for hassle-free clothes-freeness. The online travel guide for nudists, www.FKK-reisefuehrer.de lists the top sites in Germany; at number thirteen is a place called Büsum. Meanwhile the nudist equivalent of the German Youth Hostel Association, FKK-Jugend (FKK Youth!), lists, like a manifesto, 'Sixty-five arguments for nudism', among them (and their powers of translation have uncharacteristically let them down): 'nudism raises metal health' (surely 'mental', unless they mean piercing as well?); 'the naturists haven't as much stress as the people wearing clothes' (this was a poor excuse for German fashion); 'naturists are rarely involved in illegitimate sex' (only rarely?); 'naturism promotes the general health and energizes the production of vitamin D' (yes, but are genitalia really instrumental in this?); and lastly, 'FKK supports the toolism and the fight for the liberty of the women'. I cannot think what the word 'toolism' was mistranslated from.

Philosophy or no philosophy, it was hard to turn a blind eye to the specimens on parade before us. But could I bring myself to join them?

'You must go naked,' Manny ordered me.

Part of the art of being German? Probably! But a cure for *Weltschmerz*?

'You have to get closer to what you do not know.'

I did eventually summon up the courage to go FKK, later on, in the reassuring seclusion of an island called Hiddensee. The beach didn't actually say 'FKK' but I figured, 'Who's going to complain in this country?' Besides, there was already an elderly couple striding in up to their knees starkers, and a family with two children running around naked.

Now my curiosity was pricked and I wanted to ask them about FKK; why they felt the urge and was it something cultural to Germans? But did I have the balls? Maybe nudists didn't talk to one another, and in its openness maybe FKK was also very private. Or maybe there was a Masonic code of conduct? I hadn't been so nervous since trying to pluck up the courage to talk to girls in discos aged thirteen. But at least back then I was wearing clothes. And so were they. And you were allowed to look too. But how on earth could I start this conversation? 'Do you come here often naked?'

Like a spotty teenager I fluffed my line. Something silly about it being my first time and how, as an Englishman, this was all rather difficult. But far from affronted, Wolfgang and Sabine looked on me with amused sympathy and were happy to open up. They were in their early forties and from Hamburg. They'd fallen in love with the Baltic and had been coming here for the past six years, since they'd had their two children. They said they'd never really given nudity any thought, at least when they were in Germany. They didn't seek out nudist resorts when they went abroad but hadn't really considered that it was something specific to Germany. Lots of their friends went naked and it wasn't an issue.

We carried on talking for a good ten minutes. They were curious to see an English couple on summer holiday in Germany and wanted to know if I was enjoying myself. I nodded and hoped that it was plain to see. They were so friendly I almost forgot I was naked. It was the kind of conversation that could easily have taken place dressed and in a café. It just happened to take place naked and on a beach. Forgetting the superficial. Wasn't that what FKK was supposed to be all about?

Feeling rather stupid, I went back to my smirking wife, tail between my legs. Then I waded into the shallows, the surface of the water goose-pimpled by a cold breeze, squelching mud and sharp pebbles beneath my feet, pretending to be German while my wife laughed and took pictures from the beach. Was this for me or for some American nutter? *Weltschmerz* didn't come close to describing my suffering now. He had better bloody well be proud! Even if I, not in any sense, was not.

The Germans actually have a word for a non-FKK beach – a *Textil-Strand* (which sounded like knitwear) – as if it had to be specified lest whole swaths of beach be covered by unfettered nudists. And there was also a *Hundebadestrand* – 'dog bathing beach', though whether anyone else was allowed on such a beach, and in what state of undress one could expect to find the German dogs, was not clear.

There could be no doubt about it: the Germans have systemised the seaside holiday. The sun-lounger is a castle, the beaches are segregated and taxed, the cyclist is not merely encouraged but recruited, homogenised and channelled into myriad cycle lanes, and the dunes are protected against erosion. As such, life in Germany didn't seem to be a beach. But at least I knew I wouldn't cut my foot open on a stray piece of broken glass, and there were no private beaches, vandalised deckchairs or invasive beach merchants selling you frozen drinks and sugared pistachios at rip-off prices.

German seaside life was very healthy and wholesome and no

stone of pragmatism has been left unturned. But in its thoroughness and its leaving nothing to chance I found a lack of spontaneity and zest for life. What about the joys and chaotic abandon of children playing by the sea? It was no surprise to read that the Germans had set up something called the German Holiday Academy. A survey of forty thousand Germans by L'Tur, one of Germany's largest tour operators, had found that the nation had lost the art of having fun at the beach. And so courses had been set up in five cities, Hamburg, Cologne, Munich, Düsseldorf and Dresden, where for two hundred pounds Germans could learn what they called 'holiday skills': dressing casually (any clothes at all would be good!), dancing and applying a partner's sun lotion; and 'social integration skills' such as building sandcastles with children (the only attempts I'd seen were the fantasy turrets on some of the local residences). According to the instructors, 'Releasing the inner child is heartily encouraged', and at the end of the course the rejuvenated Germans were awarded a certificate and, wittily, a beach towel displaying the word '*besetzt*' – 'occupied'.

That the Germans should have forgotten to have fun was no surprise. That there should also be an academy to analyse and rectify this was equally typical. In fact it was so German it was almost American. And, in the form of consultant-types like Manny, probably on its way over here.

The Germans could do with learning how to let some of their famous hair down. And this conclusion was confirmed by a wild end-of-summer Saturday night out in downtown Kühlungsborn. A convivial party with a live band and sausage and beer stalls – free, courtesy of our *Kurtax* – suddenly wound up at ten o'clock, just when it was getting going. Half-man, half-bike, everyone disappeared into the night and the whole town, like a German philosopher, retreated into itself. This was apparently Germany's famous *Sperrstunde*, whereby it is forbidden to serve food or drink or play music outdoors after ten.

Britain used to be ridiculed by continentals for its pub closing time but what about this? Within half an hour there was as good as no one about and only one bar open for anyone wanting a risqué 'late' drink. There was no question of any public transport or a taxi – both are, I'm sure, unheard of in Kühlungsborn – and I walked back along deserted, shuttered streets. I felt like an outsider and a prowler. A sensation which was confirmed by my being totally shut out of the hotel, without hope of raising anyone, including my wife, so that I had to sleep in the hire car. If only everything in life was as reliable as a Volkswagen.

Too much cerebral nudism and you get a castrated nightlife.

They say the past is another country. In England they call it the Isle of Wight. Already, back in nineteenth-century Germany, Bismarck (ancestor of the eponymous London bon viveur) is reputed to have said, 'When the end of the world comes, I shall go to Mecklenburg because there everything happens a hundred years later.' I couldn't wait.

Apart from a brief moment in the sun following reunification – and fuelled by the curiosity of trendy Berliners – most of the Baltic Riviera had never been chic. Aristocratic briefly but never chic. No, the place where it's at on the German coast is apparently Sylt, northernmost of a group of German islands in the North Sea I had never heard of, called the Friesians – like the cows. Sylt, appropriately pronounced 'silt', is a long, thin and car-less sandbar of shifting, grassy dunes just south of Danish water, again criss-crossed by health-inducing cycle paths and with beaches arranged as theatres of *Strandkörber*. For all its northern-ness and pristine nature, it is a largely featureless but eerily elusive and captivating place. It sounded beautiful. But Manny reassured me. Well provided with gourmet restaurants, it has also taken on the status, with prices to match, of an exclusive resort, the German equivalent of Capri where chic

Hamburgers and Münchners have holiday villas and recreate their city life on the beach. 'Very Condé Nast.' And that would never do!

Never mind whether Germany had a coastline, I had never imagined it had any islands. Except for Mallorca, which is virtually a German island complete with DJs and rave scene – a German Ibiza.

'But in fact Germans have a great innate love of islands, as symbols of Romantic exile!' Manny declared.

No doubt also because of the sense of demarcated *Lebensraum* they inspire.

'Did you know Germany used to own Zanzibar?'

Luckily the British got it back in 1890 in return for a small but strategic piece of red granite in the North Sea called Heligoland. Thank God, otherwise the spicy dream destination of honeymooners and birthplace of Freddie Mercury would have been German. Imagine how the course of German music might have been changed by songs like 'Vee Are Ze Champions' and 'I Like To Ride My Bicycle'.

Sylt and Heligoland loom large in the German consciousness, along with the lush inland islands of Mainau and Reichenau on Lake Constance in the south-west corner of the country. But bigger in every way than all of these, and occupying the role in German minds of a paradise of unspoilt nature, is the island of Rügen, the country's most north-easterly outpost. That was, until the recent bird flu epidemic put the island on the map for the wrong reasons, when the *Sun* was quick to publish a cartoon showing a Second World War map with a big arrow and swastika sweeping over to Britain from Rügen.

Before Rügen, though, we found ourselves in Darss and Zingst, a mini archipelago of pristine peninsulas connected by thin strips of land which ring-fenced densely reeded lakes dotted with fishing villages set against ethereal vast northern skies. This was a nature reserve of stunning, unsuspected and untouched beauty but, as ever in Germany, only the most dedicated civilisation was allowed to encroach and these areas could only be fully enjoyed by getting out of your car and walking through nature. Half-timber had given way to small, white-washed thatched cottages that were irregular in shape and size and less vainglorious than the footballers' villas of Kühlungsborn, and whose subsidence over the years had humanised into dwellings of character. Once or twice we rounded a corner to find such houses grouped around a lush, central green, with duck-filled pond and space big enough to put a small eccentric cricket ground complete with oak tree within the boundary rope. Ah, if only the Germans played cricket! They don't know what they're missing. But then again they'd be far too good. Just the right kind of relentless philosopher's patience for the five-day game, and surely masters of the square cut and the swinger. I thought I'd even read somewhere that Shane Warne, the Goebbels of spin, had German ancestry.

Rügen was separated from the mainland by a strait of water on which sat the pretty and lively university town of Stralsund, owned for two hundred years by the Swedes, and, like Lübeck, full of bombastic and austere red-brick Gothic buildings, tall, staunch and rich. From the island, Stralsund looked in silhouette like seaside cities such as Oslo or Stockholm, so low on the horizon as to look submerged or like a battleship at sea.

'The village is hidden in the wood, away up to the left. It consists almost entirely of boarding-houses, in various styles of seaside architecture – sham Moorish, old Bavarian, Taj Mahal, and the old rococo doll's house, with white fretwork balconies.' Thus wrote Christopher Isherwood about Rügen in the detached series of vignettes entitled Goodbye to Berlin which were the basis for the film and principal prism through which I perceived Germany: *Cabaret*. What was true for Isherwood in 1931 was still true now. We were staying in one such 'old Bavarian'-style tree-cutters' lodge in the middle of a beech forest in the north-east corner of the island and in the middle of the Jasmund National park. It looked more like an alpine chalet and felt inappropriately cosy for the middle of the summer. But, far from displaying the banality of Kühlungsborn, Rügen, like some awkward prodigy, turned out to be blessed with all sorts of curiosities and mystical surprises.

In the nineteenth century the attractively named town of Binz became Rügen's principal seaside resort for the masses. Before that the Count of Rügen had commissioned a summer residence in the inland town of Putbus, from where, also by narrow-gauge steam train – the Germans loved their toy trains – he could reach the sea at his leisure. Sadly, thanks to the East German government's view of burdensome architectural heritage, nothing is left of the magnificent *Schloss* he commissioned, but the sizeable stables and orangery remain and these made for a surprising, Mediterranean sight: blazing-white stonework in a neo-classical style and with the sleepy, timeless and hazy atmosphere of a Spanish *pueblo blanco*; and gardens and outbuildings laid out in the French formal style with symmetrical rows of topiaried trees, hedges arranged in hemispheres around tended lawns casting a play of shadows in the midday sun.

Binz was also the first and only place on the German Baltic coast where I witnessed a genuine holiday bustle, a sense of liveliness, youth and widespread attempts at Mediterranean glamour. Throughout the Cold War Binz attracted over a million East Germans every year and it seems as popular today. With its cafés, ice-cream parlours, tree-lined pedestrian avenues and the neo-classical architecture, it could have been Nice or Cannes or any one of many interchangeable Mediterranean seafronts. All it was missing were the palm trees, sausage dogs and mutton dressed as lamb. Perhaps here at last was the chic I had been missing in Kühlungsborn. But almost at once it felt as hollow as it always had. Was I really developing FKK sympathies, an aversion to what was only skin deep?

But it wasn't half as hollow as the building we were about to stumble upon and whose existence I was not at all prepared for. I had promised Manny I would try to avoid thinking about Hitler during my treatment. But how could he expect me to ignore the sight that greeted me now? Four and a half thousand metres of bald, browning and solid continuous concrete, six storeys high and forming thousands of identical apartments set 150 metres back from the beach. A building that could be measured in kilometres, this was the Prora, a massive seaside housing complex set amid the trees, the Nazi equivalent of Butlins, built by the Nazis' Kraft durch Freude (Strength through Joy) workers' union and designed to give war workers a well-earned free holiday by the sea.

When the completed plans for the Prora were presented at the 1937 World Fair in Paris their architect, Clemens Klotz, was awarded the Grand Prix d'Architecture. The completed complex was to include a theatre to seat twenty thousand and a similarly sized cinema and festival hall as well as two wave-pools (decades before Center Parcs). But, interrupted by the outbreak of war, it was never finished and what was built was never used. Today it stands empty, not particularly decaying, but simply too much concrete for anyone to know what to do with and a curiosity for visitors.

No matter how much the British history curriculum may have been 'Hitlerised', I had never heard of the Kraft durch Freude (KdF) union and had Manny to thank for filling in this important gap. The KdF definitely put the socialism into the national socialism (*Nazionalsozialismus*) movement, which I was used to reducing to just 'Nazism'. In some dimension some of them were probably a well-meaning, socially committed bunch. The idea of low-cost holidays for workers was certainly a good one. It was just in other areas they went a bit too far. You didn't need a Hitler to dream up either the concept or the bland architecture. Just look at the Costa del Sol.

As well as holiday camps the KdF built ships for low-cost cruises, and the KdF-Wagen was later to become the VW Beetle (Volkswagen, 'the car of the people') built at the KdF-Stadt, now the VW factory in Wolfsburg. In a way the KdF leaders were the Stelios Haji-Ioannou of their age. Nazi brown even shares something of the sickliness of easyJet orange. And if they were around today? Well, they'd probably be setting up something like the German Holiday Academy.

The flagship of the KdF cruise fleet, I learnt from Manny's notes, was the *Wilhelm Gustloff*, the original mass-market liner, complete with swimming pools, built to carry two thousand passengers but carrying nearer nine thousand when she was torpedoed while returning refugees, mostly civilian evacuees of ethnic German origin, from places like Königsberg on the Eastern front, in the closing months of the war. Little reported it seems, and completely unknown to me until that moment, is that some six thousand people are thought to have gone down with the *Wilhelm Gustloff*, possibly the greatest loss of life at sea ever from a single vessel. More than the *Titanic*, but Hollywood has so far chosen to ignore it.

I found the Prora fascinating but was aware of being seduced by some perverse magnetism. It was not a place of pilgrimage, but undeniably an object of interest to travellers and not just war tourists or historians. In a macabre way the draw of any remaining trappings of Nazi Germany is not an interest in history and I was aware of not being drawn by history now.

'We live in the age of the war tourist wanting to catch the coat-tails of a more visceral elsewhere,' declared Manny triumphantly, his eyes lighting up. 'Yes, evil and suffering past and present are as much part of the magic of travel, the stirring of the soul. That is why people like you are drawn to the poverty of the developing world which you find so beautiful and innocent! But you are nothing but a voyeur!'

Well, if relics of evil were part of my rehab, Germany had

them in spades. But it was an uneasy thought and I felt it was time to leave the Prora.

Rügen's most famous asset is its white chalk cliffs. Which is fine unless you've been to Dover, in which case they are something of an anti-climax. Except that Rügen's white cliffs are not reached by a rusty Sealink ferry. Moreover they are a series of wild chalk crags with fearsome fantastical spikes and are a place of spiritual pilgrimage seared into the German nation's consciousness. This is down to the painter Caspar David Friedrich, a local to these parts who in 1818 painted *Kreidefelsen auf Rügen* (Chalk Cliffs on Rügen), a copy of which I remembered seeing on the walls of Manny's offices. In it three figures look out over the edge of the cliff, from beneath the windswept fronds of a beech tree, to a vast, seemingly limitless horizon. Below them dramatic stalagmites of chalk hewn over the centuries point up at them menacingly and wildly. The picture does not represent, it moves, suggests and symbolises: among other things the oneness of man with nature and the smallness of man in the universe.

As always, the money shot in Germany was not reachable by car. You had to earn your view and ensure your closeness to nature through some sweat. A series of *Wanderwege* (trails) led through the beech forest. The sun shone brightly, creating pillars of dusty sunlight between the columns of the trees. The forest sang with birds while our fifteen-month-old boy ran ahead. It was primevally beautiful.

We were joined by lots of Germans kitted out in serious rambling gear who had left their camper vans in the car park and set out in search of some Kraft durch Freude and the highlight of the eleven-kilometre stretch of chalk cliffs: a needle just like the Needles off the Isle of Wight, called the *Königstuhl*, the King's Seat. Legend has it that a Swedish king is supposed to have commissioned a viewing seat here from which to control and survey a naval defeat of the Danes in 1715. It was not easy to imagine oneself as either the Swedish king or Caspar David Friedrich, artist, philosopher, traveller, communing with nature. The masses with their bicycles and easyJet *Freude,* together with the inevitable visitors' centre, rather ruled out any peaceful meditation.

Rügen had a fragile, almost mystical air about it. Perhaps it was the combination of the Prora, the Romantic cliffs and the unspoilt patchwork of glades and fields of gold wheat rippling in the wind, seemingly alive. Or the knowledge that the forests were full of Stone Age burial mounds carried here by Ice Age glaciers. The spidery island was a mirage of flats and coves that hung together by threads of sandbanks and at times appeared to have splintered apart. In the delusional hyper-clear northern sunlight I half-expected to see windmills.

The next morning we checked out of the woodcutters' lodge. In the visitors' book I found a recent message from a Bavarian couple, 'We have discovered a second Mallorca!' and groaned.

So, all in all, turned out nice again, surely! Well, contrary to all expectations, the weather had been surprisingly hot. I even had a German tan! The countryside had been beautiful beyond my imagining. My eyes had been opened to an unknown corner of a country that maybe I knew even less about than I originally thought. 'Unknown', 'off the beaten track' – these were the holy grails of travel. Was I beginning to feel good about Germany and German life beginning to rub off on me? I was already dressing and undressing like a German. I had even grown some rather attractive facial hair.

But what was that gremlin in my mind holding me back from complete rapture?

There was nothing wrong with a place that worked, was clean, environmentally sensitive, quiet, wholesome and healthy. Indeed perhaps it was a little strange that these attributes in Germany should be seen as negative. If the weather could be guaranteed it might not even be long before Club Med opened up its first German resort on the Baltic. But it simply wasn't sexy or seductive, and I now realised I liked a bit more decadence, randomness and ruin on my travels.

'This is the problem. You are taking yourself with you, and all your problems and urban trappings. When you travel, you don't see the place, you are just trying to flee the polish of your first-world offices and identikit high streets.'

Of course, the problem lay at home, with me.

How do you make what is systemised, clean, honest and eco-logically sound – something yellow, even – seductive and sexy? If you were to personify most of the places we'd seen, Kühlungsborn in particular, they would be the unmade-up, frumpy German girl with practical clothes and pudding-bowl haircut (and maybe called Sigrun) who made people want to avoid sixth-form German exchanges. Protestant and laid bare; an open book and a *Fräulein* far from *fatale*.

'You see, holidays are like one-night stands! You are in thrall to the mystery and exoticism of the new. How often do you go back to places you've been before?

You generally like to use and abuse each new place, and move on to the next one lest some thread of mystery it might still retain disappears under the crowds of like-minded traveller-rapists.'

The German Baltic coast would be where I would want to return if I were a painter, a rambler, a naturalist or even a natur-ist – in search of isolation and purity. Its beauty was far superior to the Floridian banality of palm trees and starched aridity of much of the Med. And maybe climate change would work in its favour.

But for me it didn't deal enough in mystery and embrace baser metropolitan instincts, however crass. Although Italy, like most of the Mediterranean basin, was generally over made-up and superficially seductive, it kind of worked. And just as it was easy to tire of the Italians' obsession with '*figura*' and all that flattered to be what it was not, I now knew that it is also possible to tire of the honest German resistance to all things superficial. It was an earthy, anaemic, mustard yellow peasant-like rejection of urban gloss, the very opposite of '*figura*', that I had generally experienced at the German seaside. What might that be called? I asked myself. How about *Freikörperkultur*?

3

Selbstwahrnehmung

nf, *the search for oneself, becoming self-aware*

Manny greeted my return with characteristic effervescence.

'You see how the world opens up again once you have re-awoken your own self-awareness. There is no more efficient branding than personal experience.'

So maybe I was intrigued, perhaps for the first time in my life, by Germany. And perhaps my mind was a little more open. But so far it was hardly the vaunted lost horizon Manny had sold me, nor was I about to brag or evangelise about the virtues of bathing in the nude.

'Do you know the legend of Faust?' enquired Manny, moving on, changing suddenly to a tone of fragile calm.

Clearly I was about to hear it . . .

'Faust was a deep-thinking but frustrated man, looking for a secret that would unlock some greater understanding of the world. He was also, incidentally, German. It's the same for you. Your endless travelling is also a search for some greater understanding, of yourself and the world.'

Manny pointed to some lines of German verse on the wall of his office. It was a quotation from a guy called Goethe.

'But while Faust spent his time pursuing absolute knowledge through study' – and now Manny recited from memory, in German, his eyes closed in ecstasy – 'so you think you have travelled to every horizon. Or more likely to the limits of your own horizon. And you have both arrived at the same point: where you realise' – Manny continued to intersperse German quotes – 'you know nothing more than before. Despite all Faust's reading and despite all your movement, they have become just that – words and movement. There is still a missing link, a metaphysical void you need to fill. Faust was fed up with playing around with meaningless words, just as you are afraid that the world, by being so be-travelled by the masses, has ceased to have any meaning.'

He paused. This was getting too deep and abstract for me.

'Never mind this Faust bloke. I still don't see how Germany is going to help me with my . . . my Worldschmooze-thing!'

'Well, Faust tried to find a solution,' Manny persevered, 'by delving into black magic, and selling his soul to the devil . . .'

This was getting weird. Not just bare my body; did Manny now want me to sell my soul to Germany? I remembered my uneasiness standing by the Prora on Rügen and suddenly didn't much like my supposed *Doppelgänger* in *Weltschmerz*.

'But ultimately it was by learning to fall in love, by succumbing to the temptation of uncontrolled emotion, that Faust attained true understanding, and with it inner peace.'

Manny surely didn't think the secret lay in holiday romances! Although I liked the way he was thinking. Maybe I was supposed to find myself a pretty *Fräulein*?

'No!' exclaimed Manny, seeing my mind wander. 'The object of Faust's love, Margarete, was merely the gateway for discovering the passion, the violence and the suffering at the heart of an absolute, all-encompassing idea of love which in turn revealed the quintessent tragedy of the world.'

Blimey! But I wasn't looking for tragedy any more than I was

Germany. I was depressed enough as it was. But now Manny leant forward and stared demonically into my eyes. It seemed he might be liable to frequent mood swings.

'I am not talking about ordinary love. I am talking about the ability to wonder, exalt and be consumed and swept away by absolute Love, be it in the form of a person, a country or anything; and thereby reawaken your jaded soul!'

Manny's arm swept to another verse on the wall and his eyes closed in incantation: '"*By giving what is commonplace an exalted meaning, to what is ordinary a mysterious aspect, to what is familiar the impressiveness of the unfamiliar, to the finite an appearance of infinity;*"' then he slowed and clenched his eyes, measuring out the syllables as he uttered the last words, '"*thus I romanticise it.*"'

I coughed nervously.

'Romanticise!' shouted Manny. 'Novalis tells us we need to romanticise.'

Manny regained himself.

'You want me to romanticise Germany?' I said, sitting up and barely restraining a snigger. 'Romantic weekend in Frankfurt, anyone?'

'Typical!' Manny cried defensively. 'This is just part of the hypocrisy and prejudice with which you are spending the post-war package-tour age viewing Germany. Germany is simply off the map you tourists seek to conquer like it was some kind of world war.'

Steady on, Manny, I thought. Did you have to bring up the war? I was doing so well.

'Germany is a country that has had to bear the weight of over half a century of post-war British prejudice as outdated as a John Mills Christmas movie.'

There was something about Manny that didn't quite add up. He was no 'normal' consultant or shrink. There seemed to be some private agenda, some personal crusade. And then there were these funny mood swings between passion and clinical coldness.

'If you want to learn how to goosestep, come to Britain!' he continued, apparently incensed.

The theme from Mel Brooks's *The Producers* popped into my head: '*Springtime for Hitler and Germany/Goosestep's the new step today . . .*'

'You just can't seem to move on and can't resist an opportunity to scaremonger. With your clever reviews of German-built Minis with sat-nav that leads straight to Poland . . .'

I could do better than that. How about Bette Midler's line, 'I married a German. Every night I dress up as Poland and he invades me!'

Even in these castrated, politically correct times I felt bound to defend a proud British tradition of nation-bashing and playful xenophobia.

'They are only harmless jokes,' I pleaded.

'But it amounts to a racist slur! It is not tolerated to joke about Jews, Muslims or disabled people. But the Germans are clearly an *Untermensch*. And on the rare occasion someone does take offence at a Hitler joke it is on behalf of Jewish people! No, for you Brits Boche-bashing is a Pavlovian reflex.'

This wasn't just clinical diagnosis now. He sounded like a German foreign minister. Was Manny making a bid from his basement bunker to be the next German ambassador? Forget *Weltschmerz*. Manny seemed to want to cure me of some British psychosis about Germany.

'You Brits have so much baggage with Germany, it amounts to a special relationship! If you must have your stereotypes, then you should see them as indicators of a long, rich and healthy culture. Far better to be a nation with stereotypes than none at all.'

It was true. What did the world know of Paraguay or Taiwan? But Manny now wanted me not just to go on holiday to Germany but to romanticise it, to render Germany impressive and unfamiliar; when it was precisely a very accepted kind of familiarity and ordinariness about Germany, like the newfound unsexiness of its nudist beaches, that had probably bred such indifference among travellers.

'The point is,' insisted Manny, 'that however unique you are considering each of your previous travel experiences, they can all be reduced to a system of desires and prejudices. It is not Germany that is the problem. It is you and your system. This is why the magic and romance have disappeared. You need to desystematise yourself.'

How German! How *Vorsprung durch Technik*.

'I can help you firstly understand the system and in a series of steps unravel it. And at the same time I can help you re-learn the language of romance, re-romanticise your vision of the world and re-spark your wanderlust. You will go again to Germany, to where *Wanderlust* was invented. You will learn, as Novalis entreats, *"to give what is ordinary a mysterious aspect"*. Trust me. *Weltschmerz* will be cured. You will cast Germany in a new, exalted and unfamiliar light. And then you will see the world as new once again.'

Let me get this straight: so if I could enjoy Germany, then I could enjoy anything! Well, that figured.

Manny wandered over to the other side of the room, humming again under his breath, *"'What good's a first impression? It's just a first impression. If you knew her like I do. You would change your point of view.'"*

What was that tune? It was really bugging me now. Of course! It was one of the songs from *Cabaret*. '*Willkommen, bienvenue, velcome, to cabaret . . .*' Germany is a cabaret. Is that what he was saying? Of course, the quotation writ large in his reception, '*Leave your troubles outside.*' That was Joel Grey's camp MC at the beginning. '*"Life is disappointing?"*' he carried on. '*"Forget it! In Germany, life is bioodiful . . ."*' Was that the point? Manny made an unlikely conferencier! Unless they were doing a C&A night at the Kit Kat Klub.

'And in order to do so,' Manny continued, 'you have first to know the system!'

I was miles away in Bob Fosse's Berlin.

'As I said before, the Germans call it *Selbstwahrnehmung*.'

Manny's prosaic talk of systems brought me back down to earth.

'In a series of modules I am going to deconstruct the ingredients that make up the branding of nations, and the values which you as the modern, young, affluent consumer – for, believe me, you are no real Traveller, not yet! – require from your travel experiences: sun, good food, parties, humour, sex, beautiful nature, pop culture, health, child-friendliness and escape. That's all there is to you at the moment. You unconsciously seek all these "values" on your travels and score countries by them like on some travel index.'

Now I didn't just have *Weltschmerz*. A throb in my head told me I had *Kopfschmerz*.

'It is ridiculous to reduce a nation – particularly Germany! – a whole culture, thousands of years, to a formula. But, you see, this is the very system which you have to cast off. Remember Goethe and Novalis. Romance is the only commandment. If you can walk out with magic in your heart, then you will have been through more transformation than any brand can give you. If you want a bit of *Sturm und Drang* back in your life, then go to Germany!'

Who were Sturm and Drang? Didn't they make hi-fis?

'I am going to set you on a journey of German self-awakening; a journey to the source and meaning of the great life concepts and ideas the great German mind has bequeathed to the world. Are you ready?'

Did I have a choice?

'Then take this.'

Manny handed over a thick folder. Not surprisingly, it was yellow.

'In here is a map and a series of modules, each a separate journey dealing with one of the Values of Travel, those prejudices you have to deconstruct. You have already done the first module, about your dependence on sun, sea and sand. And so maybe you will see that Germany can be judged favourably by the rest of them also.'

I looked with dread at my homework.

'Each module contains a suggested itinerary and some historical and cultural references you must explore.'

'Suggested itinerary', 'historical fact boxes', 'must-see sights'. Manny was to be my *Baedeker*. But I loathed guidebooks!

'I want you to write down your thoughts and experiences for each module so we can analyse them together as you go along.'

Wasn't that what Freud did with his patients? I really was becoming a case. What did he have in mind? Not *Das Boot* but *Das Buch*? Or perhaps *My Struggle with Germany*.

'Trust me.'

Surely a clear sign that I should do the opposite.

Was I, who prided myself on keeping the most open of minds, volunteering to go on holiday to Germany not just once, but several times? Well, now, after a bit of enforced reflection, I knew that Mercedes cars were being slammed for their unreliability and shoddy workmanship. Meanwhile at VW there were stories of backhanders between top executives and union leaders, and junkets to Paris hotels in order to bed Brazilian prostitutes. There was even a referee corruption scandal in German football. What was happening to those boring German qualities of precision and honesty? More to the point, where had all this Latin flair for creative accounting and mistresses suddenly come from? The VW bosses and Boris Becker's antics in a restaurant broom cupboard had probably done more than any marketeering to make

Germany seem a more colourful place. Maybe Germany was a fun place after all?

But really, a cabaret? As Sally Bowles would say in her own darkest moments of *Weltschmerz*, 'What good is sitting alone in your room . . .' It was time to face the German music. Painfully I dredged up the title of my German grammar book at school: *Los!*

4

Angst

nf, *fear, anxiety, anguish*

'So, you have done the warm-up. Like any physical exercise, *Wanderlust* requires a little stretching in order to open the mind.'

What was this? Pilates for travellers?

'Now perhaps you are ready for some serious mental exercise?' said Manny, raising a patronising eyebrow and pausing portentously.

'Is the Pope German?' I said under my breath.

'Germany is a land of great thinkers,' declared Manny.

I couldn't help thinking of that joke: a young German coastguard recruit nervously takes over the shift in the control room. Almost immediately the tannoy emits a call for help from an English ship. 'May Day, May Day! We are sinking!' The spotty new boy composes himself and leans towards the microphone and stammers his response: 'Er . . . vot are you sinking . . . about?'

'A country of big ideas . . .'

And didn't the world know it!

'And the greatest of these ideas was Romanticism.'

I had already witnessed nudism. Now I saw visions of leather and thigh-slapping. I couldn't think of a less romantic place.

'Nowadays "romantic" means a candlelit dinner for two, a slow squeeze to "Careless Whisper" on the dancefloor, roses sold by restaurant hawkers, or a dirty weekend by the sea. "Romantic" has become the bleeding-heart strains of the latest boy-band ballad, the pre-inscribed platitudes on greetings cards or the toilet graffiti of adolescent boys and girls. But this is not what it was originally.'

And so Manny sent me to where it all began.

Heidelberg sits nestled in a thickly wooded valley at the northern edge of the Black Forest in the south-west corner of Germany. The River Neckar flows serenely past the old city walls, drops mellifluously over a weir and carries swans and maybe an early morning scull under a rhythmic sequence of ornate stone bridges. Behind verdant screens of trees nest the turrets, gables and follies of aristocratic villas. On the other side the city's Altstadt is laid out in layers of cobbled streets, squares of neatly pollarded plane trees and secretive back alleys, all lined by a mix of grand classical public buildings and the warped but beautifully maintained beams of half-timbered houses, these housing the succession of bars that lubricate the lively student population. The Altstadt is but the foreground for the city's centrepiece. More grand and fanciful villas climb the steep hillside, as if standing on top of one another, until a plateau is reached. Here stand the pinky-grey sandstone ruins of Heidelberg's once great and still imperious castle, a long, asymmetrical and *trompe l'oeil* accumulation of turreted fortress, complete with dungeons and cellars, fallen towers and hollow shells. The wind whistles through façades where the rest of the construction has fallen away, leaving only a screen of gargoyles and statuary; the whole thing draped in the ivy of centuries and the jewellery of neglect, such is the accidental splendour with which nature is able to adorn man's most planned but otherwise naked designs. I was becoming a bit gushing and romantic already, just looking at it!

This was the seductively decaying state in which a group of Germany's poets discovered it at the end of the eighteenth century. Twice sacked by the French and abandoned as a seat of power, the castle possessed a languour, through its setting of river, cliffs and forests, that was to become the founding image of the Romantic soul and artistic movement. What Manny referred to in his notes as the Romantics' *Sinnbild*: '*The eighteenth century was the age of the Enlightenment, an age dominated by reason, science, the birth of the dictionary and the encyclopedia, and by an intellectual elite who applied rigid thought systems to ethics, aesthetics and logic. Emotions were suppressed.*'

That all changed when in 1774 a book was published by an unknown young German author called Johann Wolfgang von Goethe. It was entitled *The Sorrows of the Young Werther* and through a series of letters to a friend it told the story of a young man, Werther, and his unrequited and all-consuming adolescent love for a woman he could not possess. It ended with Werther taking his own life at the injustice and misery of it all. Based on the author's own love for the attractively named Charlotte Buff, it was an overnight best-seller and spawned a generation of adolescents who paraded around in the flowing bohemian clothes the dapper Werther wore in the book. It wasn't the subject matter of love that was new. This gushing, populist and comparatively lightweight tale was the first Mills & Boon, the Bridget Jones of the eighteenth century. It was the first Romantic novel. There were a reported two thousand suicides in what must surely be the first instance of copycat self-immolation. Goethe went on to write up the legend of my companion-in-anguish, Faust. But he had opened the emotional sluice gates for a generation of artists who put teenage *Angst* at the heart of their every work. They were the Romantics. And they were German.

So here I stood, at the wonderwall of the first Romantics, blushing in the late evening light. In previous centuries this had been one of Germany's star attractions, which had made it a once-beloved destination of travellers.

'Did you know that Germany was the first overseas package tour destination of the English?' Manny's words rang in my ear.

Surely not!

But it was true. Before becoming a travel agent Thomas Cook was a Baptist lay preacher big on temperance. He thought people should get out more to stop them drinking and so harnessed the transport innovations of the Industrial Revolution to offer cultural excursions for the masses. The nightmare of modern tourism started as social reform.

It began with local and national trips, to places such as the 1851 Great Exhibition at London's Crystal Palace. Then in 1855 the temperate one realised he could make a mint out of social reform. He offered his disciples the possibility, for the princely sum of eight pounds, of taking a trip down the River Rhine past Cologne to Mainz and thereafter to Heidelberg, the spa resort of Baden-Baden and Strasbourg, which was then a German city. Destinations previously accessible only to aristos on their Victorian Grand Tour now became accessible to the masses. Paris, Switzerland, Italy and Egypt all came later.

Thomas Cook was to blame for my *Weltschmerz*, for the traffic jams of tacky cruise ships down the Nile and queues along the Inca Trail!

The British love affair with Germany did not end with the Great War. Germany was given the benefit of the doubt and people did not quite believe the war had been Germany's fault, nor (yet) that war was an endemic German trait. Inspired by their romance, Heidelberg and other places in Germany had become favourite haunts and stop-offs of English-speaking writers and painters. Turner was bewitched by Heidelberg's light, the constantly changing hues of its buildings and the variety of picturesque perspectives afforded by the bridges and hills. When in 1880 Mark Twain tramped through he wrote, 'One thinks Heidelberg by day the last possibility of the beautiful, but when he sees Heidelberg by night, a fallen Milky Way, he requires time to consider upon the verdict.'

As in Oxford or Cambridge and other university towns in Britain, student life in Heidelberg is apt to take over the town. Heidelberg's *Kneipe* (pubs) are generally packed with eternal students slaking their insatiable thirsts. That night I witnessed a British-style drinking session, complete with drinking games, tactical chundering and, for the last man left standing, the title of Bierkönig: king of the beers. There wasn't much *Angst* on display among these heirs of the young Werther.

Heidelberg's students seem to have earned themselves a wide berth from the local constabulary too. The party atmosphere, complete with vomit and rattling bottles, spilt out on to the streets as rowdy cliques sung their way home, supporting one another on their shoulders. Bikes were strung up on lamp-posts, friends dared one another to car-walk along entire streets. There was even a healthy queue at a midnight kebab shop. I could have been back in England. And it would have been rude not to join in. I fell in with a group of raucous revellers celebrating a birthday. They put their arms around me and didn't seem to care who or what nationality I was, let alone what language I spoke. As long as I could say 'Cheers' and keep up with the beers. They invited me to gatecrash a party in one of the old town's half-timbered houses. Except access couldn't be gained by the front door. So I found myself indulging in a local tradition of night-walking, halfway up a drainpipe above a wheelie bin, being pushed and pulled in hysterics through a half-open lavatory window.

The next morning I was tickled to see that the staff of one of the statues in the ruined shell of the castle had been replaced by the leg of a chair, the original presumably standing as a drinking trophy in some student's rooms. It reminded me of the chair leg that sits in the right hand of Henry VIII above the entrance to Trinity College, Cambridge.

Slightly the worse for wear the next morning I returned, with a large black coffee, to Manny's notes: '*Romantic artists sought to provoke strong responses in their audiences by summoning emotions such as horror, joy, fear and trepidation. This they did with a technique they called* Sturm und Drang.' Ah, so it was the artistic equivalent of George W. Bush's 'shock and awe', but for the creation of forceful poetry, not the ousting of dictators. '*At the end of the eighteenth century it was a radical change from the reserve of the Enlightenment. It expressed rebellion against authority, disillusionment with society.*' Long before the 1960s there was an *Angst*-ridden teenager stalking behind a hoodie in Heidelberg.

So the Romantics were all about the enormity of the universe and the minuscule importance of man. They also had a cheerful view of the essential tragedy and futility of human existence. '*Hitherto the world had been conveniently explained by one thought system or another which always contained a God. This God stood outside the human plane and was a fundamentally benign reference point. The Romantics, asked "What if there is no God? You might have found a way to explain the outside world, but what is this void, this infinity inside my heart?"*' Insperience. Infinity. I recalled Manny's therapy practice. He really was a true Romantic!

'*The Romantics found in Mother Nature the symbols of their simultaneous woe and elation.*' I'd seen the great German love of nature in the ramblers and environmentalism on the Baltic coast. Now Manny was sending me on a tour of three 'paradigms of nature' that were apparently seared into the German consciousness: a mountain, a river and a forest.

There was a mountain whose bare name causes a stir in the souls and *Lederhosen* of Germans. It rises in the forested Harz mountains at the country's very heart. As long as the German Democratic Republic existed it lay tantalisingly beyond the reach of so many Germans but nowadays they flock to its bare peak as if it were a Croatian nudist beach.

The Brocken is only 1142 metres high, but it symbolises to Germans a pagan and peasant-like tree-hugging past and it is here on its peak that every year on the night of 30 April they celebrate the pagan festival of Walpurgisnacht, which heralds the arrival of 'nature's greatest moment', spring. They celebrate by lighting bonfires on top of the mountain and recreating the dancing and revelry of the witches who, legend has it, met there to commune with their gods. The whole festival is a celebration of ghosts and the supernatural, of emotion over reason. Fittingly, as I gathered from an excerpt Manny had kindly quoted for me in his dossier, it takes centre stage in Goethe's *Faust* as the poet-protagonist seeks to abandon reason and knowledge in search of the quintessence of the world and true Love.

Then there was the Rhine *'with its legends of hidden gold, dwarves, giants and heroes, and the forces of love, jealousy and power which Wagner turned into the ultimate Romantic work in his epic opera, the Ring'*. On one particularly postcard-worthy horseshoe bend of the river near the city of Koblenz stands the Lorelei rock, *'a cornerstone of the romantic imagination and immortalised by the poet Heinrich Heine'*, but now, for my money, an unremarkable mound and more cornerstone of mass tourism. The rock takes its name from the nymph *fatale* 'with golden comb so lustrous' who is supposed to have lured sailors to their death on her treacherous rocks with her tuneful murmuring. Surely another incarnation of our anti-hero Werther's impossible love. But now she just lures hapless boat- and busloads of rucksacked and fluoro-gear-clad tourists into her midst and sadly there is no danger of the polluting excursion boats floundering. If anything, the Lorelei had reawoken my *Weltschmerz*. Nevertheless, with its castles, ravines, forests and legends, and still today the huge, heavily-laden cargo barges ploughing their way up and down at the slow pace of a bygone Romantic age, the Rhine was a river to fire the imagination.

And finally there was the great and noble tree, not just a symbol of Romanticism but a symbol of the beginning of the German nation.

For Germany, I now learnt, was born in a forest. Near Detmold, south of Hanover, to be precise. Here lies a dense swath of forest known as the Teutoburger Wald where a battle took place that is considered by Germans as the moment the German people was born.

Unwittingly, I had already seen many times over the Oscar-nominated Hollywood version of this battle. *Gladiator* opens with the words, 'In the winter of AD 180 Emperor Marcus Aurelius' twelve-year campaign against the barbarian tribes in Germania was drawing to a close.' We then go to a close-up on Russell Crowe, a member of that other barbarian tribe, the Australians, with a stylish stole of wolf skin round his shoulders. He has sent a messenger into the forest to offer the Germans the chance to negotiate. But the messenger is returned minus his head and the leader of the Germans, a leather-clad and hairy giant swinging a mace in one hand and the severed head in the other, emerges before the Roman front line making defiant bellowing calls in words of one syllable and decidedly low German. Whatever he's saying he means war and from the forests come the supporting cries and grunts of a ramshackle army of other Germans, all with clubs and luxuriant facial hair and showing the same early propensity for leather. 'At my signal unleash hell'. Fireballs and ignited arrows rain down in a blitz of high-budget pyrotechnics, the Germans are slain and the battle is won.

The film's extended blood-curdling action tells the story of what was surely the first bout of Boche-bashing in history. Would that it had actually turned out that way. As usual, Hollywood has a loose relationship with the facts. The truth is that the Romans never really got to grips with the Germanic tribes on the margins of their empire and never would.

It was AD 9. In what is now Germany, on the fringes of Gaul

and the north-eastern edge of their empire, the Romans had established colonies in what are now Mainz, Trier and Cologne. Beyond the Rhine lay a thick, dark forest which was a bit scary. It was full of barbarians, as the Romans called anyone who was not within their control and only capable of stringing together the syllables 'bar-bar-bar'.

A brown-nosing Roman apparatchik named Publius Quinctilius Varus took the position of governor of Germania and proceeded to order the Germans around, extracting money from them as if they were vassals. But those cunning Germans decided to feign deference to Roman civilisation and lull the Romans into thinking they were educating their witless and uncultured subjects. This was all the masterplan of one general, Arminius, chief of one of the tribes, the Cheruschi. Crucially, he spoke fluent Latin, thereby displaying an early German flair for others' languages. And this enabled him to be taken into the enemy's confidence. Until the right moment arrived . . .

Arminius told Varus of an imaginary rebellion that was being planned by the Chauci, a barbarian tribe in the north-west. Varus salivated at the prospect of a glorious victory and more crucial brownie points in Rome. And so he dispatched three of his strongest legions, the SAS of Roman soldiers, to show them who was boss.

The Kalkriese is nowadays a harmless-looking meadow surrounded by gently undulating hills in the heart of the featureless state of Niedersachsen. But two thousand years ago it was boggy and surrounded by trees that were perfect for an ambush. Arminius had rounded up all his various Germanic tribesmen with their assorted weaponry and they attacked mercilessly, egged on from the touchlines, according to observers, by women baring their chests at any sign of flagging to encourage their menfolk to earn the carnal spoils of war.

The battle was a bloody one that did much to form the image of Germans as barbaric and bloodthirsty thugs. The Roman writer Tacitus wrote an account of Germany which conveys the Asterix-like view of the life forms that lived across the Rhine and this would have been doing the rounds of the Romans baths. The natives were a bunch of uncouth, hirsute, leather jock-strap sporting and tree-hugging Neanderthals a long way from inventing the Audi. He writes of their 'wild blue eyes, reddish hair and huge frames that excel only in violent effort'. Boris Becker? And he commented on their bellicose tendencies – 'no form of approval can carry more honour than praise expressed by arms' – and the fact that they had 'no taste for peace'. 'Who would leave Asia, Africa or Italy to visit Germany, with its unlovely scenery, its bitter climate, its general dreariness to sense and eye?' Clearly, as long ago as two millennia Germany was struggling to attract tourists.

But the Kalkriese witnessed the biggest single defeat ever suffered by the Romans – some thirty thousand soldiers and Roman civilians perished – and afterwards Rome never attempted to subdue the *Schwein* beyond the Rhine ever again. Ridley Scott's battle of AD 190 (filmed in quietest Surrey) never took place. If the *Daily Mirror* had been writing the headlines the next morning it would surely have read, 'For you, Varus, ze vor is over.' And, like the paper's editor Piers Morgan, Varus fell on his sword.

'The Teutoburger Wald is important because eighteen hundred years later, in the era of the Romantics, it would be identified by Romantic nation-makers as the beginning of the idea of a German nation.'

Today in the middle of the Teutoburger forest rises a twenty-eight-metre, copper-green statue of Arminius, now Hermann, to mark the Hermannsschlacht (Hermann's Slaughter). Dressed in a leather skirt and showing a bit of thigh, with his sword raised he faces south, in defiance of Rome. Standing on a bombastic gazebo-like stone plinth at least as high as the statue itself, the Hermannsdenkmal is as bold a statement of German nationalism as you can find in Germany (or indeed in America, where the identical New Ulm Hermann monument in Minnesota – much bigger than the original, of course – is the adopted symbol of all Americans of German descent). It is the German equivalent of Nelson's column.

So the forest was a symbol of Romanticism but also one of German nationhood. And the same was therefore true of Heidelberg castle, the Rhine, the Lorelei rock and the Brocken. They were the ingredients of a mythology for a nation not yet born.

'*The desire for a German nation did not exist until the end of the eighteenth century and it was very much a by-product of Romanticism. Hitherto the Germans had been a collection of disparate feuding states fighting wars among themselves. Germans envied France its patrie, and Britain's long-established kingdom. Spain and Portugal, although in relative meltdown, had both had empires. Now they'd seen the French revolution and how people power could work, why couldn't they have a Heimat themselves?*'

Heimat. Wasn't that the name of an interminable German film saga? Yes, and the word for a sense of homeland, belonging, nostalgia and national identity. Yet it was, at the time it was first coined, in the late eighteenth century, a place that didn't exist. *Heimat* is an abstract place, the refuge for a lost soul, lost people, and a shrine made up of symbols and imaginary tales. It sounded a bit like the Promised Land.

Suddenly every German tree came to symbolise *Heimat* and none more so than the Deutsche Eiche, or German Oak. Germany's architecture, like the grandiose villas above Heidelberg's old town, went through a crazed and flamboyant Historicist phase of appropriating details – towers, turrets, neo-Gothic buttresses and spikes – thought to belong to Germany's quintessential past. The confluence of the Rhine and the Moselle at Koblenz, in the heart of the Rhine valley, was named the

Deutsches Eck, the most German corner of Germany and the ultimate German sight, complete with a statue of the Kaiser. And near Regensburg, in deepest, forested Bavaria, Germany's most wilful attempt to make a play for an ancient, classical heritage was constructed: the Walhalla, a German Hall of Fame built in marble in the style of the Parthenon in Athens. Except that inside are not mythical, pagan gods and goddesses, but the marble busts of the deities of German Romantic myth-making, the people who sum up what it is to be German: Martin Luther, Albert Einstein, Konrad Adenauer, Kaiser Willy.

A contemporary and instrumental part of Germany's push to become a nation were the Heidelberg *Burschenschaften*. These were closed student societies each representing a different region of Germany and reflecting the respective provenance of the students who flocked to the city's fabled university. The *Burschenschaften* were set up after the liberation of large parts of Germany from Napoleon in the early nineteenth century and became politically active and physically militant bodies in favour of a united nation of German peoples. In his sojourn in Heidelberg back in 1880 Mark Twain encountered the local tradition of the *Mensur*, a form of fencing duel carried out between the various *Burschenschaften*, and commented on how it was seen as a sign of manhood and desirability to the ladies to carry a wound under the eye or on the cheek. '*Burschenschaften*' translates roughly as 'youths' association' and had overtones of later nationalist-militant German youth movements. Tacitus had noted of early Germans that 'no form of approval can carry more honour than praise expressed by arms'. We were back in the woods with the barbarians.

Either way it was clear that two fundamental events were taking place in Germany at the same time as the nineteenth century dawned. Not just the adolescent *Angst* of Werther spawning an outpouring of emotion, but the simultaneous growing pains of a nation. And the two together were a heady mix.

Today the colours and coats of arms of the *Burschenschaften* still fly above their halls of residences. They retain a masonic, old-school-tie entry policy but membership is no longer based on which part of Germany you are from. They still have their head-quarters in some of the most grandiose and florid villas in Heidelberg's Altstadt and offer student accommodation together with allegiance to one or other sporting and drinking club. It is a collegiate system unique in Germany and much closer to British university life. I wondered if I had unwittingly spent that drunken evening in the company of some of Heidelberg's true *Burschen*. It certainly explained the familiarity of the drinking games.

Was I feeling Romantic yet? There was something mysterious about this powerful and brooding sense of German nationhood attached to elemental forces. But I didn't feel comfortable exalting it. And paradoxically, having once or twice taken it a bit far, nor do the Germans any more.

When it comes to *Selbstwahrnehmung*, no nation has done more to examine its conscience about its past than Germany. In the words of the hit TV show *Yes Minister*, Britain went into the European Community 'to screw the French by splitting them off from the Germans. The French went in to protect their inefficient farmers from commercial competition. The Germans went in to cleanse themselves of genocide and apply for readmission to the human race.'

Not surprisingly for a nation of thinkers, Germans have turned self-examination into a way of life and an almost daily deconstruction of their very soul. I thought of Harry Enfield's post-war caricature of Jürgen the German, imposing himself on strangers and demanding acceptance of his apology for his nation's conduct in the war. This was self-examination taken to a fascist extreme. They even have one of their word-monuments for it: *Vergangenheitsbewältigung* (literally, 'conquering the past' but meaning 'coming to terms with the past'). No wonder psychotherapy was invented in the German language.

Germany's Nobel Prize-winning novelist Günther Grass campaigned vigorously for decades after the war for other Germans to face up to their past, only to wait until 2006 for his own personal moment of *Vergangenheitsbewältigung*, revealing in his autobiography that he was once a fully paid-up member of the SS.

Looking out from the hilltop over Heidelberg's castle and the misty Neckar valley, I recalled Manny's words: 'The true Romantic soul is a restless soul who can only find fleeting satisfaction by the journey to some other place.'

Not surprisingly for a people in search of a nation, the notion of the *Wanderer*, the Traveller, loomed large for the Romantics. The lack of a *Heimat* provoked feelings of *Heimweh*, pangs for a homeland.

Heimweh? That wasn't far off Heimway, the name of Manny's syndrome. I paused but then dismissed the thought.

'The feeling of restlessness chimed perfectly with themes of unrequited love and being misunderstood by society and the world at large.'

Did that go for the German people as a whole then? Misunderstood, searching for itself? On this basis alone Germany was most definitely Romantic.

'This state of restlessness was characterised by Sehnsucht' – another German word-concept. German was full of them – '*a longing, for something better, for completion and for some absolute state of rest and perfection that is destined not to be achieved. In 1818 Caspar David Friedrich*' – he of the 'white cliffs of Rügen' – '*painted a picture which sums up the idea of the Romantic Traveller . . .*'

I recalled that this painting had hung in Manny's office, in pride of place behind his desk. *Wanderer über dem Nebelmeer* portrayed a shaggy red-haired young man, in a three-quarter-length felt coat, staff in hand, standing astride the peak of a craggy mountain surveying a vast landscape of mountains and rocky outcrops beneath him, all covered in a swirling mist. This was presumably a Werther figure, a romantic hero, a loner and adventurer, rebellious and free, ploughing his own furrow outside society's conventions and thinking himself above them. He was also a traveller in search of the spirit of the German people. Friedrich's painting captured the paradigm of the *Wanderer* and was a *Sinnbild* of the German Romantic desire for travel. Or *Wanderlust*.

'The original Romantic *Wanderlust* was the first instance of travel for travel's sake, as opposed to pilgrimage, exile or expulsion,' said Manny later. 'The Germans were the original travellers, knapsack over the shoulder and crook in hand.'

Maybe that was why their word, '*Rucksack*', curiously spoddy and unworldly, had passed into English to mean 'backpack'.

'But originally it was not the fluorescent, multi-toggled eyesore it has become, nor the whole house you would-be trekkers carry around like snails. It was a simpler, humbler and more self-sufficient container for life's essentials. And it could be worn casually over just one shoulder, not two, as if you were going to school!'

One strap or two. That seemed like a fair distinction between tourists and real travellers!

Friedrich's Traveller was me! He encapsulated all those things Manny had accused me of in my attitude to travel: that elitist sense of having unique insight, of being above it all, a loner wanting to forge my own unique path, a path devoid of tourists.

'Ah-ha, but he was also a man looking at the world and seeing it for the first time, with wonder and awe and, perhaps most importantly of all, on foot! You see "*wandern*" means specifically "to roam about on foot". On this journey you will learn the German way. Real *Wanderlust* means picking up the electricity of Mother Earth through your body and in natural time without the distorting effects of high-speed travel. Today you just drop out of the air in a preordained place with no sense of the journey. You must learn to walk again!'

I had already seen on the Baltic coast how the Germans loved their nature trails and how so much of the country was only accessible to them. Then I recalled how envious I had always been of travellers such as Laurie Lee and Patrick Leigh Fermor, who in the 1930s had been able to walk through Europe on foot. Could that be done nowadays in the age of planes, trains and automobiles? Maybe Manny had a point.

I learnt that Goethe was arguably the first of the modern travellers, travelling to Italy long before Byron got his Inter-Rail ticket. His *Italienische Reise* unleashed German eulogies to the elusive *dolce vita* which still have not abated to this day. '*But German* Wanderlust *was not restricted to the German-speaking lands. It was also characterised by* Fernweh *(pangs for what is far away and the opposite of* Heimweh*).*' Ah, so that's why they were always invading other people's beaches. According to Manny, as if I needed confirmation that they are generally everywhere, Germans take more overseas holidays per capita than any other people in the world.

'And do you know what book those first Thomas Cook tourists used to guide them around the Rhineland and other countries outside Germany?' Manny asked proudly.

Started in 1827, the neat red volumes published by Karl Baedeker, a bookseller in Koblenz, were apparently the world's first guidebooks, not only fashionable accompaniments to leisure travellers but also synonymous with unerring German accuracy. With their crimson leather binding, gilt-edged pages and 'olde' script maps, the originals were fine objects, symbolising the civility of a golden age of cultured travel. But Baedeker had unleashed another Frankenstein's monster. The garish, photo-packed guides of today were frankly an embarrassment to be seen carrying around and a major ingredient of my *Weltschmerz*.

'*With its emphasis already on walking and respect for nature*

German Wanderlust *was also about a certain kind of self-suffi-ciency.'*

Germany's best-selling writer of all time is apparently not Goethe or some other literary giant, but a man called Karl Friedrich May (pronounced 'my'). Living in the latter half of the nineteenth century, Karl May was a teacher who spent most of his life in jail for petty theft and fraud. By all accounts he had a psychopathic, Munchausenesque tendency to lie but turned this to creative use in his prison cell, from where he imagined the whole world of the Wild West that he had never visited, nor ever would. He wrote dozens of mythical Wild West novels featuring Winnetou, the wise chief of an Apache tribe, and Old Shatterhand, his white blood-brother and May's alter ego, that are now an essential part of every German's home library. But this is not cowboys and Indians. Old Shatterhand is a Romantic hero, a noble savage full of undogmatic, Christian feelings and empathy for the Indians as the victims of white aggression. The stories are less action or adventure than contemplative, philo-sophical, even mystical tales, full of respect for nature, native culture and the need for self-sufficiency. The good guys in May's novels are also all of German descent.

By all accounts May has become a cult. There is an open-air festival in Bad Segeberg in northern Germany where every year thousands of feather-clad and painted Indians and Shatterhands meet up and May's Wild West is acted out. In 2001 *Der Schuh des Manitu*, a comedy spoof of the Karl May–Winnetou style, broke the German box-office record.

Manny had included a sample novel in my therapy pack. It was revealing. On the surface Karl May's tales had nothing to do with Germany. But in their expression of nostalgia for a purer, more innocent – barbarian? – world of self-sufficient roaming and communing with nature they seemed to paint a pretty accu-rate portrait of the German psyche.

*

So Romanticism was originally German. But what about today? Was modern Germany Romantic? I didn't see many felt-coated fops wandering around. These days Werther wears Hugo Boss. But I did sense something introverted, all-consuming and anguished.

When the Germans sat down to think about what slogan would best represent their nation to visitors to the 2006 World Cup, they came up with *Deutschland – Land der Ideen* (Germany – Land of Ideas). For this nation of *Angst*-ridden thinkers it will have been the subject of much fraught deliberation. One of them, the German philosopher Arthur Schopenhauer, noted that 'it is a curious failing in the German people that they search in the clouds for what lies at their feet,' and the image of the *Fahrradmann*, or 'bicycleman', was coined to describe a people whose thoughts and actions were disconnected. That figured, I thought, remembering all those man-bicycles on the Baltic.

'A recent Ulster University survey found Germans, at 107, have the highest average IQ in the world. Germans spend a lot of time exercising their grey matter and have consequently bequeathed to the world some of mankind's greatest ideas.'

They sure had the complex language for it. Wasn't it Twain, during his Heidelberg sojourn, who once quipped he would rather decline two drinks than one German adjective?

Following this, Manny took me on a little historical tour of the German brain: '*In 1516 the Western world looked obediently and without individual reflection towards Rome and the Pope for its guidance. Catholicism reigned supreme and a succession of corrupt Popes spinning Indulgences had grown steadily fatter and built palaces to their greed. Meanwhile the rest of Europe was poor, diseased and illiterate.*'

Up in the north-eastern German town of Wittenberg lived an educated but disaffected young monk called Martin Luther. Being German, he was 'sinking deeply', carrying the weight of

Catholic injustice on his shoulders and dreaming of a better world for all. One night in October 1517 he decided to vent his *Angst* and, using the accepted method for initiating a public debate in those days, nailed ninety-five protests against the church to the door of his local chapel. These ninety-five protests would become the foundations of Protestantism. And, in a way the young Luther could scarcely imagine, they would change the world for ever.

Luther set out a radical vision of the enlightened individual who has his own direct relationship with God in a local church without deference to Rome. He translated the Bible into German so that people could read it and for the first time think for themselves. But his actions had far-reaching ramifications. They paved the way for the challenging of all the accepted social hierarchies. This started with the Peasants' Revolt in 1524, the greatest mass rising the European continent had ever witnessed. Nations aligned themselves against one another behind either Catholicism or this new way of thinking, giving rise to the Spanish Inquisition and Monty Python's greatest sketch, the English Civil War and the sacking of Heidelberg castle. Fought out principally on German soil, this religious schism was the biggest single cause of bloodshed and strife among the country's feuding states for the next three hundred years.

The Protestant Reformation had profound effects throughout society. Books, reading and scholarship were encouraged and became more widespread. Schools flourished and the disciplines of contemplation and philosophy emerged, while scientific research, the ultimate meeting with God's own matter, became the embodiment of this newfound freedom to think. Faith was something to be experienced, not preached. This gave birth to the Romantic cult of the individual, while Protestant-powered scientific *Vorsprung* led Europe into the Enlightenment. And the sheer number of inventions the Germans bequeathed to the world was startling.

Manny had given me a copy of a little yellow book called *Fifty German inventors every German should have heard of*. It was a German joint business and government initiative aimed at jolting the German people out of the national depression they'd been wallowing in more than usual of late. It was being distributed to German schools and universities to reassure pupils that Germany invented the world and to encourage a little more inventiveness. There was Gottlieb Daimler, who invented the car; Rudolf Diesel and his engine; X-ray technology courtesy of Herr Röntgen; and the Zeppelin, the original stairway-to-heaven airship. One or two were a surprise to me: Felix Hoffmann and the first aspirin pill in 1897 and Henrich Focke's first helicopter in 1936; some controversial: apparently it was not our Alexander Graham Bell who invented the telephone but Philipp Reis in 1859; and some of dubious worth: the Berliner *Currywurst* and *Gummibärchen* jellybabies.

With Protestantism the concept of work was also revolutionised. Before Luther work was viewed merely as a way to stave off the Catholic sin of sloth. But Protestants thought you could work your way to heaven. 'Be lazy and be damned.' Not only that, reinvesting your gain and working still harder was encouraged. And thus the entrepreneurial capitalist spirit was born. It was Karl Marx, a German, who wrote *Das Kapital*. And a German, Max Weber, one of the founders of sociology in the nineteenth century, declared that Protestantism showed our universal understanding that the accumulation of wealth, the rat race, was the purpose of life. '*Arbeit macht Frei*,' as Hitler would later say. In the early seventeenth century John Winthrop and the first Protestants arrived in the United States and the whole American Constitution and indeed the go-west pioneering American Dream with its MBA-kid business geniuses is arguably underpinned by the German Protestant work ethic, as were the original white settlers and trekkers of South Africa – noted for their harsh pragmatism, the majority of whom were not Dutch but German.

How ironic that religion, normally so shy of worldly possessions, should have ultimately turned possessions into a religion in themselves. How strange that what in Luther's mouth were once radical thoughts are now the conservative dogma of George W. Bush and Bible-belt America.

Well, the Germans are famously hard-working and efficient, and now I knew why. German companies, from BMW and Bertelsmann to Deutsche Bank, seemed to rule the world. German companies own the highest percentage of real estate of any country within London's Square Mile including, most recently, Norman Foster's Gherkin. All Luther wanted was to stop having to pay the Papacy through the nose. But he has a lot to answer for!

Well! I'd scarcely thought that I would find myself musing on religion. I'd never really considered Germany to be a particularly religious place. Sure, Italy or France with their madonnas, cathedrals and more villages called 'Santa' this or that than grottoes in a Christmas shopping mall. And yet this was the country I now knew also charged its citizens a church tax. Well, if that wasn't an indulgence . . .

But this was it! I could now put my finger on that feeling I had tried to analyse at the end of my FKK holiday. FKK said that clothes could be attractive and arousing and that this was therefore bad. But wasn't that the point of a bikini, that it gave something 'an exalted meaning' or 'mysterious aspect'? FKK seemed to be the opposite of Romantic. Either way, for a German it was not a seductive state of nakedness of the flesh but an expression of philosophy and a return to a sort of fetal innocence. Certainly there was something conceptual, transparent, honest and direct – you could say straight-up – about FKK that made it sound inherently German. It was Protestantism on a sun-lounger.

The Protestant finds bland nudity instinctively preferable to the tasselled nipples of carnival dancers. And as a result the trains in his country run on time, he rides a bike, it is cleaner, people work harder and everything generally works. In contrast to Catholic countries, where that is the exception. Take Brazil, home of the carnival of carnivals. They may have the pseudo-socialist all-South American slogan '*Ordem e progreso*' on their flag, but if you're Brazilian, when it comes to actually sorting out some 'order and progress' you think, I'll leave that to somebody else. Or, in fact, as they did, why not get some Germans in to do it for us? They're good at *Vorsprung*.

Compare a Protestant church with a Catholic one. The first is austere and more simply furnished than the second. Bare, you could say naked, stonework versus saints, iconography and gold leaf. One plain, the other a bit garish. It is the difference between a revealed, exterior idea of religion and a private, cerebral one; one based on guilt, confession, forgiveness and an imagined future, the other based on personal responsibility, the tangible here and now, and working to avoid sinning in the first place. That meant the orthopaedically sound Birkenstock over the stiletto; nudism over bikinis; and an unmade-up Steffi Graf versus a glamorous Gabriella Sabatini. For a Protestant, all that glisters definitely is not gold, it is superfluous.

And this precision and normality bordering on the tedious so often came at the expense of spirit, spontaneity, decadence and human failing. Living with Protestantism seemed like hard work. It was fine for making trains and cars, but not well suited to the beach. And that, I was sure, was why Germany struggled to attract me and apparently millions of others as a travel destination, no matter how 'Romantic' its past.

But Protestantism was just the first in a long line of examples of the German mind seeking a solution for the betterment of the world and in the process turning it on its head.

The sheer number of German philosophers suggests that the German mind is peculiarly adapted for the business of contemplation. It is a mind that likes to reduce the world into neat systems so that it can be better understood and, if necessary, improved. Very like Manny and the overlapping worlds of psychiatry and business consultancy. I was not about to wade through Kant's *Critique of Pure Reason* and knew little of Hegel's slow journey to consciousness beyond my Heidelberg hangover, but Manny had kindly summarised them for me and it was clear that they all had two things in common. They sought to lend order to a chaotic world. For a German '*Ordnung muss sein*': order must prevail, with nothing left to chance. And they were all radical and absolute in scope. Luther threw down his gauntlet with the words, 'Here I stand, I can do no other.' And, as Kant wrote, 'The Germans are praised in that, when constancy and sustained diligence are demanded, they can go further than other people.' Germans didn't do things by halves.

And now I discovered from Manny that this radical quest for absolutes and systems was not a matter of history but was alive and well in the Protestant banalities of modern German life.

Germans have a deep aversion to chance and by implication anything that falls outside the control granted by a system. By contrast with the debt-happy British, they dislike credit cards and the notion of credit drawn on an unknown future. Credit cards are a bit like the Catholic practice of Indulgences, right down to the way they line others' pockets in the process. Baedeker displayed an impulse to catalogue and systemise every detail of a country, leaving no stone unturned lest the traveller be thrown by a chance event. Germans like *trempen* (hitch-hiking) and this seemed to me the modern incarnation of the *Wanderer* spirit for the age of the car. Hitch-hiking was once based around chance, but in order to reduce this the Germans have invented the *Mitfahrerzentrale*, an Internet site where drivers and lift-seekers register themselves and exchange details of planned journeys and hook up without the need to wait for hours by a traffic light with a grubby piece of cardboard (thereby also appealing to their green and efficient mentality). Surely chance meetings were a key part of real *Wanderlust*!

Then there were the systemic tendencies displayed in the staggering of the dates of school holidays from state to state in order to avoid congestion on the major holiday routes. Not for the Germans the packed motorway at the end of August. And the autobahn itself, a German invention, was a radical and yet pragmatic solution to the need to get somewhere quick and in a straight line.

And just look at the stuff they read for entertainment. I remembered how at school German magazines had always had a deceptively alluring cover only to reveal swathes of dense, pictureless and minuscule text to wade through so that after half an hour you couldn't comfort yourself that you'd even turned a page. As for German broadsheets like *Die Zeit* or the *Frankfurter Allgemeine Zeitung*, they seemed like walls of text with barely a single picture in the whole paper, let alone a paragraph break in any of the articles. And as for their equivalent of Penguin Classics, Germany's most famous Reclam series was a list of Blackberry-size yellow paperbacks with myopically small print, clearly designed for scientific analysis not lazy reading on the beach. No wonder, it seemed to me, so many Germans wore glasses.

I remembered a German wedding reception I'd once been to where, not content to allude generally to the hundred-strong wedding party by way of thanks for their presence, the bride and groom spent an hour and a half giving a little speech about every one of them; the bridesmaids sang before dinner then, between courses, showed a twenty-minute video they'd made of themselves impersonating the wedding couple; then, before the proper dancing and post-breakfast drinking could really begin, a whole mock tabloid newspaper giving behind-the-scenes details of the bride and groom's lives was handed out by the best man dressed up in fluorescent overalls as one of those vendors who sell the next day's newspapers on the road at midnight, and a whole song sheet of odes to and parodies of the wedding couple was produced for everyone to sing in unison. Then and only then could we start cutting some shapes on the dancefloor. A few stones left unturned would have made the affair a lot more relaxing!

As for absolutism, the 1960s and in particular 1968 were more systematically violent and activist in Germany than in any other place, including Paris. The punks, successors of these students that I saw in German cities, always seemed to have more radical hair, be more pierced and more goth than punks anywhere else. Perhaps only in red activist Italy of the 1970s was there an equal to the violence wrought by the left-wing terrorist Baader-Meinhof gang. The German students invented the idea of the living commune or *Wohngemeinschaft* (or WG, pronounced 'vay-gay'). More than just flat-sharing, this was a political statement of 'equal living' as against the old Protestant family unit, which young post-war Germans saw as fascist. In the process many of these communes adopted a belligerent stance towards the German state.

Back in the 1970s the chosen vehicle of German hippies and WG students was the VW Westfalia combi camper van, the ultimate living-travelling solution. Every aspect of the living space was incorporated into the environment of a vehicle, and like in a chest of drawers everything had its place. If Wagner's operas set out to be the *Gesamtkunstwerk*, the Total Work of Art, the VW camper van was the *Gesamtwagen*, or Total Car, its vehicular equivalent. In fact German cars themselves are exercises in absolutism. The technology under the bonnet of an Audi says, 'Granted, the universe is vast and chaotic but if you can imagine and design the most complicated labyrinth possible and know your way through it you will be that much nearer to an understanding of the world.' As Manny's notes explained: 'Vorsprung durch Technik *is not an idle boast of technological excellence, it is a philosophical aphorism, the equal of "Ordnung muss sein", propelling mankind along an automotive equivalent of Hegel's slow journey to consciousness, the* Weltgeist *whereby the synthesis of thesis and antithesis leads to ultimate knowledge.'*

I had to admit Manny had lost me a bit there, but I sort of knew what he meant.

And now the conflict had gone full circle. For Manny the famed German technological excellence and love of order, the German search for ultimate understanding, far from being dry, heartless and emotionless, was Romantic! An Audi, unlike a relative rust-bucket from Italy, now expressed all-consuming passion.

'*Vorsprung durch Technik* is a piece of poetry, an appeal from the heart, a declaration of humanity and an invitation to dance!' We were back in the offices of Infinity. Manny stood up and held out both arms heraldically. Or was he wanting to waltz? 'So, you see, the story of Germany and the German soul is the search for absolute solutions to the chaos of the world.'

But human beings, Germans included, succeed only occasionally, and then fleetingly, in mastering the questions posed by the universe. And sometimes they get it badly wrong. This is a source of great *Angst* to Germans. Beneath those glasses lies a restless *Wanderer*'s mind in a constant battle of understanding with the world and one that feels the world doesn't live up to its potential and needs betterment. The solution to *Angst* is *Ordnung*. Nudity alone is not enough, despite what FKK-Jugend might say. Yet the scale of this ambition and the frequency and ubiquity of the German need to apply it leads ironically to yet more *Angst*. I could see how easily Freud had invented psychotherapy by working with Germans!

Back home I found by chance a copy of the rather jingoistic pocketbook given to Allied soldiers to prepare them for the psychology of their foe before the D-Day landings in 1944. It noted of Germans their curious 'mixture of sentimentality and callousness' which 'does not show a well-balanced mind'. Oddly, I felt this also summed up Manny's own flights of emotion. 'The Germans are not good at controlling their feelings,' it went on, 'they have a streak of hysteria. You will find that Germans may often fly into a passion if some little thing goes wrong.' Well, that's because Germans are Romantics, I now understood, who want everything to be perfect.

'So, now do you know what it means to be a true Romantic?' Manny had asked me on my return.

Well, my search to understand not only Germany but also the world through travel was an essential part of being one, and that was the quest Manny had sent me on. This is what he had meant with all those comparisons with Faust. Romance had become commonplace and stale, and its currency diluted nowadays. But now I understood its German origins and its truly wild, powerful and slightly tragic original meaning. I resolved that when I next saw a German 'sinking' and labouring over every detail with myopic intensity, wanting to be over-precise and logical, or even scoring another efficient precision penalty, I wouldn't dismiss it as pedantic, dry and cerebral but as Romantic and coming from deep in the soul; as the expression of an innate philosophical need – which appears to be greater in Germans than any other people – to understand and improve the world. For better or for worse, Germans have made more such attempts than most peoples and it goes hand in hand with an admirable desire to treat every day as a new day and to see things, as I was beginning to see Germany, for the first time. To wonder, and in wonder, to wander the earth.

5

Gemütlichkeit

nf, *comfort, cosiness, joviality, sociability*

Once again in the cinnamon-flavoured comfort of Infinity's therapy rooms I recounted to Manny my own general sense of *Vorsprung*.

'You are indeed making good progress,' he said. 'But enough thinking for a bit. It's time to loosen up. You tourists are always in search of fun and festivals. Well, Germany is also a party land.'

It was time to get my German party gear on. And that could surely mean only one thing. Leather.

Munich, so Manny claimed, is the northernmost city of Italy. By which he meant the locals are easy-going and have a flair and spirit normally seen as the sole preserve of Latin lands. But I'd also heard Milan described as the southernmost city of Germany for the very opposite reason. Either way Bavarians clearly saw themselves as a cut looser, if not above, their fellow Germans. At times they had considered themselves hardly German at all and spent much of their history either forming alliances against fellow Germanic regions or trying to maintain their independence from them. And yet at others they saw themselves as the most German of Germans. Certainly Hitler thought so, having busked around the city for a few months in 1913 as a street artist before pursuing an alternative career; so much so that he made Munich the headquarters of the Nazi Party and always had a certain awe for all that hailed from this most German of cities. 'I belong to that town more than to any spot in the world, inseparably bound up with my own development,' he wrote in his semi-literate 'autobiography' *Mein Kampf* (or *Me in Kamp F* as I'd heard it parodied), a book which, along with Nazi salutes, Holocaust denial and David Irving, is illegal in Germany. So much for the claim of being an easy-going city. You could hardly call Hitler 'easy-going' or 'Latin' (unless you're Mussolini). Nor could you really call voting him in as leader of Germany an example of Münchners having an eye for a good party – unless the dress code was brown shirts or you had the same taste in fancy dress as Prince Harry (himself more than a fraction German).

I say all this knowledgeably now, but before my treatment with Manny Munich was just a German city I'd visited several times fleetingly on business without ever getting to know much more than the duty-free shops at Franz-Joseph Strauss airport (apparently nothing to do with the 'Blue Danube' waltz). Munich epitomised the contemptuous familiarity in which I held Germany: important as an export market but nothing more. I had vague images of tatty, overcoated eternal students with leather satchels on more of those upright Baltic bicycles. But through a combination of strong regional identity and cultural ignorance on my part Munich was still now for me what it had always been: oompah bands, silly hats with feathers, much beer and much slapping of thighs dressed, of course, in leather trousers. *Lederhosen* are surely the most mocked skeleton in every German's presumed wardrobe. The lower echelons of English television comedy would be lost without them (without the *Lederhosen*, that is – not the Germans). If *'Allo 'Allo*'s Herr

Flick hinted at a link between German militarism and sex, *Lederhosen* were proof of the bond between Germans and fetishism.

But now, at Manny's behest, I was in Munich and willing to have my worn-leather prejudices ripped to shreds. And yet now I found *Lederhosen* being held up by be-breeched Münchners as the symbol of the city that was also supposed to be Germany's fashion capital. Local politicians hailed Munich as the city of 'Laptops und *Lederhosen*'. How could we travellers have ignored it for so long? But what was that about 'Germany' and 'fashion'? I wasn't sure I'd ever put those two words in the same sentence any more than 'Germany' and 'humour'. Even Jean-Paul Gaultier has steered clear of chafing hide.

But apparently Germany had made considerable *Vorsprung* in matters sartorial and in fact has a buoyant non-leather fashion industry. This reputation is carried not just on the pedestrian soles of Birkenstocks but on the shoulder pads of Jil Sander, Escada, Wolfgang Joop and Hugo Boss; not forgetting Chanel's chief designer, Karl Lagerfeld.

What I had to understand was that while Munich symbolises much of the tradition that the idea of Germany is founded upon, it is also a very modern and wealthy city, nicknamed *Millionendorf*, not just because it claims to be a 'town of a million (friendly) souls' but because it is where many of Germany's millionaires live. A quick glance at the hi-tech Olympic Park built for the 1974 Games, or the translucent Alliance Arena stadium, home to Bayern Munich and Munich 1860 football clubs, confirmed this. And when local leather was not being used to warm Bavarian bottoms it was being used to upholster the insides of the ultimate driving machines local to these parts: BMWs.

Munich had a cosmopolitan air about it that evening. And no wonder. For the world and his first and second wives had descended on the city for its most famous party; the party that

most of all accounted for the beer-swilling, thigh-slapping stereotype I carried in my mind: the Oktoberfest. In fact when Manny
had first said he was sending me to the Oktoberfest I was doubtful whether it would prove the existence of a German party
spirit. There were so many imitations of the original around the
world that I felt it was over-familiar, even though I'd never been
before, and had been pretty much de-Germanised and appropriated by Australians.

'Ah, you have hit the nail on the head,' Many had replied
when I put this to him. 'This is the problem with the party culture. Visitors don't feel the need to understand their roots or
even explore the rest of the country. But don't worry. Germany
has fun festivals in buckets and I'll show you others.'
Meanwhile, he'd assured me, the Oktoberfest would reveal itself
as impressive and unfamiliar.

The party had already been underway for a number of days
and as the evening drew on so the bar and surrounding streets
grew fuller of swaying revellers of all nationalities, draped over
one another and in fine voice (if not tune) returning from the
beer tents. A huge amount of leather was on display and now
that I looked with a more critical eye I caught myself thinking
that in fact they looked, well, rather natty. There were full-
length, slightly baggy trousers, three-quarter-length, slightly
tighter ones, and then the shorts that matched the stereotype in
my mind. There were dark brown, light brown and sort of
murky green; shiny and well-worn or soft and suede. And there
was an infinite variety of styles of embroidery on the seams and
hems: from leaf motifs and feathers to scrolls and wistful twirls.
Nor were the *Lederhosen* worn in isolation. They were just one
element of what goes together to form the *Tracht* or *Volkstracht*
(folk costume). You had to have the right shirt: baggy, white
cotton with long sleeves, embroidered around the neck, where
four buttons open to show a manly chest or an optional red
neckerchief. There were thick, cream-coloured woollen socks

too, and if you were being really fussy, clogs. Only the older generation seemed to go for the full jacket, either short and midriff-hugging or long and flowing, and feathered cap that made them look like Beethoven on a hunting trip.

And what about the women? I had in my mind huge, slightly hirsute, buxom waitresses of indeterminate sex, looking mostly like eastern European weightlifters and dressed in lace-fringed gingham tablecloths, their considerable embonpoint to the fore and used for parting the crowds. What girl would wear a *Dirndl* – the word means both the costume and a girl in Bavaria – by choice? Surely it could not be made to look flattering or sexy? Well, clearly these things were a matter of personal taste. But, looking more closely at Munich's young wenches dressed in their traditional finery, I saw I had been wrong. The lace and the check patterns had a childishness that on the adult female form oozed a naughty, Heidi-like innocence, especially given the plunging neckline and trussed-up chest *à la Liaisons Dangereuses*. The European Union, that great leveller and arbiter of fun and good taste, had in 2004 threatened to make excessively décolleté necklines illegal at the Oktoberfest. Munich's mayor was so outraged he is reported to have said, 'A waitress is no longer allowed to wander round a Biergarten with a plunging neckline? I would not enter a Biergarten under these conditions.' Like the mayor I was now convinced the *Dirndl* was in fact made for frolicking. The more ties there were to pull, the sexier. In our flesh-obsessed age – and no more so than on the Baltic coast – I sensed that previous, more conservative eras had a better understanding of the power of suggestion. A thought that was no doubt anathema to members of FKK-Jugend!

So, was I becoming a *Lederhosen* convert, or just a fetishist?

All in context, of course. You wouldn't want to be seen dead in *Lederhosen* outside the Oktoberfest. For this latest generation of partying Münchners, *Lederhosen* were just a party uniform.

And this had rubbed off on international visitors. While there were plenty of boring party-poopers in normal clothes, a huge majority of non-German party-goers treated the Oktoberfest as an excuse to dress up in one form of national costume or another.

Ubiquitous among these was the kilt, which, it occurred to me, is the British equivalent of *Lederhosen*: faintly ridiculous, outmoded and full of sexual connotation, pointlessly patriotic and so displayed with great pride by natives, but much parodied or worn as mocking fancy dress by the rest. Standing next to me was a case in point: a group of five fat blokes dressed in those identical one-clan-fits-all tartan kilts you can buy on Oxford Street. On the front of their boys-on-tour T-shirts they had had printed, 'Bangor Gynaecology Hospital – Oktoberfest 2005' and on the back, 'Jesus Loves You – the rest of us think you're a twat'.

But there were other more erudite takes on national dress. I saw several groups of English people dressed up like toffs out for a day's fly-fishing or grouse-shooting: plus fours, yards of tweed, Sherlock Holmes cap and the same hues of brown and murky green. On first sight I was inclined to agree with the boys from Bangor. But on reflection I found their attire to be quite a good judgement of equivalent sartorial cultures. Like tweed plus fours and their associated jackets and hats, *Lederhosen,* I now knew, have their origins in hunting and country pursuits. If anything, this was proof of a link, not a difference, between Germany and Britain. I thought of those market towns in England with their timeless sporting shops, 4x4s parked outside, that sell Barbour gear, Pringle jumpers, check tweed and unspeakable red corduroy trousers better suited for reading the property section of the *Sunday Times*. The clothes were always window-dressed with the veneer of guns, fishing rods and a plethora of other sporting accessories equally unlikely ever to be purchased. This nostalgia for a more rural and noble hunting past seemed to be common to both countries.

Apparently no evidence can be found that Bavarians wore *Lederhosen* any earlier than the late eighteenth century. So their invention seemed to me more the fruit of Romantic nation-building. Germans looking back into the mists of their past saw a forest-dwelling nation of hunters. They needed an outfit that could be identified with their past, and also serve as a *Volkstracht,* a national uniform. And so they had cobbled together a peasant's costume that seemed plausible. Those tall, strapping young Germans in *Lederhosen* were the modern incarnation, with a Texan cowboy strut, of the militant youth of old Heidelberg, ready to re-forge the German nation.

So here I was, one of the new, sober and underdressed arrivals. But I knew that tomorrow I would be one of *them*.

Manny had arranged for me to go to the party with some German friends of his, true Münchner! It was clear that I had to go dressed up as a German. There was nothing for it but to buy my very own pair of *Lederhosen*. What were they actually like to wear? Did they in fact chafe? Did you get sweaty underneath? Who could know until I'd actually tried them. Manny would like the way I was thinking. But where could I get an authentic pair? There were lots of cut-price shops near the station selling ersatz *Lederhosen* for twenty quid. They would never do. I found a few flyers and brochures for shops showing Aryan Bavarians sporting discounted leatherware. But these outlets turned out to be miles away. Eventually I was told that one of the city's main department stores stocked a wide variety.

And so it was that the next morning I found myself in the 'folkwear' section of the Adler department store on one of Munich's main drags. Imagine a 'folkwear' section at your local M&S. At first I was doubtful, as it looked like a pretty plain store full of insipid clothes for C&A man – Manny would have been at home shopping here – and the average age of the clientele was pushing sixty. But up on the second floor things changed dramatically. Before me stretched out a whole tannery of leather, lace and felt: surely an English toff's paradise. But there were so many cuts, colours and designs – more than I had ever imagined – that I felt hopelessly out of my depth. And not just in terms of making an informed choice but also of cost. You could spend anything up to five hundred euros on the full monty, including jacket. And just a pair of *Lederhosen* at the top end could set you back as much as two hundred.

For a while I browsed aimlessly, not knowing what I was looking for, confused by the sizes and nervous of looking an idiot. Eventually, seeing me flummoxed, a couple of formidable German housewives in their mid-forties, themselves dressed in *Dirndl* and every bit the buxom stereotype, took pity on me and enveloped me under their sizeable wings. I had only discreetly enquired as to whether the shorts I held in my hand might fit me, but they had taken me by the arm and were soon pulling me up and down aisles and thrusting garments into my arms. They were looking for folk clothing for their husbands but I was their temporary toyboy and they were relishing it. 'There you are, a nice pair of shorts to show off those young legs,' they cackled, more to each other than to me. 'Here you go, you'll have ladies falling at your feet with this,' and an embroidered cotton shirt was held up in front of me. When I was piled high with leather they shoved me into a changing booth and declared they would wait until I came out leather-clad to give me their Bavarian fashion advice.

Putting on a pair of *Lederhosen* was like getting into a bucket with two holes in the bottom, the leather was so stiff. It was also like getting into a climbing harness. There were straps everywhere that were easy to get tangled and several times I put my two feet through the same hole. Eventually, after ten Mr Bean minutes, I managed to corset myself up correctly in a pair of light brown suede shorts and braces, white shirt and thick cream socks. These were authentic *Lederhosen* all right. The pockets hung out of the front in a pouch rather like a codpiece. I was rather pleased. It was easy to look like Linford Christie in *Lederhosen*.

Blushing and self-conscious, I walked out to meet my Bavarian Trinny and Susannah, who greeted me with flattering swoons. They then took pleasure in fiddling around with the buckles and straps, some of which lay near quite private parts of my anatomy, before announcing that my *Lederhosen* would need adjusting. They were too loose around the waist and over the shoulders. Obviously I did not have the average Bavarian girth. So they whisked me off to the fitting room, explained to the tailor exactly what needed doing and bade me farewell and '*Frohes Fest!*' ('Happy partying!'). Friendly folk, these Germans, I thought. The tailoring was all part of the service and that afternoon I went back to Adler to pick up my new prized possession. For eighty euros, a mere fifty quid, I had my very own piece of rawhide. Smooth, warm and very comfortable, they instinctively made me want to go, 'Yee-hah!' and I could see how thigh-slapping might come naturally in them.

That evening I met up with Manny's friends, still feeling self-conscious but thinking I was doing the right thing, albeit looking forward to some safety in numbers. And luckily, as genuine locals Bettina, Gert, Monika and Bernhard were all kitted up in their traditional finery. Gert and Bernhard's *Lederhosen* looked as if they'd seen many years' use, worn shiny behind by the polish of so many sittings. I could only admire how well they fitted their much-maligned costumes.

By now I had convinced myself that *Lederhosen* and *Dirndl* were fashionable and cool in a retro kind of way. Or maybe I was just trying to feel good and kidding myself. But my wearing *Lederhosen* was a symbol of how they had lost their tradition.

'As the world becomes more globalised, so its oppressed local traditions grow back all the more strongly,' Manny had declared.

Yes, but in an overblown, non-traditional and non-local way that takes the best bits and adapts them to modern trends.

Either way, Manny's young lady friends Monika and Bettina looked not only a million Deutschmarks in their tight décolleté pink lace-edged *Dirndl* but, with white Puma trainers, also the height of fashion.

We headed off to the *Wiesn*, as the Oktoberfest is locally known; so named after the 'meadows' where it takes place and which once lay outside the city walls.

I had always imagined the Oktoberfest was a festival designed to celebrate its main ingredient: beer. 'Beer is a Munich, if not German, religion!' Manny had said proudly. And Munich's architectural symbol may be the twin onion-dome towers of its famous baroque Church of Our Lady but on the evidence of the Oktoberfest I could be forgiven for thinking that by far the city's largest congregation belonged to the Church of Our Next Pint.

If not beer, I had always assumed the Oktoberfest at least had something to do with the harvest and the sense of plenty at the end of the summer. Nothing so seasonal, it turned out. The Oktoberfest is actually a wedding-anniversary party. On 17 October 1810 the crown prince of Bavaria, who would become Ludwig I, married his princess, Therese Sachsen-Hildburghausen. Bavaria had allied itself with Napoleon and the Bavarians had had to endure much war with their Germanic neighbours and hardship as a result. So the Bavarian prince, full of the status won him by this alliance, and also to thank the people for their support, decided to lay on a big bash to which all inhabitants of the city were invited. At the time Munich numbered just forty thousand inhabitants and it is said that about three-quarters of them turned out for the five-day festival. The celebration was repeated on the first anniversary and so it carried on year after year, despite Ludwig's subsequent infidelity with a buxom dancer, and slowly but surely acquired more and more local characteristics, such as the traditional dress and the oompah bands, to become Bavaria's greatest showcase.

Later, in the mid-nineteenth century, before Athens was a twinkle in anyone's eye, there were even attempts to revive the Ancient Olympic Games at the Oktoberfest. But it was found that traditional Olympic disciplines were incompatible with inebriation, and that the Olympic motto of pushing yourself 'higher, faster and further' was only applicable to beer consumption and its effects.

As German troops were sent into the trenches of the First World War the Oktoberfest was banned on the grounds that its congenial atmosphere cultivated a dangerous fellowship with strangers. Then in 1920, as the Bolsheviks in Russia were pursuing their own October revolution, the Oktoberfest was reinstated; only to be cancelled in 1923 as the inter-war Weimar Republic spiralled into debt and the cost of a litre of beer reached twenty-one million marks. Thomas Mann, from conservative, mercantile northern Lübeck, described the Oktoberfest as 'a monstrous event where a defiant people corrupted by modern mass movements celebrate their saturnalia'. And certainly the pliability of inebriated masses high on nostalgia for tradition made it a prize for the Nazis, who were quick to appropriate it as a symbol of their thousand-year Reich. Hitler was famously a teetotaller but that did not stop him from targeting a Munich beer cellar, the Feldherrnhalle, in 1923 for his failed first attempt to seize power. Resembling a bunch of English football hooligans, they trashed 143 steins, 98 stools and two music bandstands. The debt remains still unpaid.

In 1949, after the Second World War, the Oktoberfest was successfully revived, remarkably with no Nazi association, so that the party I was heading for was in effect the 172nd wedding anniversary of Ludwig and Therese. The Oktoberfest was surely Germany's most remarkable export in that, despite the stereotypical images, through its international popularity it has transcended cultural boundaries and, more uniquely, Germany's past.

I found the Oktoberfest truly medieval in size. It basically consisted of a giant funfair set amid fourteen enormous beer tents the size of football pitches, each belonging to one of the big Munich breweries. The Theresienwiese occupied forty-two hectares and the tents together offered some 100,000 places to park your bum with a pint. It was like a giant holiday camp, a canvas version of the concrete Prora on Rügen. Not so much *Kraft durch Freude* as *Freude durch Bier* (joy through beer).

Munich is no more the capital of German beer than any other of the country's great brewing cities. But I discovered it takes its name from the Benedictine monks, or *Munichen*, who had a monastery here, along with about three hundred nearby monasteries who specialised in brewing the stuff, when it was declared a town in 1138. The city accounts for many of the great German brewery houses, six of which take part in a harvest parade of shire-horse-drawn carts before the festivities begin; a piece of tradition lost on most of the six million visitors. The six breweries include Löwenbräu. Now what was the correct pronunciation for that beer? I had heard so many variants down the years. Well, apparently, thanks to those dots above the vowels called umlauts, it was 'lurven-broy', not 'lowen-brow', and means 'lion's brew'.

Each of the tents has a specific reputation. The Löwenbräu tent has become the favoured haunt of Antipodean revellers and is the most international tent. At the other end, the Schottenhammel tent is the most traditional. And it is here, after a cannon fires twelve times, that the festival is always opened by the mayor of Munich ramming a stake into a keg and shouting, '*Ozapft ist!*' – 'It is tapped!' He gets the first *Mas* (Bavarian for 'pint') and then everyone can stop being thirsty. No mention is made of the wedding all those years ago. Just get on and drink up!

No matter what Manny had said, this was refreshing proof that most of the world's famous festivals, from the running of the bulls in Pamplona to the Rio Carnival, are now just an excuse for one giant piss-up.

Contrary to what I thought, you can't just turn up and expect to get a seat. Just like with the *Strandkörber* on the beaches of Sylt and Binz, you have to reserve a table at the Oktoberfest months in advance to avoid disappointment. Each tent had large but friendly bouncers at each entrance checking we had the right badge or arm tag to prove we had a seat. And there were constantly people trying it on with a bit of imaginative chat trying to gatecrash. 'Honest, I've got my towel on a sun-lounger somewhere in there!' It was part of the fun of the fair and many of them seemed to be succeeding. But, generally speaking, I reckoned you didn't mess with a rotund Bavarian farmer in his *Lederhosen*.

So I was truly honoured to be sitting at a table of Germans in one of the more traditional tents, the Hofbräuzelt. I had thought the festival would have been taken over by the British, Italians and Australians, and although there were many about it was pleasing to see that it was still very much a local, or at least a German, affair. According to Monika, only a tiny 15 per cent of *fest*-goers come from abroad. The Herr Brents of German companies are encouraged to take their employees and, once a year, rather like at office Christmas parties in the UK, 'get down' with the staff, do away with the formal '*Sie*' form of address, sit among them without hierarchy and do silly jigs in their funny trousers.

The atmosphere inside an Oktoberfest beer tent was all the things I'd expected: packed, noisy, smoky and sweaty but somehow, owing to the gigantic proportions of the hangar-like constructions, it was possible to sit comfortably without having to jostle, to hear yourself think and other people talk, and not to feel suffocated, overheated and claustrophobic. In fact moving around was remarkably easy as long as you were prepared to be spun forward like a fairground waltzer. The atmosphere was close and so were my neighbours. This was one instance of Germans not demanding *Lebensraum*. And random friskiness seemed to be par for the course. As I had witnessed on the Baltic coast, Germans like to sit together at benches in a way that is classless, friendly, humble and inclusive. I also found it quite medieval and primitive. If you imagine Asterix and Obelix sitting down in a pub full of convivial but slightly brutish Goths to eat a couple of boars after bashing up some Romans, that would pretty much be it. Breaking bread (or a boar's neck) and drinking for Germans is something to be done communally. In fact I learnt from Berny (as I now knew him) that the Bavarians say, '*Nur ein Schwein, drinkt allein*' – 'Only a pig drinks alone.'

Our tent, I imagine like most of the tents (and you don't tent-crawl as I had thought), was low-lit like the inside of some of the traditional *Bierkeller* that I remembered going in on business trips. It was festooned with the imagery of the forest and of hunting. There were boars' heads, stags' antlers and images of eagles, and the stanchions that held up the tents were dressed up as oak trunks wrapped in creepers and flowers. The intention seemed to be not just to evoke tradition but to take revellers into a fairytale forest where they could suspend reality. The words of the compère in *Cabaret* came to mind: '*Leave your trubbles outzide.*' If Munich has a chic, modern and stylish side, it was not to be seen here. There was no room for laptops in the beer tent.

As for 'ze orchestra', they were far from 'bioodiful'. But they were rather talented. Set up on a bandstand like a boxing ring in the centre of the tent they were a twelve-or-more-piece band all dressed in full leather gear and comprising predominantly brass instruments with various unusually shaped bells – some of them entwining the significant girth of their players – which, even as a former member of the brass section of various orchestras, I had never seen. I presumed these were hunting horns of some description, rooted in Germany's fine tradition of hunting and horn-making. The band was like an English marching band but their vernacular was not 'Pomp and Circumstance' or the theme from *The Dambusters*, nor even 'Deutschland über alles'. Instead it was a rather generic, cheery, up-and-down, oompah repertoire that could only be described as *Stimmungsmusik*, background music. When required, as they often were, however they turned to the chorus that was the quarter-hourly refrain of the Oktoberfest and which sparked cordiality like a recurring crap joke that everybody knows and loves. Whenever you had a new beer in your hand – which seemed to be about every fifteen minutes; or whenever the bandleader didn't know what to play next or thought the atmosphere in the tent needed a bit of livening up (which it never did but it was a good excuse) he would strike up the anthem, which all visitors, even the most tone-deaf and linguistically challenged foreigner, could eventually get the hang of. To a tune sounding not dissimilar to the theme from *Blackadder* the whole tent would stand up and sing and sway in unison to the words:

> '*Ein Prozit*
> *Ein Prozit*
> *Zu der Gemütlichkeit*
> (and repeat).'

ending with a huge clinking of steins that should have shattered more glasses than it did.

This basically translated as 'cheers' – the Bavarian for 'cheers' is '*Prost*' – to 'cosiness and friendship'. '*Gemütlichkeit*' was another German concept-noun for which I could find no single-word satisfactory translation into English. 'Yes, it means cosiness, friendship, comfort and oneness – all of these,' Manny's notes clarified. 'But it also has a ring of tradition and nostalgia, and is a core sentiment at the heart of the German Romantic soul.'

Gemütlichkeit was in the boars' heads, the stags' antlers and the trunks and tree-creepers of the beer tents. It was in the music, the smiles and half-lit communal joviality. It was in the folk costumes of the formidable waitresses and their laden trays of beers. Was that *Gemütlichkeit* in my *Lederhosen*? Or was I just happy to be there?

Gemütlichkeit was therefore a state of suspended reality. Suspended not just with braces, but with a belief in tradition and myth. Romantic but therefore emotional and also dangerous. Hitler abused and appropriated *Gemütlichkeit* for his ends, and it was what I thought of when the beautiful Aryan boy stands up to sing 'Tomorrow Belongs to Me' in the beer garden in *Cabaret*:

> *The sun on the meadow is summery warm*
> *The stag in the forest runs free . . .*
> *The branch of the Linden is leafy and green*
> *The Rhine gives its gold to the sea.*

In 1945 the idea of *Gemütlichkeit* was tarnished with war-time connotations and for decades of *Vergangenheitsbewältigung*, or coming to terms with the past, many Germans resisted its return. The Green Party, the 1968 student rioters and the violent left-wing gangs of the 1970s saw danger in the nostalgia for tradition that was inherent in feelings of *Gemütlichkeit* and railed against anything they perceived to symbolise it lest it return to Germany. In the ultimate German form of protest they eschewed *Lederhosen* in favour of nudity.

Until recently Germans didn't even allow themselves to have a national anthem. You don't have to be German to know the tune or opening words to *Das Lied der Deutschen* (The Song of the Germans): '*Deutschland, Deutschland über alles*'.

'It has long raised heckles on you Brits' necks even though it's a tune to which you sometimes sing, "Glorious things of thee are spoken" at Sunday service.'

Maybe, but I'd sure grown sick of hearing the tune every Sunday as Michael Schumacher was fêted for yet another ritual Formula 1 victory.

Since 1945 the Allies had apparently banned the German anthem, afraid of its ability to inspire dangerous national pride in its countrymen. So what did Germans sing when their sportsmen walked out on to the field, for example to lose to the English in 1966?

'The post-war Chancellor, Konrad Adenauer, obtained unofficial permission for the tune to be used. But only with the third verse and only on special occasions. And this was only formalised in 1990.' Manny explained.

Why only the third stanza, which speaks of 'Unity and justice and freedom for the German fatherland'? I doubt many Ing-gur-land football fans know the words to the second verse to 'God Save the Queen', or even that it exists.

'Well, just think about the words of the first two stanzas! They translate as "Germany, Germany above all, Above everything in the world" and go on to talk about the borders of a former larger country.'

'Ah but they were actually written in 1841, at a time when Germany did not yet exist and was merely a vague geographic area containing over thirty quarrelsome Germanic city-states, monarchies and republics. The words of the hymn are an appeal to the monarchs of these German states to put to one side their local feuds and concentrate "über alles", "above all", on creating a unified nation.'

I see. They'd just got rid of Napoleon and becoming a nation state – Greece and Italy were about to do it – was trendy.

'What's more, the tune, composed by Haydn, was in fact used as the Austrian, not German, national anthem until 1918. And only in 1922 did it become the anthem of Weimar Germany. Meanwhile, do you know what the tune was for the first-ever German anthem following the creation of the country in 1873? Your very own "God Save the King".'

I had been disabused. Even so, it seemed that the Germans themselves hadn't been convinced and shrank from singing their national anthem. Since 1945 they had been nervous about being proud of their nation, which I found rather annoying given their economic post-war achievements. Even if they had no tourist industry.

And so in its absence they sang the '*Gemütlichkeit*' anthem I heard at the Oktoberfest to celebrate something more abstract, a form of unpatriotic nationalism and tradition shorn of its state.

Another perennial of the festival's soundtrack was 'Viva Colonia', sung to a tune similar to 'Viva España', and a nod to one of Germany's other party towns, Cologne. But occasionally the band would take a breather – it was thirsty work, all that blowing – and the woofers of a giant Rottweiler of a German hi-fi would take its place, blasting out a limited range of lo-fi eurohits such as DJ Ötzi's 'Ooh! Ah! I wanna know-oh-oh if you'll be my girl', – one of the few pop songs in German that had ever made it in the UK.

The Oktoberfest was an amazing feat of organisation and pragmatism. It was, in effect a piss-up in twelve breweries, and on this basis alone I reckoned you would definitely want Germans to be in charge of organising any major party. They even understood and catered for the collateral damage of excessive beer consumption. There was a special *Bierleichenzelt* (beer corpse tent) for those who'd arrived too early and treated this drinkathon as a sprint. And there was in total over a half a mile of dedicated urinary space. As the festival organiser, a prosperous Frau Weishäupl, put it, 'All that beer has to come back out somewhere sooner or later', displaying an earthy lack of prudishness; the same that led people to go FKK.

Courtesy of a rather understaffed tourist office (many staff were apparently 'off sick', which I took to mean 'hung-over' – it was refreshing to see Germans chucking a sicky) I learnt some statistics about the event that emphasised its outlandish, medieval proportions. These had been accounted for and noted down to the last Romantic detail.

In the sample year of 2004: a total of six million people had attended and a total of 6.2 million litres of beer had been drunk. Just over one litre a head – not bad when you consider the high percentage of visitors who are children. The attendees had consumed 481,649 chickens, 55,089 pork knuckles and 89 oxen. Eighty-eight thousand and twenty-three cubic metres of water had been used (and recycled), 2.4 million kilowatts of power consumed and a total of 647 tonnes of waste produced, of which 32 tonnes were paper (recycled) and 311 tonnes food waste. Four thousand items of property had been lost, divided into categories including glasses, wallets, credit cards and clothes. There was even a column for 'exceptional items': like 'one arm of a doll', '1 x Bach (J. S.) sheet music' and an 'unknown bird'. That year the total monetary value of the event to the city's coffers, including the whole visitor infrastructure (hotels and so on), was €954 million, with the festival alone accounting for €449 million of that. Again, I thought, the Germans don't do things by halves, and in just two weeks make up for their lack of popularity during the rest of the year.

I discovered the Oktoberfest also had a social conscience. In 2005 the organisers prohibited the playing of 'party music' before six o'clock in the evening, to keep a lid on otherwise premature *Gemütlichkeit*, and also imposed a decibel restriction on bands. Over the last few years they had taken measures to ensure that all those oxen, chicken and pigs were organic, free-range, fresh and locally sourced. Besides this, all the electricity was now produced by water turbines and all the water recycled (and the washing-up water used as 'grey water' for the toilet facilities); cans were *verboten* and a deposit was required for all crockery to encourage returns; all waste was meticulously sorted, having already been divided at the point of disposal, and stalls, breweries, rides and all businesses on the grounds were awarded marks each year so that the public could see how eco-friendly they'd been. In addition, each year 250 pensioners were invited without charge to the Schottenhammel tent, 2250 seats were given to people in need and there were discounts on 'family days'. The whole event had been approached with a scarily exhaustive mindset I now understood to be Romantic, such that it ran with the smoothness and efficiency of an Audi engine.

I had never imagined the Oktoberfest was also a giant funfair. This element is almost as old as the festival's very origins, dating back to the 1880s and the time when the pursuit of fun and leisure met the Industrial Revolution, bringing about the kind of grand exhibitions that begat the Eiffel Tower and the Ferris wheel in Vienna's Prater. Perhaps to help with digestion, and in tune with the festival's obsession with size and superlatives, every year there are modern additions to the array of rides, each going faster and higher and so inducing more vertigo, dizziness and vomiting. Imagine Alton Towers on ten pints. And aside from the rides there has long been a tradition of mazes, puppet shows, theatre acts and photo stalls, all dating back to the late nineteenth century. I was in a kind of Disneyland, a concept of which the Oktoberfest was surely the forerunner. Fun for all the family – something, I was fast observing, the Germans are rather good at.

The whole Oktoberfest was in fact a paradise for children and a celebration of the childish in the adult mind. On the top of all the beer tents were giant plastic automata, effigies to the religion of epicureanism: moving lions to symbolise Löwenbräu, huge steins being lifted to sculptures of huge mouths and massive Dirndl-clad legs rising like the legs of Parisian can-can girls.

There were shades of carnival in these imposing models: fun but slightly menacing and doomsday-ish. And everything was supersize, from giant pretzels to gingerbread hearts the size of dinner plates inscribed with icing and twee phrases like '*I mog di*': Bavarian for '*Ich mag dich*', 'I love you'. Primary-coloured and made of elementary shapes, it was simple, childish gigantism. In Lübeck I had observed gingerbread houses fit for miniature men in a miniature world. Here it was the reverse. Like Gulliver on his travels, I had been transported from Lilliput to Blefuscu and could now have been wandering around some giant's nursery.

I was surprised to find they stopped serving beer at eleven o'clock. Oh no, not the infamous *Sperrstunde* Baltic closing time again! I'd thought the festival must be an all-night party. What was the point of getting hammered only to go home in the evening? But sure enough, safe in the company of locals with inside knowledge and who knew how to party, I discovered that leaving the Theresienwiese site was just the beginning. For young and trendy Münchners, such as Manny's friends were turning out to be, it was all about the 'After-Wiesn Party'.

And so it was that I found myself on the guest list of the Lenbachkeller nightclub, one of the hottest After-Wiesn addresses in town, jumping ahead of a queue of energetic party-goers anxiously waiting to continue their revelry. Inside on three floors the tables and chairs of one of Munich's biggest bars had been cleared to make a continuous dancefloor, seething with members of the city's beautiful set, casting their affections indiscriminately between friends and strangers. On each floor different music was playing, but gone now were the traditional folksongs. Just as the beer had been replaced by vodka, and the canvas and tree motifs by mirrors and aluminium, this was from the other end of the spectrum of German musical excellence: Ibiza-style house music, techno, trance and electronica, with 'ze veels of steel' being spun by would-be Sven Vaths and Paul van

Dyks. We could have been on Mallorca or on the après-ski slopes of St Anton. *Lederhosen* were still *de rigueur*, and to see Münchners through the strobe, red and blue neon and dry ice, cutting disco shapes in all that leather, confirmed my view that the best of this traditional costume had claimed a place in present-day German culture. We were back in the land of laptops and iTunes.

Outside, beyond the After-Wiesn club scene, the party atmosphere had spread out into the streets and no citizen, *fest*-goer or not, was left untouched by the joking and pranks of revellers. It reminded me of my student days and my night out among the Burschenschaft crowd in Heidelberg. Gatecrashing balls would have been the equivalent of gatecrashing those beer tents. And even the *Lederhosen* were akin to dressing up in a form of purposely destructible black tie. Clive James wrote a hilarious account of his days at Cambridge entitled *May Week was in June*. May Week in Cambridge was the week of frenzied partying and ball-going that followed the end-of-term exams in June. Just as eccentrically, the Oktoberfest was in September. But it lasted a good deal longer than a week. Starting on the penultimate weekend of September, it ran for sixteen successive days, twelve hours at a time, and ended on Ludwig and Therese's wedding anniversary on the first Sunday of October. This year, because of an additional public holiday, it was due to last a massive, stomach-stretching seventeen days. No wonder Germany has the oldest students, the shortest working week and the longest holidays.

There was no doubt about it: the Oktoberfest united the world around beer. What's more, it was proof, 5.5 per cent alcohol proof, of a strong link between the Germans and the British: the basic drinking songs, the love of fancy dress, the huge window-dressing for what is simply an excuse to drink, the sheer enjoyment of beer not because you need it or are thirsty but for beer's sake, and the unashamed mutual acceptance of becoming publicly dishevelled, losing control of the bladder, suffering from 'backwash' or just lying around comatose.

And yet the Oktoberfest has not been able to contribute significantly to changing the general view of Germany and Germans. So maybe there are differences after all. The Oktoberfest takes place with a peacefulness and inoffensiveness that would be nigh impossible in Britain. Nazi putsches aside, there are rarely any fights, no chairs, tables or punches are thrown and the rest of the city doesn't wake up the next day strewn with evidence of a party turned violent: broken windows, smashed-in cars or victims of assault. *Gemütlichkeit* prevents this. Any injuries suffered are purely drinking injuries and casualties alcohol-induced. The whole two-week party I saw was a celebration of congeniality, with a numb peace and a gentle tipsy smile pervading the whole city, whether you partook of a beer or two in a tent or not. This was apparently the essence of *Gemütlichkeit*.

Munich is Germany's second city. Hold the Oktoberfest on the outskirts of Birmingham and what would happen?

'Already in Roman times Tacitus remarked that "no nation abandons itself more completely to banqueting and entertainment than the Germans",' Manny's notes reminded me. Well now I'd had first-hand experience of this. But apparently there was a lot more fun to be had in Germany than just Oktoberfest. I'd never had it down as a carnival country but now I learnt that there were carnivals large and small all over those parts of modern Germany that the Romans were able to reach and refresh with their pagan festivals. And later the Catholics came up with the whole un-Roman and frankly German idea that taking a break from excess was spiritually healthy.

The Romans settled along the Rhine and set up a colony in a place whose name means just that: Cologne. I remembered the other Oktoberfest anthem, 'Viva Colonia'. They apparently had fun there too. Cologne vies with the cities of Mainz to its south and Düsseldorf to its north for holding the best party on the Rhine. But none of them is Rio or Port of Spain and, as with anything organised by Germans, the formalisation of fun displays a particularly Teutonic character, its enjoyment being taken very seriously indeed. Look no further than the organisation of Cologne's carnival, which begins every year on the dot at eleven minutes past the eleventh hour on the eleventh day of the eleventh month. Then woe betide you if you are wearing a tie on the first Thursday before Mardi Gras as this is this *Weiberfestnacht*, 'Wenches' Day', when any woman has licence to cut it off in what is presumably a symbol of emasculation. More pleasurably and less damaging to your Hugo Boss wardrobe, they are also free to give anyone a *Bützjer* (kiss), and this licence, as I found out on my arrival, was even enjoyed by the hostesses on Lufthansa flights coming into Cologne. Thereafter the city seemed to me a huge street party with some people dressed up as clowns, like convicts, in the red and white stripes that are its colours, while the sight of a fair few *Lederhosen* confirmed my long-held suspicion that there must be a pair in every German wardrobe.

'Traditions of Fasching' – German for 'carnival', apparently, and nothing to do with Fascism – 'were important for Germans in the creation of the their newfound national identity in the nineteenth century. Many of the traditions developed out of a need to mock their French overlords.'

Mainz, Cologne and Düsseldorf, as large cities, could do this with confidence. But towns and villages evidently felt the need to enshrine their costumes, pageantry and traditions as museums. In these places festivals were celebrated in an elitist and exclusive fashion and I found myself unenthralled. Carnivals here were to be watched, like a nativity play or the enactment of a piece of history, and only true locals could really take part. It was the opposite of my notion of carnival and hardly a blow-out. The aim might have been to cement the traditions, as if the locals were aware of their mortality in a globalising world. But this had robbed the festivals of their life and ability to evolve, and they had become rather twee and fake.

Only one, in Rottweil in the Black Forest, leapt out; the town after which were named the stocky dogs, surely the canine incarnation of German Bight that were once used to draw local farmers' carts. Even so, I found Rottweil's claim to possess a world-famous carnival rather toothless.

There was one exception, Manny's notes said, to all this folklore, costumes, nostalgia, tradition and all-round *Gemütlichkeit*. The Berlin Love Parade was an annual summer street party that honoured true diversity – sexual, sartorial, religious and national – by contrast with the Oktoberfest's celebration of a single nostalgic ideal. The Love Parade was deliberately rootless and anti-tradition (though its participants still wore leather, albeit a different, shinier variety) and celebrated the hopes of the '68ers for a multicultural and more tolerant post-war Germany.

But that, stressed Manny, was an exception and for another of my therapy courses entirely. Still, I reflected, either with so much regional folklore or even without it, as in Berlin, Germans obviously loved dressing up. Folklore was just that: lore. A collection of ideas as opposed to real, lived-in tradition. Festivals led to the simplification, exaggeration and idealisation of these ideas. Germany, I had learnt, was precisely that at its beginning: an idea. And every detail of the country's folklore was based on ideas rather than reality. *Gemütlichkeit* was the comfort, but also the simplification, exaggeration and idealisation, of the idea of Germany. And, in the nation's priorities, it came before pure fun.

As always, too much 'sinking' and not enough sinking of pints.

6

Gesundheit
nf, *health*

'Today's world is obsessed with wellness.'

I couldn't stand that dreadful word. How could you make a noun out of an adverb? It was almost German in its American-ness. What was wrong with 'health'?

'It has turned into one of the biggest sectors of the tourist industry,' Manny continued, as we sat in his luxurious office once again.

Yes. And his type were the biggest beneficiaries of this obsession.

'But you don't have to go to some five-star hotel in Thailand or India. Go . . .' Manny's nose started to quiver and his eyes squinted, brows arching.

'Go to Germany!'

He sneezed. As if by magic, from some stirring linguistic recess of my brain, I retrieved a fragment of O-level German.

'*Gesundheit!*' I said.

'Exactly!' said Manny, surprised.

'Germans take their *Gesundheit* very seriously indeed. They were finding ways of practising daily good health long before the days of leotards, leg-warmers and Jane Fonda exercise videos. And light-years before Bikram yoga. You are now going to partake of an experience that is core to German life. *Das Bad*.'

Das Boot? No, it was bathtime.

How could a bath reawaken my *Wanderlust*? What could be so culturally significant about getting wet? I had already seen aspects of the German health obsession in the *Kur* resorts of the Baltic coast, the cycling, the accent on walking everywhere, and of course the nudity, and I was curious to know what Manny had in store for me.

And that was why I found myself back in Bavaria the very next day. It was time to undergo Manny's next module and exorcise my body in the serenity of a German swimming pool; a timely piece of biological *Selbstwahrnehmung*, after the vicissitudes of the copious and unquenchable German party spirit.

Munich has not one *Bad* (pronounced 'baht') but nine. Manny's notes directed me towards its most famous, the Müllersches Volksbad, Müller's People's Bath. It sounded like something from the *Kraft durch Freude* era. Sort of easyBath.

From outside I would never have imagined the building was a public bath. A mellow light-brown sandstone colour, it had a neo-classical, temple-like façade with ionic columns and a triangular pediment. From afar its entrance resembled that of an art gallery or museum. Behind the façade it stretched back in a long rectangle like the nave of a church, but with the tall, thin, arched windows of the more beautiful examples of nineteenth-century industrial buildings, such as railway sheds or waterworks. Above the nave sat a large dome and what could have been the twin bell-towers of a baroque church. But this was not a church. Sitting slightly sunken down near a bridge crossing the River Isar, where in summer Münchners like to bathe, no doubt naked, it was nothing other than a giant cathedral to the flesh. Not the Frauenkirche, Church of Our Lady, but the Bath of Our Lady.

Although it was drizzling outside, already the fresh air had begun to work its magic and I felt a glow of satisfaction. Going to a public pool and getting to know the bus routes, I felt like a local, part of the fabric of the place. Just what a real traveller wanted to feel.

Speaking of fabric, I had no swimming trunks, or *Textil*, whatsoever, and hoped I could buy a pair at the entrance desk. But part of me also thought there was a small chance I would not need any.

The Müllersches Volksbad was teeming with people young and old. It was as if the whole of Munich, after the recent demands of the Oktoberfest, had come to do penance at the altar, or rather sauna, of God. I passed through a beautiful, huge five-metre-high wooden revolving door with curvaceous brass handles. It was rush hour and so I had to take a number, like at a deli counter, and wait my turn. Meanwhile, I was in luck. The reception desk had a small selection of trunks which mercifully included a pair of baggy blue Bermuda shorts. After the *Lederhosen* of my last trip a pair of Speedos would have been wounding to the pride.

At last, after I had spent some twenty minutes admiring the gently rounded Jugendstil of this altogether sensual building, I heard my number called out on the tannoy.

'*Schwitzerbad* or *Hallenbad*?' the cashier asked me.

On entering a public pool in Germany the bather is presented with a fundamental choice: either a normal pool, with diving boards and lanes, or the so-called 'sweating bath' of saunas, steam rooms and hot and cold pools. You can go to both. But the two are separate. A 'sweating bath' sounded like just what I needed to expunge the alcohol of the Oktoberfest from my system.

'How long would you like?'

I asked for what I guessed was a normal length of time.

'An hour? Hour and a half?'

'The minimum is four hours,' came the reply.

Four hours! How can people sit around for four hours in a sauna? Don't they get bored? Haven't they got anything better to do?

My surprise must have been written all over my face.

'Some people find this is not enough,' said the woman pointedly.

I took the proffered four-hour ticket and followed the signs up the stairs to the first floor.

There was just one entrance. I put my ticket in the turnstile, which clocked my entry time like a parking meter. Then I went in search of the men's changing room.

But between the rows of clothes pegs and lockers I couldn't see any doors that obviously indicated a partitioning of the changing area on lines of gender.

I found myself in the ancient baths of the imagination: labyrinthine, with stairs and corridors everywhere, around which echoed disembodied murmuring, groans and cries. There were musty wooden lockers and dinky wooden drawers with big, dangly keys for storing valuables. The air hung thick with an earthy, dank smell of wet stone. Occasionally I could hear people changing and caught glimpses of bodies. Was that a woman? Yes, it was. And quite an attractive one at that. And now she was coming towards me in an eye-catching combination of tights and flip-flops and nothing on top. She walked straight past me to a row of hairdryers and began drying her hair, oblivious to my presence.

It wasn't just the unisex changing or the upfront nudity that threw me. It was also not knowing what to do next. My whole surroundings were geared towards a service I didn't know how to use. I had never felt so foreign and out of place so relatively near to home. Manny would have been gratified to see me, the self-proclaimed jaded traveller, so far out of my comfort zone.

'Ah yes,' he had challenged me, 'you see, in your average Holmes Place in England you have begun to have saunas and steam rooms. But they are small, pathetic things in comparison; curious little add-ons to the main pool area that you don't really know how to use. Maybe spend a few minutes in each before getting bored and impatient.'

I decided to ask the *Bademeister*, who in Germany is more than merely the equivalent of a pool attendant. He is the resident healer, in charge of both running the place and administering treatments.

Ulli, as his badge read, was a cuddly man dressed in a white T-shirt and shorts, plastic flip-flops and white socks, and had a bushy black moustache. Hardly the picture of health, despite his ruddy cheeks and smiley demeanour, he sat at a reception desk like a janitor. I didn't like to disturb him, particularly not with such idiotic questions. But he seemed only too happy to help Johnny foreigner in his obvious bafflement and showed me where to change, what not to wear – for indeed I would not be needing my new trunks – and where to shower before I entered the sauna complex. He then advised me, as a complete new-comer, what routine I should observe.

'First shower and then go to the first sauna, the lower-temperature one. Spend maybe eight to ten minutes there and then take a cold shower or go in the cold pool. Then walk around a little to relax but keep the circulation going. And then repeat. As you're not used to it, don't stay too long in the sauna. And as soon as you feel uncomfortable you must come out.'

I had my orders.

Self-consciously I stripped and went into the shower. I was slowly getting my head around the whole thing, but was still taken aback when I turned and saw two women naked in the shower next to me. It was that British prudishness again, which Manny had so derided. One was in her toned mid-forties, the other nearing her seventies and, from the voluminous folds of her body, had clearly invested heavily in insulation over the years. What would she look like in a *Dirndl*? She had a mischievous grin and, seeing my obvious surprise, cackled, 'It's all right, we won't do anything to you!' I managed a smile and, slightly missing the moment, replied, 'That's what I'm afraid of.'

We all towelled down and, to avoid doing anything wrong, I followed them, towel firmly around waist, out into the communal area.

The centrepiece of the Müllersches Volksbad, sited beneath the frescoed dome I had seen from the outside, was a warm wallowing pool made of stone, where everyone was hanging out between doses of hot or cold punishment. It was quite a shock to the eyes. The circular pool was packed with cooing couples draped naked over one another, and I could barely see the people for the flesh. It was as if we were in some fairly early circle of the Inferno. Either that or I'd walked in on some huge swingers' party.

I recoiled and went on a tour, at the very least to find a place where I wouldn't feel like a naked gooseberry. There were many saunas of varying temperatures and, as Ulli had recommended, I plumped for the least hot.

Seven bodies now sat together in total silence, like sweating melons. I found myself with my two earlier lady friends, one of whom had now joined her male partner, another couple, and an old man. While I sat prudishly with my towel over my lap, all my other co-sweaters had their towels laid out beneath them and sat or lay with their legs at varying degrees of openness, from the discreet five-to-eleven to the full-frontal quarter to three. They could have been posing for *Déjeuner sur l'herbe*.

For Germans, sauna nudity is a matter of serious hygiene. Indeed they can't understand why the British insist on wearing a swimming costume. According to them, the sweaty costume contaminates the wooden rungs of the sauna benches and so instead you should lay your towel down underneath you and sweat naked. That's about as poor an excuse for nudity as I've heard.

Whatever the rights and wrongs, it was like being in a very long lift. It was simply impossible to keep your eyes focused on nothing or the vague middle distance. So they started to wander. But, aware that mine were the only wandering ones, I began to feel even more uncomfortable. Before long it was hard to suppress the nervous schoolboy giggles that were gurgling up inside me.

I decided I needed to cool off. The place had all manner of contraptions for giving yourself a cold shock. 'Vee haf vayz . . .' There was a cold pool, a traditional 'vertical' cold shower and a shower that sprayed cold water sideways at all heights of the body. But I went for a cold bucket that was constantly refilled from a pipe in the ceiling and which, when you yanked a cord, emptied freezing water on your head from a great height like a watery guillotine.

Now I needed to warm up again, but not overheat, and so felt obliged to join the mass love-in in the main waterhole. That was it, yes. It was a bit like a safari. There were hippos and elephants, tall, spindly giraffes and one or two lithe gazelles. I found myself a discreet place on the steps of the warm pool and attempted to relax. But again my position also turned into an involuntary vantage point. What could I do with my eyes, short of closing them?

A word or two about hair. Other than on our head, hair is not something humans generally find attractive. It overheats, smells, carries dirt and grows where you don't want it to. Unless you're German, in which case you love it everywhere. At least that was what I thought. I'd grown up with images of hirsute East German female athletes like Marita Koch who, whenever they won (which they did with suspicious frequency), would raise their arms to reveal Black Forests of hair. And when Nena, she of '99 Red Balloons', appeared on *Top of the Pops* I was shocked to see her raucous, sexy voice belonged, yes, to a sexy body but one with armpits memorably described as looking like 'ZZ Top in a headlock'. There was old Adolf himself, of course, with his postage stamp. And who could forget footballer Rudi Völler's moustache and perm? The ultimate porn star look, it further cemented everything *Lederhosen* had done to link Germans and sex.

Rudi had what we call a mullet and the Germans call a *VoKuHiLa*. This is not a Glaswegian expletive but short for '*Vorne Kurz Hinten Lang*', or 'short at the front, long at the back'. I was glad to hear the Germans had acknowledged it as a hairstyle, for while hair in Britain went from Flock of Seagulls to Rick Astley, the *VoKuHiLa* had seemingly remained pre-eminent in Germany from the 1970s to the 1990s.

With his moustache Rudi had actually had a full-on '*VoKuHiLa Überlippen*' – 'above the lips'. But call it what they like – '*Rotzbremsen*', 'bogie barriers', for moustaches or '*Pornobalken*', 'porno handlebars', for sideburns – German men (and so, I suppose, German women) loved a bit of facial hair. In the 2005 World Beard Championship held in Berlin the Germans mopped up fourteen out of seventeen categories, including 'Musketeer', 'Wild West', 'Imperial Austrian' and 'Dalí'. And in Germany they even have a National Federation of Beard Clubs. As a diversion from my therapy I decided to make a study down at the local supermarket. After half an hour of time-and-motion follicle research I concluded that a massive one-third of German males over eighteen had a moustache of one form or other.

Why? I could only conclude that, along with trees, antlers, *Lederhosen* and kegs of beer in half-timbered pubs, hair for a German was *gemütlich*. I don't mean the 'comfortable' part but certainly the warmth and nostalgia parts. Arminius and the lot from *Gladiator* all sported facial hair. A moustache for a German seemed to be part of the mythology of a longed-for national rural tradition.

But what about down below? Whatever Marita Koch and Nena might have been hiding in their tight trousers, what were today's young German women like? I would not even have been thinking about this had I not by now, after an hour or so in Müller's People's Bath, involuntarily accumulated some evidence. All I can say is that if I had recently learnt about a little-suspected German community in Brazil, now I could vouch for the presence of 'Brazilians' in Germany.

In my mind I was trying to make everything I learnt about Germany fit together. Was this further proof of a German love of *Ordnung* in matters of personal grooming? The pubic trim as a metaphor for the German mindset? More likely a case of German over-analysis. The evidence was a little thin . . .

Some bathers had clearly come better prepared than me and with something to focus their gaze on. It wasn't all lovers. There were students studying novels or textbooks, naked or with a tactically draped towel. What had FKK-Jugend said about nudity freeing the mind? Others chatted with their mates as if down at the pub. Others again sat reading the weekend papers, some of them at a mosaic-tiled circular plinth at the foot of which were tiled footbaths which could be filled with hot water. The idea was that while you sat and relaxed, reading the paper, your feet were kept warm and your circulation stimulated. It was almost normal and I suddenly wanted to be here with a friend too, chewing the fat or conducting a post-mortem of the night before. Or, if I had been better prepared, I could have brought my own newspapers or a book. It was a great way to chill out and pass the afternoon, as if you were in a library, albeit an FKK library.

The most spectacular room in the Müllersches Volksbad was the steam room, entered through a heavy iron door like that of a vault, and as I stepped inside I was met by a huge jet of steam. The whole room, barely lit, was full of a grey-white fog like the dry ice in a cheesy eighties pop video, through which it was just possible to glimpse other people moving around like pink shadows. This seemed to be the favourite room and against the low, hypnotic roar of the steam jet people were trying to converse. A hard core of bathers did stretches and exercises right up in front of the jet, while others either stood in its wake or sat on stone walls at its edge. Along one side lay three tiers of sarcophagal stone shelves, like bunk beds in a school dormitory, on which it was possible to lie or even sleep. These were the spa equivalent of sun-loungers or *Strandkörber* and there was fierce competition for them. After waiting patiently I at last got my turn on one and would have fallen asleep but for the fact that there was something unsettling about being amassed naked in a dark room full of Germans with steam being pumped in.

As I wandered between pools, saunas, showers and the steam room I began to see the same people and recognise their faces in a way for which my English sense of etiquette was not equipped. I wasn't quite sure if I should now start hailing them, or even engage them in conversation. I retreated into British reserve and isolation. And a little paranoia. Was that man following me?

I was in one of the saunas when suddenly there was a huge rush of people crushing one another to get in. What was going on? It was like the Carling Black Label ad all over again. 'How many naked bodies can we fit in the sauna?' seemed to be the game of the day, as more and more people arrived and squeezed their sweaty naked behinds on to any spare bit of bench. Some even sat on others. There was something quite primitive about it all and I was really beginning to doubt the hygiene supremacy argument.

Why all the kerfuffle? It was time for the *Aufguss*, or 'topping up', of the sauna coals with whatever curative potion was on the menu.

Had I been more observant or expert in the art of the *Schwitzerbad* I would have seen the clock above Ulli's desk, which had shown the time of the next *Aufguss*. This was clearly a ritual no serious 'sweater' wanted to miss and so it was no wonder they were running, as if after sun-loungers. And I, a Brit, had unwittingly got there early – again.

The sauna can only have been about three or four metres square but I counted more than thirty people jammed inside it. It was no longer the empty-lift scenario. This was like one of those packed commuter lifts I was sure was overloaded and where there was no option but to stare at whatever part of someone's body was directly in front of me.

Then Ulli appeared, like a master of ceremonies. German life is not a cabaret but a sauna, I thought.

'So, everybody. It's *Aufguss* time.'

Then, as if reeling off a choice of teas, he offered us, 'Jasmine, eucalyptus, mandarin or rose?'

Mandarin seemed to be the unanimous verdict and so, like a high priest, the *Bademeister* began ladling it on to the coals, which gave a pleasing fizz and sent clouds of fragrant steam into the air. I thought that was it. But no, Ulli took the sodden towel from over his shoulder, which I had presumed was to mop his brow, and proceeded to flick it about violently, driving the fresh, flavoured vapour in our direction, as if it were incense and he were blessing us: 'The steam of Christ, the steam of Christ.' Then he began to whip the towel around more wildly, like swinging a cat, and with a mischievous grin said, 'Let's get rid of all that beer then, hey!' One by one he went round all of us, giving us each ten lashes with the towel. People lifted their arms to let all the vapours waft over them, grimacing with the concentration and the intense heat, and all around there was a sound of deep breathing in. It was a form of masochism and self-flagellation – military and fetishistic and peculiarly German – and I felt as if I was chastising myself for my sins. Those who couldn't hack the heat got up and left immediately. Then, when Ulli had finished, he gave a quick Hispanic flourish, as if to say, '*Olé*', and there was a round of applause. I lasted another five or six minutes, breathing in the vapour as if drawing on a hubble-bubble pipe, before rushing out. Never had I been so glad of a pool of freezing water.

I'd had enough long before the full four hours were up. But by the time I handed back my swimming costume, unused, at reception I'd been there nearly two hours. I felt a new man, cleansed and a bizarre combination of invigorated and exhausted, as if I had actually done some exercise. There was no denying the Müllersches Volksbad was an all-German health experience and the sensuous building had added a sense of the heritage behind the tradition. I felt almost uplifted by my discovery of the *Schwitzerbad* and glad that I would now know what I was actually supposed to do with the saunas and steam rooms in my local gym.

And yet I couldn't quite evangelise. There had been something dehumanising about the lack of sexuality. In a bizarre twist it was a case of 'No sex, please, we're German'. In the sauna, gender seemed to disappear behind the health philosophy. A sort of 'Strength through Nudity' took precedence over reality. The mind of a levelling ideology triumphed over matter. Yet surely gender was an essential part of human dignity. The Germans had taken the Roman orgy and turned it into a Tupperware party. It was like the beach: for Germans the nude body was again not to be treated with carnal joy but with earnestness. The sauna was all about the importance of being naked and healthy.

It was impossible to ignore the Aryan connotations of this emphasis on purity and hygiene, like the perverted megalomaniac general in *Dr Strangelove*, bent on nuking the Russkies in order to preserve the purity of America's 'precious bodily fluids'.

'*In Germany a spa town is denoted by the prefix "Bad", meaning "Bath", just like the Wiltshire town. Except that you Brits have so few that the word "Bath" is enough to single out one solitary place's bathing virtues*,' Manny's notes admonished me.

Whereas Germany is littered with them. There are the famous ones, Baden-Baden and Wiesbaden. But also tens of smaller ones: Bad Homburg, Bad Doberan, Bad Wimpfen and so on. In order for a German town to earn itself the prefix '*Bad*' it has to satisfy certain criteria in terms of the purity of its air and water. Technically speaking it should also be founded on an area of natural springs. But equally a town can lose its *Bad* status for being, well, bad. In a country where even a mediocre hotel will have a sauna and pool in the basement, the spa is clearly an important part of German life. And, given the current explosion in health tourism, I thought, Germany is surely well placed to benefit. If only people could be sold the nudity angle . . .

At the core of the *Bad* experience is the whole idea of the hot-cold routine and how this stimulates what the Germans hold most dear in their bodies: *der Kreislauf*, the circulation. Countries seem to have favourite ailments and favourite parts of the body they consider should be nurtured as the root of all health. The French are obsessed by '*l'estomac*' and you will frequently find them in thrall to all that is gastric, from gastronomy itself to the pain caused by its excesses. For the Italians it is '*il fegato*', the liver, which is why they are fairly hopeless participants in the Oktoberfest. And the English are always obsessed by headaches and migraines. But the German's most-feared ailment is *Kreislaufstörung*: disturbance of the circulation. And so to prevent this, although they invented aspirin, they nurture the heart, the motor of circulation, as a preventative cure as much as possible, through sweat-bathing and all types of exercise, seemingly into their seventies. Hence the seventy-year-olds on rambling and bike treks along the Baltic and the tendency of older German males to suffer from competitive-dad syndrome. Can you imagine having Oliver Kahn as your dad? I also remembered watching the Olympics as a child there was always one relentless German slaving away amid a pack of far more natural African athletes and he just wouldn't lie down.

But not content with identifying *Kreislaufstörung* as their own nemesis the Germans, so I now learnt, had to go and systemise ways to ward it off. Here was Manny's Romantic German spirit entering even the bathroom! For, just as nudism in Germany had its Great Educator in Heinrich Pudor, so there would emerge, in the early nineteenth century, which was just learning to be Romantic, a German high priest of bathtime: Dr Sebastian Kneipp. Kneipp was indeed a real priest as well as a Bavarian, and in the first half of the century he was one of the founders of naturopathic medicine.

Neither Kneipp nor the Germans claim to have discovered the healthy qualities of baths. But what Kneipp did was to turn bathing from a social pastime into a philosophy. His lasting legacy was the *Kneipp Kur* or *Kneipp-Bad*, a system of hydrotherapeutic healing involving the application of water through various methods, temperatures and pressures, which is what I had experienced in the Müllersches Volksbad. For his books such as *My Water Cure* and his work as an early Manny-type counsellor Kneipp was considered a global authority on health and tens of thousands flocked from all over the world to the little Bavarian spa town of Bad Wärishofen to seek his healing advice. Water was central to his philosophy but he also had progressive theories on exercise, herbalism and nutrition. In Norway they even named a type of bread after him.

According to Manny, if I was to be a *Kneipp-Bad* convert I had to visit the mecca of German wellness (or 'vellness' as they inevitably called it): the town of Baden-Baden on the edge of the Black Forest in south-west Germany. So clean they named it twice.

Baden-Baden was on the route of the first Thomas Cook tours in the 1850s, although it had long been a playground for Europe's royals and aristocracy. This landlocked Monte Carlo, branded by tourism boards as 'the summer capital of Europe', was known for the healing waters the Romans had discovered there and also for its gambling, which at the time was banned in France. By sacking Heidelberg's castle, occupying large tracts of Germany and banning first carnivals and now gambling, France was fast approaching par with Germany as one of history's most churlish neighbours.

The legacy of so much upper-class fun is a Parisian-style city of boutiques, villas, cafés, gourmet restaurants and Europe's oldest casino; of private roads and an infernal traffic-calming one-way system. There were even neat symmetrical rows of pollarded dwarf plane trees *à la* Tuileries and the greyish buildings with iron balconies and grey mansards that are such a feature of the French capital.

The town is set deep in a valley of rolling hills and has the air of a posh alpine resort, like St Moritz without the Alps, lots of fur and mutton dressed as lamb, and too much Louis Vuitton for my liking. I was in good company. According to Mark Twain, 'it is an inane town, full of sham, and petty fraud, and snobbery, but the baths are good . . .' But the beautiful and fragrant lawns laid out along the banks of the trickling River Oosbach did remind me of the Cambridge Backs.

Baden-Baden has a sense of style, or rather an abandonment to the superfluous and the superficial, that, recalling the pragmatism of the Baltic resorts, I found very un-German. The Kempinski Hotel at Heiligendamm aside, you were unlikely to find a casino on Germany's Baltic coast.

Nowadays I reckoned not many people went to Baden-Baden for the casino, however therapeutic it might be to throw away large sums of money. The glamorous image of the idealist artist-gambler helplessly hell-bent on self-destruction and penury seemed to be a thing of the past and even black tie and evening dress are no longer *de rigueur* in these naff times full of *Weltschmerz*.

But whereas the casino seemed a hollow symbol of a bygone age, the magnificent bathing buildings of Baden-Baden were still hanging in there. The Trinkhalle (drinking hall), now the tourist office and a café serving delicious Black Forest gateau, had the original natural spring issuing a foul-tasting but reputedly health-enhancing mineral-rich water. The building itself was an amazing Valhalla-style Parthenon of neo-classical columns and arcades hewn in a mixture of red and gold sandstone, and decorated with huge frescoes. But in a Teutonic rehash of the Renaissance, where these frescoes might normally have depicted the hands of God, blue skies, cherubs and madonnas, here, as on the Baltic coast, they showed Romantic Wagnerian hunting scenes, suggestive moonlit landscapes and nature at its most tempestuous.

Many new and new-fangled baths had sprung up on the coattails of the original but the *pièce de résistance*, the Friedrichsbad, with its majestic red-white sandstone neo-Renaissance façade, sea-green cupola and, inside, a labyrinth of columns, arches and mosaic tiles, still took centre stage. Built in 1877, this was a museum, a temple to *Gesundheit*, inspired by the Romans. But also a temple to the foundation of the German nation and its accompanying mottoes of nudity and water therapy.

The Friedrichsbad, I was reliably informed, was the bath of all baths. It went with the snobbery of the town's name: aristocratic and double-barrelled, so permitting its residents to distinguish themselves from other spa towns, as if theirs was the real McCoy.

I walked, belittled, through the entrance arch inscribed with poetry by Goethe. It was that man again. Something about the mind becoming freer and blood being renewed, the lady on reception told me. It was clearly an exaltation, a case of 'Reinheit macht frei', or 'Purity makes you free'. Bathtime was supposed to be a Romantic experience!

This time I'd come prepared. Remembering Munich, I wanted someone to chat to, who could share with me this whole German bathing lark as a partly social thing. My therapy didn't have to be so lonely. So I'd brought with me a sweat-bathing novice in the form of a doctor friend of mine. But no Kneipp, he was about as English an Englishman as you could get.

I had obviously become inured – you might say brainwashed – to the whole nudity and mixed-bathing phenomenon. So as we embarked it was amusing to see an Englishman exactly where I had been before my first German bath experience. Here the whole healing process was much more ordered and sequential than in other German baths, and we were moved from room to pool, from pool to room on a course of fifteen steps to purity timed to last two hours. As a sweat-bather – we English really don't do compound nouns comfortably – now of some intermediate experience I thought this was a bit on the light side. I was also surprised to learn that, in a rare concession to gender, men and women were segregated, only coming face to face in a pool in the middle at the end of the treatment. Surely not very German.

The high point came about halfway, when we were given the option of a scrub-down by a couple of apathetic-looking *Bademeister* who looked more like disaffected male nurses. I thought nothing of it – or at least gave them the benefit of the doubt – and lay starkers first on my front and then on my back as the attendant lathered and rubbed my body. But my friend, being the type who would wear plus fours up a Scottish mountain, was having none of it. 'Just my back and legs' he said firmly, as his man attempted to turn him over. 'That'll do fine!' Out of the corner of my eye I could see the *Bademeister*'s look of amused perplexity at this prudish Englishman and it was all I could do to suppress my sniggers.

We left the Friedrichsbad revived if not relieved and comforted by Twain's double-edged words on his bathing experiences: 'I fully believe I left my rheumatism in Baden-Baden. B-B is welcome to it. It was little, but it was all I had to give. I would have preferred to leave something that was catching, but it was not in my power.'

So I was now fully versed in the German obsession with the spa. They hadn't invented it but they had made it their own. The *Kur* was a core part of German life and I now understood its many-layered meanings of care, cure, life philosophy and spiritualism. Every German is entitled to a week a year free at a *Kurort*, or 'wellness centre', as part of their national insurance if they have some indefinable illness and are unable to work. Like *Weltschmerz*? I wondered. But my journey into German wellness wasn't over yet.

'For a German *Gesundheit* is not some form of hypochondria that relies on a quick-fix, on-demand cure. It is life philosophy that pervades all aspects of living and stems from a respect for and closeness to Mother Nature.'

A German's health is affected by the health of nature herself. He can't bear to see her abused. This idea appears to go back way beyond the Romantics, who found nature the most perfect instrument for describing their inner state. Whether or not the early Germans were barbarians, the Romans had observed their tendency to hug their national symbol. According to Tacitus, 'they consecrate whole woods and groves, and by the names of the gods they call these recesses; divinities these'.

Early travel writers visiting Germany also found it worthy of comment. In *Peeps at Germany* of 1911 the writer describes the concept of the *Waldschule*, a primary school in the forest: 'all the winter the children who are lucky enough to go to the *Waldschule* look forward to April, when they will leave their stuffy homes every morning early and for six months will spend the whole day in the forest.'

'Did you know,' said Manny, 'that a version of the *Waldschule* was exported to Britain by the German Jew Kurt Hahn? Another of Germany's great educators, he believed in the value of outdoor pursuits as a cornerstone of education and in forming leaders. He set up a number of schools in Germany, typically in abandoned castles in the middle of nowhere, and when pursued by the Nazis' – Manny neglected to reveal Hahn initially sympathised with them and included Hitler Youth teachings in his syllabuses – 'he came to Britain. His legacy is schools such as Gordonstoun in Scotland, Atlantic College in Wales and various dedicated Outward Bound schools around the country.'

Two millennia later little had changed. The ancient Germans' love of nature underpinned modern Germany's attitude to *Gesundheit* and its Protestant approach to social responsibility.

'The Germans were the original eco-warriors,' declared Manny. 'Pioneers of how every day every individual can do their bit to save the environment. The environment is now the biggest problem facing humanity and the Germans have taken the lead. You tourists globalise the world in your jumbo jets instead of walking amid cultural gems such as Germany that are on your doorstep. Modern tourism is nothing but ethnic cleansing that destroys cultural diversity both on the ground and in the mind. Hence your Syndrome.'

Manny then listed Germany's green achievements.

The Germans had catalytically converted their cars and started recycling long before anyone else. They'd invented the *Grüne Welle* (green wave) traffic light to keep city traffic moving and limit the time cars spent motionless pouring out fumes. Germany's Green Party was the first environmental party to win any significant voice in any European national parliament. The long-awaited autobahn linking Hamburg to the north-east of Germany was delayed and re-routed several times in response to ecological campaigns on behalf of a rare German frog. All over the Baltic coast I had seen huge utopian wind farms and, said Manny, in terms of total wattage Germany produces the most wind power of any country in the world. The Germans being past masters at segregation, where in most other countries there would be one rubbish bin, in Germany there seemed to be ten, each for a different type of waste. I remembered hearing an amusing anecdote about German troops stationed in Afghanistan who went to great lengths to separate all their waste into categories for recycling. But no sooner did it leave their compound than it was mixed up with all the other rubbish collected from the compounds of their less environmentally aware allies. While the US was fighting the War on Terror, the Germans were fighting the War on Waste in a coalition with nature all of their own.

Manny's notes finished with a flourish: 'And in the USA it has taken an Austrian as Governor of California to see the "inconvenient truth" and pledge "I'll be green!"'

Even if you didn't actually see Germans worshipping trees nowadays, *der Wald*, the forest, was still clearly an object of veneration. Out of respect for the environment Germans have now invented Peace Forests where, instead of paying for a grave in a cemetery for a departed loved one, they can 'buy' a tree for them and have a plaque dedicated to them nailed to it. The German Romantics spoke of the *Waldespracht*, the splendour of the forest, and imbued it not just with national symbolism but also notions of justice, knowledge and uncontrollable wildness. All contradictory human facets, I reckoned. Germany was still full of the woods and forests that scared the Romans: the Teutoburger Wald, the Thüringer Wald, the Pfalzer Wald, the Oberpfalzer Wald and, of course, the Schwarzwald, the Black Forest. Together the combined forests of Germany and Austria represent the largest wooded surface area in Europe, with as much as 33 per cent of German *Lebensraum* still forest, compared with just over 10 per cent of the UK. Thirty-three per cent? That was the same as the percentage of bearded Germans. The tree was not only healthy, it was as *gemütlich* as facial hair on German men and as much a symbol of German nationalism as Arminius, the original Hermann the German.

Ironic then, that politically Germany's Green movement was the legacy of the angry, sometimes murderous '68ers and their opposition to a post-war return to German *Gemütlichkeit*. Being *umweltfreundlich*, friendly to the environment, like going naked, was supposed to symbolise a tolerant, pacifist, compassionate, left-wing and anti-fascist stance. At the same time Germany did, I learnt, have a track record of deregulation remarkable in these nanny-state PC times. In contrast to the anti-nicotine fascism of most of Europe, Germany is still set to remain a smoker's paradise. And famously there is no speed limit (*Geschwindigkeitsbeschränkung*) on most of its autobahns. It takes an age of studying and practical exams to qualify to drive in Germany, so it was assumed that after this a driver could handle a car at ridiculously high speeds. The alternative, to regulate, was seen as plunging back into their dark past.

So, as it was for Karl May and his fictitious eco-warrior Old Shatterhand, I now understood that German life was something that took place very much outside, amid nature. *Gesundheit* was a metaphor for a Zen-like harmony with the world. It was based on what could be harnessed from nature and used, through a suitable way of life, in order to prevent rather than cure. Granted, an innate disposition to *Angst* ensured a near-permanent state of cerebral hypochondria. But not for Germans just a bathroom cabinet full of potions and pills or a living room full of the bizarre fitness equipment advertised at midnight on cable channels. The *Angst* had to be fought by the mind, by an idea. Again it was the Protestant hard-work ethic versus the aspirin indulgence of a Catholic confessional.

On the Baltic I had seen how Germans of all ages liked to get kitted up like ramblers, complete with crooks like Caspar David Friedrich's *Wanderer*, and walk everywhere when on holiday, using their vast network of *Wanderwege*. This was far too serious and geeky for the average English person who sees a far greater virtue in phlegmatism. But now I understood that it was all at the service of the old *Kreislauf* (circulation).

Old travel books which Manny quoted noted how Germans loved to walk. 'It is one of Germany's peculiar virtues that her sons and daughters use their feet, and the visitor who wishes to know the German character must study the process at first hand [. . .] wherever there is beautiful country in Germany there are the walkers in their thousands.' And German schools quite often had *Wandertage*, or walking days, when children would simply roam about the countryside because it was both good for the soul and taught them about nature. In the Rhine valley I had experienced for myself a short piece of the spectacular Rheinsteig, 320 kilometres of narrow, precipitous trail following the river past castles on cliff edges and rolling vineyards, and passing through dense German forest. The Germans claim this is the best and most Romantic walk in Europe.

In Germany there was no debating a person's right to roam: it was a birthright if not a national duty.

Then I learnt that the Germans had invented the *Barfusspark* – barefoot parks where you divest yourself of shoes as a barrier between you and nature; hadn't the same excuse been used for nudity by German sun-worshippers? – and wander barefoot among the woods and meadows, feeling the electricity and wisdom of Mother Earth coming up through your feet.

And in the hills around Baden-Baden I could see that the Germans even treated skiing, especially *Langlauf*, or cross-country skiing, as a tour through nature: all kitted out with fitness-freak/fetishist tight catsuit trousers, techno aerating top, woolly bobble hat and a rucksack full of assorted hunter-gatherer necessities to keep them going for weeks, I observed tens of Jürgen-the-Germans setting out on circuits through the forest to commune with nature, birdsong and fresh animal tracks.

And not surprisingly, I found there were educators at the root of all this lifestyle – social engineers, systemisers and Romantics in search of a better world.

The Germans call this kind of exercise circuit a *Trimmdichpfad*, or 'trim-yourself path'. It is usually a marked run through a forest with various exercise bars and rings for the runner to do at varying intervals. At each station a sign indicates how many repetitions you should do according to whether you are a man, woman or training as a family. But the *Trimmdichpfad* is more than just a normal training circuit, like something you might do on various bits of apparatus in an indoor gym. The whole point is that you should be outside, smell the pine and feel the spring of Mother Earth under your every step. Every German village has one and they are to be found on the outskirts of most towns and in some big city parks.

The *Trimmdichpfad* is the legacy of one Friedrich Ludwig Jahn. He invented and institutionalised *Turnen* (gymnastics) in Germany and is affectionately known as 'Turnvater Jahn': Jahn, Daddy of PE.

In the early nineteenth century, when Germany was a disorderly collection of city states largely under Napoleonic rule, Jahn was a political activist and a forefather not just of PE but of the concept of a united German state. A true revolutionary, he failed exams and entry to various institutions and became a maverick and marginalised teacher of radical ideas. In his first *magnum opus, Das Deutsche Volkstum* (German Nationhood), he took the line that 'the small city-stateness of Germany constrains Germany's size in the world. Whoever lets their children learn French is a madman who in doing so stands against the holy spirit. If he lets his daughter learn French, he might as well be teaching her to be a whore.' So, all in all, quite a mild man.

In mass physical education Jahn saw a means to an end: the freeing of Germany from French rule by an athletic and fit people, and the establishment of a German state. The Heidelberg *Burschenschaften* were an embodiment of Jahn's teachings. And I wondered whether the German word for secondary school, '*Gymnasium*', had anything to do with Jahn-influenced physical education. Fitness and health were political, as they would be again in the 1930s, when Hitler appropriated much of Jahn's theories.

Jahn was imprisoned by the French and then the Prussians as a pariah of the state, and it was only in 1840, when doctors started taking note of the health benefits of his teachings, as expressed in his book of 1816 *Die Deustsche Turnkunst* (The German Art of Physical Education), that his name was cleared and his *Turnplätze* (gyms) started to become a feature of German life. Jahn would eventually be regarded as a national treasure, credited with equipping the common people with the strength to overthrow the authorities in the 1848 revolution that finally won them social freedoms and launched the rise of the German middle class.

It was at roughly the same time that another of Germany's social educators – there were quite a lot of them – was talking up the health benefits of another outdoor space that is now dear to all Germans: the garden. But not the English rose garden; instead the *Kleingarten* or *Schrebergarten*, named after Dr Daniel Schreber.

In Britain we would call this kind of garden an allotment. Colonies of these small, often rectangular green spaces are found on the outskirts of towns and cities, where they are dedicated to the cultivation of fruit and vegetables. And ultimately the allotment and the *Schrebergarten* share the same aim. An admirer of Charles Dickens (the social progressive more than the novelist) Schreber was concerned about the lifestyle and education of young German Oliver Twists. He wanted to bring the young closer to nature and outdoor spaces. To this end he promoted the conversion of urban wasteland into recreational areas, and his legacy is that today Germany has 1.3 million *Schrebergarten*.

So far so normal. Schreber sounded like a decent sort of bloke, keen to give the country's children green fingers, and, being German, keen to advocate gardening as a nature-loving activity good for the circulation. But that is where the link with the Garden of England ends.

For Schreber was no gentle Alan Titchmarsh, and far from being a pastime for the cultivation of sweet peas for the village fête, gardening in Germany became a method of social engineering. Like Turnvater Jahn, Schreber was an exercise fanatic who thought his fledgling nation needed toughening up. His gardens were places where the urban youth could be forced to practise his strenuous exercise regime. Schreber's book *How to Achieve Happiness and Bliss through Physical Exercise* was once to be found on the bookshelves of most German families. It recommended, among other things, the daily immersion of children in cold water, the encouraging of girls to carry dolls in their right hand in order to prevent 'onesidedness', the improvement of children's postures with various torturous machines, and an anti-masturbation strap (Schreber saw masturbation as enfeebling) which would pierce the skin of a boy's penis should he dare to have a nocturnal erection or *Morgenlatte*, 'morning glory'. I took it as read that Schreber was an avid FKK supporter and opposed to the arousal caused by clothing.

Some idea of happiness. Life in Schreber's garden was definitely not a bed of roses. Imagine an average child emerging from this kind of moulding – upright and mechanical as a robot, pure but with too much repressed testosterone – and you have your average Nazi. Schreber practised on his own family and, not surprisingly, his first son shot himself and his second was admitted to an asylum.

Like FKK the *Schrebergarten* was an outlet of freedom in the former East Germany, a place where they could avoid surveillance and to a certain extent live out a fantasy life. But there was a rule book with strict regulations on everything from the number of trees that had to be planted and the maximum height of raspberry canes to the forbidding of walnuts and rhubarb, strict curfews and the acceptable days for hanging out washing.

If you planted only flowers and no vegetables, you paid double the usual rent because you were contributing to the queues in the shops. But if you had a *Schrebergarten* at all, you didn't even have to queue for beetroot.

Not exactly 'How to Be a Gardener'. And presumably the Stasi had a special 'Garden Branch' checking that every blade of grass was precisely the same length.

'But you see gardens are something you have in common with the Germans. You live outside your city centres, and in houses rather than apartment blocks. The layout of residential roads is everywhere quite similar. And you love your front lawns and like to establish boundaries with hedges and the like.'

Was Manny saying the garden was a metaphor for that Anglo-German obsession, the sun-lounger?

I had learnt a fair deal of German history, and not the stuff taught at school. I now knew a bit about Bismarck, Kaiser Willy and Hitler. But here were Hahn, Jahn, Kneipp and Schreber, four nature-loving social engineers working more or less in the same era that coincided with Goethe and the birth of the Romantic ideal and who were in their respective ways also responsible for the creation of the German nation. Luckily only the best bits of their legacies remained: that's to say, the basic health and outdoor disciplines without the nationalism or penis piercing.

So far, I had been for a number of swims in Germany, both clothed and unclothed, several saunas and steam baths (unclothed), bike rides and walks. I hadn't done any gardening but had seen plenty of *Schrebergarten*. What's more, back in England allotments and going green were now trendy, or in Romantic vernacular, 'exalted'. And I now saw modern Germany as one of the most tolerant and liberal countries in post-war Europe with a smaller, more rolled-back state than I had imagined.

'How are you feeling?' Manny asked the next time we met.

Pretty detoxed, in touch with nature and invigorated, I told him. Surprisingly pleased, all in all. Could I have simply sweated out my *Weltschmerz*, discarded it like clothes on a beach? Was what I was beginning to feel the uncovering of that holy grail of travellers: an undiscovered destination at the start of an upward curve of cool? In Manny's brand world, Germany might be beginning 'to deliver value'. Certainly if I needed an explanation as to why Germans were so resilient and good at penalties after 120 minutes of semi-final, now I had it: they took lots of baths (like all the best philosophers), didn't masturbate, walked or cycled everywhere, liked gardening and indulged in lots of liberating and empowering nakedness.

And I was about to learn that *Gesundheit* even extended into the German bedroom.

7

Grossmannsucht

nf, *megalomania, the desire to be the big man*

'What is travel if not a metaphor for sex?'

Was he talking about sex tourism? Or that hope of the serendipitous meeting with an exotic other that was so often the titillating delight of true travel? Or for Manny, a true Californian, did travel begin in the bedroom?

'For you other countries are potential conquests. You have already said so yourself. And thereby you turn countries into prostitutes.'

Now he was putting words into my mouth. But from the little I knew about Freud and therapy, wasn't it all supposed to revolve around sex?

'Sex, or at least sexiness, is one of the key prejudices you judge a country by. And Germany is perhaps not sexy enough? Well, you are wrong!'

Well, on the evidence of the FKK beaches of the Baltic, no. Leather trousers and *Dirndl* skirts at the Oktoberfest? Maybe. And in the sweat-baths of Munich and Baden-Baden? Not really. Klum and Schiffer aside, Germany did not seem a land to conjure Überbabes and Miss Worlds. Germans were too busy thinking about the *idea* of sex.

Not even German car manufacturers took advantage of their national prowess to market their cars as sexy. In France cars were all 'Nicole?' 'Papa!' pert French sexiness and love triangles. Italian car ads never failed to linger in a piazza with some smoky *signorina* sipping coffee in a café the driver wished he was in instead. But German cars, they were always portrayed in some neutral, neutered surrounding: a laboratory, sometimes just a black background like outer space. Perfect for demonstrating traction control, but where were the girls? Not Billy Ocean's 'Get out of my dreams and into my car'. More 'Get out of my car, you are ruining ze experiment!'

Was Manny trying to sex Germany up? Nothing so limp. He was even proposing to show me how Germany could sex up my life. I was about to discover that for Germans sex put the lust in *Wanderlust*.

If ever there was a language barrier, German is it. The Spanish King, Charles V, famously said, 'I speak Spanish to God, Italian to women, French to men, and German to my horse.' However Romantic, *Vorsprung durch Technik* is hardly pillow talk. Musing on its use of the neuter, Twain joked: 'In German, a young lady has no sex, while a turnip has. Think what over-wrought reverence that shows for the turnip, and what callous disrespect for the girl.' Suffice to say, most people hate the German language, dismiss it as ugly, harsh, full of ridiculously long words and more useful for invading countries than making either passionate or subtle love.

At school most of my peers, given the choice, wanted to study French or Spanish before German, and for some extra physics might even have come first – which is more than you could say for German verbs. Even if that was what they did in Latin, putting the German verb at the end was just that for many – the end of their interest in the language. Furthermore, when the mind fast-forwarded to school exchanges the prospect of square-haired Heidi from Hanover was much less seductive than rebellious, mysterious Sophie from Paris. To the teenage mind how could a girl called Heidi possibly be fit? (Unless, of course, her surname is Klum . . .)

The German language also sounded comically naughty to the pubescent English ear. Any language where a motorway exit was an *Ausfahrt* and jewellery *Schmuck*, was bound to produce titters at the back of the class. While words like *Funk* (radio) just sounded plain stupid. Christian names appeared to be no better: Helmut, Fritz, Ludwig, Wolfgang . . . all sounded invented. And even in my professional life, when I've had dealings with Germans the amusement has scarcely abated as I have met Germans who insisted on calling themselves variously Frau Koch, Herr Wank and Herr Bonk.

But if German was an unlikely language of love, it was certainly the language of lurv. Maybe it was the Rudi Völler *VoKuHiLa*, the perms and the tashes but somehow I had grown up believing that the words 'porn movie' and 'German' went together. Like a pair of *Lederhosen*, the German language itself had been fetishised. Without ever checking it was correct, the one German phrase everyone knew at school was '*Ich habe einen grossen Pimmel*', and while '*Schnell, schnell!*' was an order to go faster learnt from a host of war films, we assumed it was regularly shouted in equally military fashion in German bedrooms.

The first porn videos I ever saw were at school and in German and, as one of the few still trying to study it, I was called upon to translate. There was a surprising use of the subjunctive 'if you were to . . .', which sent a surge of verbs to the end of the sentence. But by the time the end was reached the action was pretty much complete. My vocabulary definitely benefited, even if none of the new words cropped up in any exams. Furthermore, German and Californian seemed to be the preferred language of the erotic films on offer in business hotels around the world. which suggested there was a productive porn industry in the Bundesrepublik.

In fact, as I had seen from some of my visits to Germany so far, the sex industry was well and truly, well, in your face.

Munich, said to be the city of 'Laptops and *Lederhosen*', was more like the city of 'Lapdancing and *Lederhosen*'. Every second shop near my hotel was a live show, sex shop or sex cinema and in other areas of the city I'd seen sex shops on main streets next to supermarkets, clothes shops, toyshops (for children), hardware stores, cafés and restaurants. It was a frank, Protestant juxtaposition. In England, with the exception of Soho, sex shops are mainly confined to side streets and referred to as 'private shops', their windows blank and their entrances covered by strips of plastic curtain. Ann Summers went some way to redress the balance but the chain's idea of erotica was about as naughty as one of the French waitresses in *'Allo 'Allo*.

German sex shops were invariably called 'Dr Müller's,' as if prescribing a cure like a pharmacist. Who was this Dr Müller? Some modern-day Daniel Schreber? Some German Kinsey? Or, more likely, a doctor-cum-porn star? Was going into a sex shop in Germany like going into Boots to ask a girl with a white lab coat, specs and red nails for your medicine, to be taken four times daily? And sex seen as a cure?

'Well, you may well scoff,' said Manny, shaking his head, 'but the thought is not such a laughable one for Germans.'

One chain of sex shop seemed to crop up more than others, presenting a polished and stylised, porn-free front. They were called Beate Uhse shops. Who was she? None other, it turned out, than Germany's Queen of Sex.

'But she was no Ann Summers. Beate Uhse was another of Germany's great educators. When West Germany celebrated fifty years of existence she was awarded a cross, the equivalent of your OBE, for services to Germany.' Manny coughed before clarifying, 'Er, through her contribution towards the German economic miracle . . . She became a national treasure, nicknamed by the German tabloids "*Frau Oberst der Lustwaffe*"',

Lady Wing Commander of the Loveforce, or '*Orgas-Muse*' (pronounced 'orgas-moozer' and a pun on her juicy surname and the
German word for 'muse'), and '*Schlummermutter*', 'pillow
mother', to the Federal Republic.

Pretty good puns for being German, I thought. And 'worthy'
of the *Sun*.

Then I realised I'd seen her name elsewhere on my travels, on
some campaign called '*Du bist Deutschland*'. What had all that
been about?

Well, the Germany I was discovering was apparently in a pretty
morose mood. It was a country with its own *Weltschmerz* and
that had sent a nation of traditional pessimists and introspectives
into a Freudian spin of *Selbstwahrnehmung*. A reserved purring
pride like a Mercedes engine was fine while things were going
well, but now the unemployment rate had hit double figures and
the economy that during my childhood had always been such an
impregnable Colditz had been stagnating for many years. The
world's economic analysts now laughed at Germany's inability to
compete on the world stage and accused it of 'Waiting for a
Wunder'. German economists themselves accused the *Vaterland* of
being a *Warteland*, a 'waiting-room country'. Then there was the
indecisive election that went to extra time and penalties before
eventually being won by Germany's first female and first East
German Chancellor, Angela Merkel, a dry and featureless physi-
cist whom the *Sun* promptly photographed naked on holiday and
gave the headline 'I'm Big in the Bumdestag'. And to cap it all the
German football team had even lost 5-1 to the English in *die
Schande* (the disgrace) of Munich.

Now Germany's main cultural magazines wrote cultural
essays of self-examination and self-flagellation. Remember, this
was a nation that still felt nervous about its flag and national
anthem. What do people think about Germans? How do we get
ourselves out of this mess? What does this thing called *Heimat*
actually mean now and dare we be proud of it again? And there

were television studio debates called '*Was ist typisch Deutsch?*' that tried to define and reaffirm a sense of national identity.

The '*Du Bist Deutschland*' campaign was the largest, most public of all these attempts to instil a feel-good factor in the German people. This multi-million-pound programme, funded by the German government and business, bombarded Germans from 8.13 p.m. on 26 September 2005 on billboards, in magazines and in cinemas, across all nine terrestrial television channels and on the Internet. It consisted of short films and adverts intended to get Germans off their backsides and start making the country great again. A farmer would be seen chugging his tractor down a country road and the viewer would be told, '*Du bist Michael Schumacher*', 'You can be Michael Schumacher'. A sweaty would-be rock singer would be told, '*Du bist Beethoven*', or a lab technician, '*Du bist Albert Einstein*', and among the forty German celebrities used, most of whom I didn't know, was a sultry model, all red lips and eyes hidden under the brim of a hat. '*Du bist Beate Uhse.*' Well if anyone could get Germany up again it was her.

The campaign had a manifesto-like voice-over that sounded like pastiche Romantic poetry and this was meant to instil in the public a sense of *Sturm und Drang*. It spoke of the wondrous, far-reaching impact and fruits of what began as merely the flapping of a butterfly's wing.

To me this piece of propaganda might have had a sinister ring. But in fact it was a German, a typical past-conquering, over-analysing historian, who pointed out to the mass media that the slogan was almost identical to one used by the Nazis outside a 1935 party convention saying, '*Denn du bist Deutschland*' (Because you are Germany), with above it a picture of the Führer. Various marketeers hired by the government and business community, shocked on to the defensive, pointed out that the idea of the campaign was meant to be the opposite of Nazism: they had deliberately used Germans from different ethnic backgrounds in the films and one was even shot among the granite slabs of the new Holocaust memorial in Berlin. 'Surely it cannot be,' complained one executive, 'that the use of the word and concept "Germany" be restricted only to references to the past?'

Oh yes it can!

'"But there is where the dog lies buried,"' said Manny, somewhat deflated, 'as the Germans say. If you're German, even if you do win, you can never really win. Someone will always dredge up your past.'

So now I knew who Frau Uhse was and why she was big for Germans. But Manny wanted me to find out what lay behind her story and gave me a translation of her autobiography, *Ich will Freiheit für die Liebe*, or 'I want freedom for love'. If I'd had fantasies of some leather-trousered dominatrix, the cover showed instead Beate Uhse as a toothy, short-haired but probably sexually active seventy-year-old, shortly before her death at the dawn of the millennium.

She was raised the daughter of a priest in hyper-strict Königsberg in former East Prussia, now Russian Kaliningrad. She served in the Second World War as a courier pilot and afterwards ended up in Flensburg, lodging with the local priest and his family. Flensburg was the most northerly town in Germany, on the border with Denmark; and also the German equivalent of Swansea, being the home of the German DVLA, with whom I now had four points logged for speeding on the Baltic coast.

Frau Uhse was by now a mature and experienced woman. But by no means a nymphomaniac. She had lost one husband in the war and would marry again and always remain faithful. But the Germany in which she now found herself was one not only of rations, poverty and torn-apart families but a society still imbued with the castrating values of people like Schreber and Hitler. None of the women or men knew what they were doing when it came to things like menstrual cycles and natural contraception; only that they could not afford any accidental children. In comparison with the womenfolk of Flensburg, Uhse was a woman of the world and word soon spread. People looked to her to solve their sexual queries about anything from contraception to how to enjoy both one's partner and one's own body. The woman who ended up as a porn magnate had started as an agony aunt.

More significantly, when dispensing sexual advice she always placed it in the context of health. She genuinely believed that sex lay at the root of a healthy relationship and she received only confirmation of this from her customers – for that is what they had become – as they expressed their satisfaction.

Beate Uhse's entrepreneurial spirit prompted her to formalise her advice into a direct-mail subscription newsletter on family planning. The trouble was, she lived with a priest, so she made sure all copies went out in nondescript brown envelopes. The newsletter grew into a magazine of sex tips. Then the supply of condoms and other prophylactics was added to the service, and later other 'marital aids' for the maintenance of regular, healthy sexual relations. A conviction about the health benefits of sex was always central to any extension of her services.

It was not long before her mailing list encompassed residents from all over the Bundesrepublik. Then she licensed other magazines. After this came the first shop, and not far behind it the network of shops I had seen in frank evidence on the German high street (where 'Dr Müller' was just one of Uhse's invented sub-brand names). So she was immaculately positioned – you might say 'on top' – come the global sexual revolution of the sixties.

Living in Flensburg, Beate – we were on first name terms by now – had access to the films produced by the Scandinavian porn industry that occasionally slipped through the net into Germany, where they were still banned. She found them poorly made, to say nothing of plotless, and thought she could do better. By the time she died she was overseeing the production of videos to suit every proclivity, persuasion and fetish. But in her autobiography she found anecdotes and statistics from national surveys to emphasise that this 'variety' was in response to requests from both the men and women of Germany. I found this a bit far-fetched. Beate Uhse's original well-meaning advice on sexual health had miraculously transformed into an excuse for German gang bangs. One nation's pornography was another's healing. It was 'Strength through Sex' and Frau Uhse was its prime mover. Everything 'sex' about Germany could not only be traced back to Beate Uhse but also purported to be motivated by health!

This was a stimulating introduction to German attitudes to sex, if not a justification for them. But Manny was keen that I witness them first-hand, that I get to the bottom of the German relationship with sex and find out why, unless you were Boris Becker, a German's sex was not confined to his closet. And for this he was sending me to Hamburg, home of the original meat sandwich.

Like dope in Amsterdam earlier, prostitution was decriminalised throughout Germany in 2002. But the north-western city of Hamburg, like its Dutch neighbour, had apparently already long been the sex capital of its country, principally because of its red-light district, Sankt Pauli – a German version of New Orleans's Storeyville – and in particular its main drag, the Reeperbahn (pronounced 'raper-bahn'), named after the rope-makers who used to live and work there. Hamburg was another Hanseatic city with a proud maritime tradition, and a constant influx of seamen, excitable after months at sea single-handedly (or perhaps with no hands at all) sustained the Reeperbahn for decades.

As if trying to further endear it to me, Manny described Hamburg as the most British of German cities. Its civic buildings and leafier suburbs with their grand townhouses, he said, exuded a sense of old money, merchant dynasties and a naval aristocracy, just like the offices of the great shipping lines and the old family houses around London's Pall Mall.

In some bizarre display of local aspirations and love of the British, I discovered Hamburgers even held a yearly British Day in the nearby countryside. Here Germans could try to play cricket, eat many flavours of Walker's crisps and chocolate bars, dress up in blazers and sip warm beer and Pimms. I had unlikely visions of a German Henley.

In a bid for a place in global pop culture Hamburg also seemed to want a slice of the Beatles, making out that the city was the Fab Four's second home. John Lennon might once have casually said, 'I grew up in Hamburg, not in Liverpool,' but Hamburgers have never forgotten it. What he probably meant was, 'There wasn't such a good red-light district in Liverpool, and in Hamburg I came of age.' The Beatles (and bands such as Cream) played at the Reeperbahn's Star Club, bashing out numbers such as 'Can't Buy Me Love', 'Love Me Do' and 'She Loves You', all of which, in that quarter of the city, had more than a hint of sexual irony.

I had taken the precaution of inviting a friend along for what might be a difficult module of my therapy. We arrived on a cold February afternoon on one of Germany's low-cost airlines, German Wings, which sounded more like a sanitary towel or something off a German fast-food menu. The plane, like many of those I'd recently taken to Germany – to Lübeck, Munich and Baden-Baden – was almost empty. And long may it stay that way, I thought, catching myself off guard. Was I a nascent Germanophile wanting to keep his discovery a secret?

I hadn't been to Hamburg since a half-term trip as a disobedient adolescent schoolboy. The weather was similar, with a biting winter wind and the River Elbe full of fragmented slabs of ice like tombstones. The city was built around two inner-city lakes and claimed to have more bridges than Venice. The streets were not as famously full of water but the reflection of so much water cast an eerie light into the northern sky. A few intrepid boats battled across the rippling water but generally the city's Helly Hansen-kitted seadogs seemed to be having a day on dry land.

It was Saturday and in this most British of German cities we spent the afternoon in one of Sankt Pauli's dodgy pubs before going to a football match. The boozer looked more like something you might find on the Kilburn High Road, and although friendly, was anything but *gemütlich*. The walls were covered with plywood and fake brick-patterned wallpaper. Very English, it was like the run-down clubhouse bar of a cash-strapped suburban football club. We were the only customers apart from a couple of regulars who played arrows with the landlord and barmaid to the accompaniment of their favourite tunes on the jukebox. These amounted to the songs of Hamburg's greatest crooner and home-grown sound of the Reeperbahn, Hans Albers. It was a kind of cross between the British music hall and songs of the Weimar era, with lyrics like '*Auf der Reeperbahn Nachts um halb Eins, ob du ein Mädel hast, oder auch keins*' ('Out on the Reeperbahn at night around half past midnight, whether you have a girl or not'). The other tunes they put on repeatedly and sang along to with gusto all took the mickey out of Düsseldorf. Guess who FC Sankt Pauli were playing at home that afternoon?

Hamburg's main football team is FC Hamburg, which once numbered Kevin Keegan (in his *VoKuHiLa* years) on its payroll. Hamburg's far cooler, laid-back and less successful club is FC Sankt Pauli, sponsored by Jack Daniel's and known more for the womanising habits of its players. In a kind of English, phlegmatic way, though, they were having a good run and having languished for years in the lower divisions were now competing with the big guys. We didn't have tickets but managed to smuggle ourselves into the decaying, all-standing stadium. As befitted their reputation the players were all shirts out and socks round their ankles, but languid, bow-legged and skilful. It finished 1-1 and we left before the end but not before getting a taste of German terrace songs. There was 'You'll Never Walk Alone' (or was that 'You never wore Cologne'?), apparently an FC Sankt Pauli song ever since the Beatles-Liverpool link. And then: *'Düsseldorf ist Scheisse/Düsseldorf ist Dreck/Eine kleine Bombe/und Düsseldorf ist weg!'* ('Düsseldorf is shit/Düsseldorf is muck/One little bomb/And Düsseldorf would disappear.')

Hang on, wasn't that our line?

The night was what Manny had sent me for and so we moved from bar to bar, homing in, in ever-decreasing circles, on the Reeperbahn.

Unbelievably for Germany, the rubbish collectors had been on strike for twenty-four hours and the cobbled streets of Sankt Pauli were littered with beer cans, broken bottles, the polystyrene boxes from countless takeaways and other assorted human detritus. The Hamburg council reputedly liked its 'sin-bin' image but this was taking the 'bin' part too far. The scene was medieval, the stench Augean. It was like San Antonio, Ibiza, after a summer of English clubbers. But this was the Germans shitting on their own doorstep and creating mess and disorder in a most un-German fashion.

The bars too were packed and sweaty, like a Munich sauna during the Oktoberfest (but with clothes on) and they were pumping out heavy metal and rock music neither of us much fancied doing battle with. Hamburg was supposed to be a media mecca, home to many of Germany's advertising firms, magazine groups and Herr Lagerfeld himself; a funky city of up-and-coming designers and hip hotels and bars. From what I could see it was pretty down and out, and had some way up still to go.

Even in the business of prostitution and in this most disorderly and British of German cities the Germans have imposed one of their Romantic systems. The three most famous streets of Sankt Pauli are three parallel, short cobbled passageways, Friedrichstrasse, Herbertstrasse and die Grosse Freiheit (not the Big Easy but the 'Big Freedom'). And, in an incredible piece of dehumanising segregation, these three streets correspond to three 'grades' of prostitute, starting with the ropiest, appropriately nearest the Reeperbahn, up through silver to gold-star quality on the Grosse Freiheit, where all or most of the women are German. The Grosse Freiheit itself is blocked at each end by a graffitied wall with a small entrance bearing a sign that says '*Frauen Verboten*'. All women, except ladies of the night, are banned from this street as a distraction from what men go there to do. Surely, if the prostitutes are gold-star standard, it would have to be a pretty major distraction. In 1944 Aldous Huxley noted 'how appallingly thorough these Germans always managed to be, how emphatic! In sex no less than in war – diving deeper than anyone else and coming up muddier.' I wondered if he'd ever been to Hamburg.

In the clichéd, rose-lit intimacy of her boudoir I met one prostitute who undressed the would-be mystery of the local sex industry, translating it into figures purer than her own. Her name, at least that night, was Anita, a bright-eyed and eloquent Austrian with a degree in political science and a steady boyfriend to go home to at the end of the night. Prostitution here was serious commercial business, raking in millions of euros in taxes each year for Hamburg and the federal government, and this was surely a large part of the reason for decriminalising it. According to Anita, most of the girls in the Grosse Freiheit were German, not eastern European, and many of them were her friends and also had academic qualifications and ambitions. Not only was German prostitution taxed, there were prostitutes' unions, but although they might ask for a rise, unlike dustbinmen I doubted they would ever go on strike – that would be like becoming housewives. It was all so frank and deadpan. They probably even had an independent regulator. What would it be called? Ofjerk?

Humbled by Anita's frankness and clear control over her life, I made my excuses and left.

Aside from these three extraordinarily German side streets the Reeperbahn was ultimately a huge bore and as lacking in originality as the human urge that spawned it. It was high-street, bargain-basement, fast-food McSex. The main drag was as tacky as Oxford Street, a would-be Elysian Fields of neon, naked automata and sleazy heckles from the girl whose turn it was to stand outside and attract customers. On this massive scale it was as if the human body, and all sense of the erotic with it, had been sent to a sex camp. This was what happened when on the beach you denied the human body its natural sexiness in a bikini.

In terms of Manny's Romantic cure, sex *à la* Reeperbahn might be an easy lay, but it was impossible to exalt. Maybe a bit of the Beatles' 'P.S. I Love You' would not go amiss here.

Before going to bed we went – passing from one stench to another – to the city's famous fish market, where late-night revellers meet with marketeers setting up their stalls in the cold morning gloaming, to sip more beer, hot chocolate and tuck into a breakfast of *Aalsuppe* (eel soup) and *Labskaus* (lobscouse), this last dish, in a final Liverpudlian link, giving us the word 'Scouser'.

We eschewed the stew and sought refuge in our designer hotel – a haven of the minimalism and the clean and hip city lines I had been told about – feeling slightly flaccid about Hamburg and its famous attributes.

Before the 2006 Football World Cup the German authorities anticipated that as many as forty thousand foreign prostitutes would descend (did they mean go down?) on Germany. No matter what *Vorsprung* those clever men at Audi might invent, man has clearly not progressed beyond his basest urges. Prostitution is legal only in designated areas in Germany and people were worried that the whole country would turn into the Grosse Freiheit. The authorities came up with two solutions. One was to put up road signs showing a red-rimmed white circle containing the crossed-out silhouette of a well-endowed woman in thigh-high boots. The other was to erect wooden 'love shacks', complete with condom machines and snack bars, close to the stadiums of host cities. The response of Andrea Petsch of the prostitute support network Hydra was: 'It sounds as if the poor women will be working in something like a toilet cabin. Working conditions at the new brothel in Berlin seem much better.'

New brothel? Berlin! The city of Sally Bowles and '*bumpsen*' from *Cabaret*, the Berlin of songs about 'two ladies' and 'each of every one of zem a wergin'? Yes, Miss Petsch was referring to the new luxury brothel or '*Puff*' (pronounced 'poof') called Artemis (after the goddess of chastity) that was built in the German capital to cater for customer-fans during the World Cup. I wondered, did Lord Coe, in his bid-winning 2012 Olympic dossier for London, account for the sexual requirements of the masses? More to the point, Miss Petsch pressed her argument by saying: 'I understand it will be more like a spa, with saunas, jacuzzis and bars.'

But Berlin, I was reliably informed by Manny, was not actually the sex capital of Germany, any more than Hamburg. No, that honour fell to Cologne, at least if you judged by the size of its biggest brothel, Pascha.

Occupying a mind-blowing seven floors, Pascha is basically an apartment block and surely the biggest brothel in Europe, let alone Germany. In addition to its 126 private rooms, which prostitutes rent on a monthly basis, it offers a restaurant, beauty centre, boutique, laundromat, tanning salon and what it calls its 'contact bistro' for extreme speed-dating. It also prides itself on its 'turnover' of around forty girls a month – was this high or low, and either way, was that good or bad? – and on being the only brothel to offer a money-back guarantee if a guest is dissatisfied with the service. Although quite how this could be proved is hard to see. I found Pascha's website detailed and bizarrely frank. It showed you around all the floors and rooms as if it were a normal three-star hotel and listed all the services and care it offered potential 'staff'. It was an almost convincing attempt to make some girls not think twice about becoming prostitutes just in order to stay there.

Cologne's city council took an estimated seven hundred thousand euros a month from Pascha. Now that was a good turnover! I could see why Beate Uhse's contribution, direct or indirect, to the German economy had been so highly valued.

But what was it with the obsession with size again? Grossen Pimmel, Grosse Freiheit, the largest brothel . . . Why did the Germans always have to have the biggest this or that? Like the Oktoberfest, it was medieval and primitive. Besides, surely size wasn't everything.

This was what the Germans, and the Prussians before them, call *Grossmannsuch*: the Texan-style desire to be the big man, the powerful member of a group, the leader of the pack. The formation of the German state was about Germany assuming its own self-perceived natural geographical size and political importance, in the wish to be the dominant force in Europe. It also seemed like a pretty good metaphor for the male desire for an erection.

Was this sexual complex, *Grossmannsucht*, more present in the German male than others? I remembered a German pop anthem that was often played in the après-ski bars of the Austrian and German Alps. It was a Stock, Aitken and Waterman-style formula-song called 'Zwanzig Zentimeter' and written for a Düsseldorf model called Möhre. In its opening verse she confessed to liking it *'lang und dick'* (no dictionary required) and the chorus went: *'Das sind nicht zwanzig*

Zentimeter/Nie im Leben kleiner, Peter' ('There's no way, little
Peter, that that thing is twenty centimetres'). I couldn't imagine
hearing a song like that in any other language. Maybe the
world's twentieth-century ills could be explained by a Daniel
Schreber-induced suppression of testosterone in Germans. If
Grossmannsucht caused two World Wars, thank God for *Puffs*.

So, I had walked down the Reeperbahn and the Grosse Freiheit
in the interests of therapy and in search of *Wanderlust* but not
seen anything to romanticise. Red-light districts were surely the
same the world over. Yes, but German attitudes to sex stood out
as more liberal than most places, and positively Californian in
comparison with Britain's. And the ambition and organisation of
Pascha and the Grosse Freiheit were on a truly German-
Romantic scale.

But Manny, I now understood, had only shown me the lowest
common denominator of the Germans' sex life. Now he wanted
to show me how German sex could be different, better, more
open, more in tune with nature and healthier. '*Puffs* like Pascha
are OK. But I like to avoid them. For a real experience of German
sexual health you have to go to an FKK club, which is different!'

FKK. Those three magic letters again. Was he suggesting I go
to a nudist club, something like the FKK-Youth club I had read
about? One of their manifesto points had been, 'children who
grow up in naturist families are more self-assured, more self-con-
fident and sexually loose than non-naturists'. Ah, so maybe that
was where the Germans got their fabled directness from. Either
way, I felt we were moving uncomfortably far away from a cure
for *Weltschmerz*. Surely Manny didn't expect me to actually
indulge in German sex! I had explained that I was married and
had children. Heimway Syndrome seemed like a poorly veiled
excuse for indulging Manny's sexual habits by proxy. Or simply
humiliating me.

I had stripped naked on a Baltic beach, I had bathed naked in a German spa after wearing *Lederhosen* I had bought and had fitted for myself. Where was all this going? I thought to myself as I stood one midnight at the entrance to a place called the FKK-Oase in the spa town of Bad Homburg. It was another of those *Bad* towns that were spas and centres of health. But with a name like an ill-fitting hat, this one really was bad.

The arrival seemed so innocent and at this stage I was genuinely still thinking I was going to a kind of naked nightclub where, in contrast to FKK on the beach, the idea was to act as you would in a normal nightclub and chat, flirt and try to pull. It was a bizarre idea but, in Germany, when it came to nudity I knew anything was possible. If not at all comfortable with the idea, I at least had some prior insight.

The entrance to the FKK-Oase was like arriving at a Best Western Golf hotel. There was an orderly customer car park with bays separated by neatly tended, low privet hedges and low-level lighting in the form of white globes. More sunken and atmospheric lighting showed the way along a neat flagstone path between a screen of hedges and down to a long, three-storey, hotel-like building with gardens and, just before reception, a well-tended clay tennis court. At the entrance were a couple of bouncers operating an intercom system and they duly let me in.

I was expecting the thud of music, dancing, disco lights and people chatting and drinking, albeit in the nude. Instead I was met by silence, a warm, disinfectant fug and a jaded madam at a high reception desk that stood between me and the rest of the club. Beyond her I could see various girls floating or lounging around in nothing but knickers.

I handed over the voucher Manny had given me in his therapy pack, stepped inside and was immediately surrounded by vulturous, half-naked furies.

This was no Best Western hotel, nor was it a nightclub. On closer inspection it revealed itself to be an erotic version of a

Holmes Place gym. The lighting was low and pink, the décor themed in the kitsch statuary of Eros. A few guys in dressing gowns lounged on stools at the bar, looking vacuously up at screens that hung from the ceilings at various angles. But whereas in your average city gym these screens would be showing CNN, BBC News or some football match, these were showing hard-core porn. Away from the bar area was a huge, low-lit lounge like a hotel lobby, complete with sensual sofas, armchairs and chaises longues and beyond that a cinema room, again showing close-up hard-core porn. And in the other direction a passage led into a covered area with two decent-length swimming pools of different temperatures, saunas and Jacuzzis. Outside there were tended gardens, accessible throughout the night, where there were more Jacuzzis, saunas, a table-tennis table and the tennis court I had seen on entering.

This was a brothel doubling up as a health club. Open from midday to the early hours, it was a place where you could eat, drink, exercise, play tennis and table tennis, swim, sweat, all the things and more that you could do in the Müllersches Volksbad in Munich, and all of them naked – as well as have sex if you wanted, as it was just one more facility the club offered. The sex itself was offered in a menu, as if each method was some Ayurvedic treatment or specialist massage.

Entry would normally have cost sixty-five euros but Manny had advanced me a voucher to cover my costs. I now had access to all the facilities and this included unlimited drinks at the non-alcoholic bar. But if you wanted any of the 'special treatments' these cost fifty euros per half hour, and the madam from reception went through these in a matter-of-fact manner as if reeling off the specials at a motorway restaurant. '*Analverkehr*' was an extra fifty, as was '*Französischer Schluss*'. What on earth were they? Well the so-called 'French finish' was, like the madam, 'in your face'. '*Analverkehr*'? Well, from German O-level the first meaning I had learnt for '*Verkehr*' was 'traffic'. 'Anal traffic'?

Was that what the Germans called it? Travel updates on German radio would never be the same again.

I took a reluctant accompanied tour in the dressing gown supplied to me, after which the madam informed me that Manny's voucher also covered the opportunity to partake of the special treatments. I looked at her in shock. How dare he? Did the German notion of sexual health encourage polygamy? I thought Beate Uhse had remained faithful throughout her life.

Needless to say, I declined and after half an hour or so, which included a hamburger and a Diet Coke on the house, there not being much on TV and little conversation to be had, I slipped out from the close atmosphere of sweat and disinfectant into the clean, fresh night air. It washed over me like a purifying lotion as, with a shudder, I put my flirtation with temptation behind me. How would Faust have reacted in my situation? Manny had momentarily turned into my Mephistopheles. But surely Faust did not seek his Margarete in an FKK club! Despite the Jacuzzis, saunas and pools, the FKK-Oase was a vacuous place devoid of seduction and mystery, stripped down to a bare Protestant work ethic and where the only *Sturm und Drang* was to be found in dirty German men's underpants.

So much for the *Freikörperkultur* 'philosophy' I had come across in the Baltic. Deep down it was just an excuse for the oldest trade in the world. I discovered there was a network of FKK clubs all over Germany, all, like Frau Uhse and Manny, purporting to be in the service of health. Do me a favour! They just confirmed what everyone else always knew: that German beaches and saunas, even the Oktoberfest, were inches away from being brothels or orgies, and that with their language, *Lederhosen* and military approach to exercise, Germans were obsessed with sex, and on a mass scale. *Grossmannsucht* was what got Germans going. It was Germany's G-spot (a term itself named after a German sex doctor, Ernst Gräfenberg). No wonder Freud thought it was all about sex. He developed his theories mostly on Germans.

8

Kindergarten

nm, *nursery*

(lit. children garden)

'The ability to return to a childish state of wonder and see each day as new is a key element of German Romanticism,' announced Manny.

Was this something to do with the releasing of the inner child that Germans had started doing at their Holiday Academy?

'I want you to remember your childhood. Imagine you are a child seeing Germany for the first time.'

Sex and now my childhood. This was classic. Was Manny going to say I had some repressed Oedipal love of Germany going back to my childhood?

But now I had to come clean. It *was* as a child that I had first seen Germany. 'When I was three I lived there for a year,' I confessed.

'Ah-ha, you see!' cried Manny, 'so deep down you know Germany!'

But I was three years old! That hardly qualified as in-depth knowledge. Nor did it necessarily mean I had latent German tendencies.

I dredged up what I knew of my fourth year on the planet.

My father, who was a teacher of French and German, had taken up an exchange position to teach English in Heidelberg. We lived in a dormitory town called Sandhausen. A German family came to stay in our house in Oxford and we stayed in theirs. It turned out to be the Popps, now famous for their son, Alexander Popp, who went on to become a German tennis star. Boris Becker came from the next town, Leimen, but sadly the tennis tradition of that corner of Germany did not rub off on either me or my brother.

By all accounts it was a happy time. It was 1975 and West Germany, as it was then, was still at the apex of its post-war economic miracle, or *Wirtschaftswunder*; a country of gleaming wealth and space-age technology that seemed other-worldly compared with seventies Britain. If it hadn't been for Dad's teaching post we might have been economic migrants.

'Well, why don't you go back?' Manny asked. 'There are other things I want you to do but I think this is important. As you know, nostalgia, youth, the past are important contributors to the state of exaltation of the true Romantic.'

I had only the vaguest of memories: of the flat where we lived, of a sledge, and come to think of it, lots of trees. That must have been the Black Forest. And for some reason the image of a rather pretty American girl called Elizabeth (also three years old), who introduced me to peanut butter. Somewhere I knew there were photos. My parents would have these and all sorts of stories and memories. I was suddenly struck by the urge to delve into my past and find out more about those times. It was all already very Freudian and German.

According to my mother, I refused point-blank to learn or speak any German while we lived there. Who knows why? Perhaps I was simply displaying some early fine judgement. They showed me a scrapbook they had kept of the year, with photos of various holidays we took around the country of which I had obviously been blissfully unaware. My father reminded me of the wood on the edge of Sandhausen where we used to go walking and where I used to be very scared. Yes, I remembered now, it seemed huge, as if we were trespassing on some giant's property. And there was one particular flea-infested clearing with wooden rings hanging down from metal bars like nooses. Of course! I now realised. The rings were part of the local *Trimmdichpfad*!

With all this Romantic reminiscing I was now officially wistful. And, armed with my new-found knowledge of Germany, I wanted to see if it was all still there. It wasn't exactly *Vergangenheitsbewältigung*, but I had to get in touch with my German past.

And so it was that one drizzly, grey morning I found myself standing outside 55 Friedrich-Ebert Strasse looking up at the balcony of the second-floor flat where, as a three-year-old, I used to live.

The apartment block was much smaller than I remembered it and I had a Gulliver-in-Lilliput moment convincing myself this could be right. But the courtyard at the back by the garages, where I learnt to ride a German bike, was just the same. And I remembered an old lady, Frau Grassinger was her name, who used to throw down sweets to us. I wondered what had happened to her. The families would surely all have died or moved on, I thought. But one familiar name was still there on the postboxes after thirty years: Herr Sommer.

My father had recalled how, when we first moved to Sandhausen for our year of being German, Herr Sommer from the flat below had taken him on a neighbourly tour of the town. Herr Sommer finished the outing with a visit to the local swimming pool and ran through the opening times. 'Monday is ladies only. Tuesday is family day, Wednesday and Friday are mixed, and so are weekends. My wife and I go on Thursdays, which is naked day.'

Would Herr Sommer remember me, or even want to see me?

I rang the bell nervously. There was no answer. I was not going to have the chance to put to him my theories on FKK and German *Gesundheit*.

Sandhausen was a quiet kind of place and the streets were deserted save for a few hardy old people grinding their way around on bikes. The postwoman looked at me strangely, as if I should have been a local. It was the kind of place where everybody knew everybody.

As I explored the centre it also seemed there were very few young people. It was a modern town, with bright-red roofs, white-weatherboarded houses and groomed streets that, like many German towns, gave the impression of a model village. But from my parents' scrapbook it seemed Sandhausen had in its day been a relatively cutting-edge town, at least in architectural terms. It had an angular modern library-cum-town hall made of concrete and glass that would once have been considered avant-garde. It had even made it on to local postcards back in the seventies. But now it would look commonplace in Milton Keynes. And yet the modernity of the place contrasted with my mother's memories of horse-drawn carts passing our apartment every week on their way to market, piled high with tobacco leaves from the local fields. That image belonged more in Cairo than Sandhausen.

Walking into the nearby woods I found the *Trimmdichpfad* immediately. At the start was an old signpost with the legend '*Errichtet zur Erholung aller, die zum Ausgleich ihrer einseitigen beruflichen Tätigkeit etwas für ihre Gesundheit tun wollen*' ('built for the use of all those who want to do something for their health in order to bring balance to their one-sided professional lives'). Back in the 1970s this would have been unheard of in Britain. The woods were, of course, much smaller than I remembered, but after wandering up and down thickly wooded paths I found many of the familiar exercise areas. There were the rings; then further on, the stumps of tree trunks used for step-ups; and a set of parallel bars, the yellow paint slightly peeling. I took a few photos to show my parents. A woman walking her Rottweiler passed me and, seeing me meticulously framing a set of rusty iron bars, asked me what on earth I was doing. Possibly some photos of installation art for my collection? I told her my story and she seemed touched by my reminiscing about a piece of iron. It turned out she had been living in Sandhausen when we had been there. Her daughter, now a lawyer in America, had gone to the same primary school there as my brother. I attended the local *Kindergarten*.

'You see, "*Kindergarten*" is a word used generically to mean "nursery" all over the world nowadays,' said Manny smugly. 'But it is, of course, a German word.'

Silly me! '*Garten*' meant 'garden' and '*Kinder*', as anyone who liked those German chocolate eggs with surprises inside will know, meant 'children'.

The *Kindergarten* was the brainchild of one Friedrich Froebel, yet another of the swelling rank of German educators and sys-temisers who lived in the early nineteenth century. Froebel was also the son of a Protestant pastor, thus continuing the tradition of Protestantism as begetter of radicalism.

His revolutionary idea, Manny explained, was to recognise the concept of play as fundamental to a child's learning. It sounds so obvious now, but there was a time when children had few if any toys and were not inspired to interact, if they were given anything to do at all. Froebel changed all that with the invention of *Froebel Gaben* (Froebel gifts), geometric blocks that could be assembled to form three-dimensional objects and basically a precursor to Denmark's Lego. The *Kindergarten* was taken to the United States not long after its invention when a student of Froebel's, Louisa Frankenberg, went to Columbus, Ohio, to spread the Froebel gospel. And so '*Kindergarten*' became a global term.

'You see, the child is another obsession of modern tourism.

Where can I holiday with my kids? Where is child-friendly or not? This is often as important as food or sex. But I'm not talking about patting on the head, cooing or spoiling with this or that toy or sweet.'

Of course not. This was the land of Daniel Schreber!

'These are all ephemeral gestures that are so superficial.'

Was this some kind of apology for German intolerance of children? I hadn't previously considered Germany particularly high on the list of child-friendly countries. And my mother had remembered how Herr Sommer generally complained at the noise, mess and general existence of her children, often saying to her, '*Zwei Kinder, viel Arbeit!*', 'Two children, hard work!'

'What you have to judge instead is whether a country understands the child at its very heart and whether in its culture the child is alive and well. Germany is that place!'

Really?

'Take, for instance, the archetypal celebration of the child, Christmas. Did you know that almost all the trappings of Christmas are German?'

For his next trick Manny was sending me into the heart of the German Christmas.

As my brother and I found out to our delight when we lived there, in Germany they celebrate Christmas twice. It had been a normal 6 December when my father answered a knock at the door to our apartment. He opened up, expecting another broadside from Herr Sommer. But there was no one at the door and instead at his feet lay a family of chocolate bunnies, a card and two beautifully wrapped parcels which we found to contain two German toys, a wooden train and a little Steiff teddy bear. They were from our neighbour, Frau Grassinger, to celebrate Sankt Niklaus Tag, after whom Santa Claus was named. From then on, and for many years after we returned from Germany, my parents had no choice but to maintain the Teutonic tradition of present-giving to children on St Nicholas's Day.

'Come the end of November the central square of every German village, town and city is given over to the *Christkindl* (Christ-child) market and this becomes the centre of civic and family life.'

The greatest of these markets is held in Nuremberg, Manny told me, and it was there that I took my wife and wide-eyed two-year-old son in my search for the child in the German soul – and to rekindle it in myself.

To me Nuremberg meant Nazi rallies and the trials where many Nazi leaders were condemned to death. Hardly toytown! But in fact Nuremberg had a far longer tradition, five hundred years or more, as the toy capital of Europe, and home in particular to those most malleable of men, Playmobil figurines. In an old travel book, *Peeps at Germany*, that my mother had dug out from her memory chest, I found this rhyme: 'The children of Nuremberg take pleasure in making/what the children of England take pleasure in breaking.' And when you considered Playmobil, Steiff teddy bears and Ravensburger puzzles, to name just a few, Nuremberg was just the capital of a whole country that loved making toys.

Nuremberg lies in a region of north Bavaria called Franconia. Away from the childishly debased classicism of Hitler's arena and congress centre at the city's limits, we found an Altstadt lovingly restored after a virtual flattening during the war, its medieval outer wall and hilltop castle rebuilt in the city's austere grey-red sandstone. Within this area stood a mixture of modern office blocks and traditional half-timbered houses with their distinctive lattices of polished wood. A few errant snowflakes eddied in the winter wind as we arrived shortly before midnight and checked into a welcoming hotel, fronted by gas lamps and Christmas bunting, just inside one of the main gates. Opposite, in this capital of toys, stood a Beate Uhse sex shop.

The following morning we wrapped up in scarves and bobble hats to visit the market in the mellow glow of a white, low sun.

There was an irresistible pull towards the main square and as we neared it the streets filled with couples, families and groups of friends. Everywhere were wooden stalls displaying meats, cheeses, cakes and biscuits, all dolled up and dressed in Christmas holly, greenery and ribbons. From street corners came the music of well-rehearsed and vigorously conducted choirs, a quartet of horn players, and the tubular wooden jingle of old, hand-turned barrel organs. Wafts of cosy, seasonal smells floated through the air. Cinnamon and orange from *Glühwein* ('wine that makes you glow') and ginger from *Lebkuchen*, the ginger-bread biscuits, individually wrapped and in beautifully Gothic-script-engraved tins, that are as essential to a German Christmas as mince pies to a British one, and which originated in Nuremberg. I recognised the smell. It was the same smell that wafted through Manny's office in London.

The market square was laid out in a honeycomb of more wooden stalls, already with their lights on and exuding warmth and *Gemütlichkeit*. At the end of each row crowds huddled around the steaming food and drink stalls selling local bratwurst sausages, mugs of *Glühwein* and honey wine clasped with both hands. *Glühwein* was also sold *'mit oder ohne Schuss'* (with or without a shot of schnapps) in little china elfin boots.

'There is no nation in the world that makes such a charming feast of Christmas as the Germans do,' were the opening words of a chapter on Christmas in *Peeps at Germany*. The stalls were stocked high with carefully laid out craftware and although there was some overlap in the wares most of the stalls seemed unique. There were tree decorations in all forms, from painted glass balls to tiny wooden sleighs, puppets, dolls and figurines and all manner of toys, planes and trains, cars and helicopters, all made of wood.

Call me old-fashioned but wooden toys are preferable to plastic. Unlike the garish and shiny merchandising of the brand world, wood was soft and smooth, and natural and earthy to the touch, its corners more rounded and it could be painted in mellow hues. There was not a brand in sight. But wood required craft, not just a mould and a factory. A forest-dwelling people, the Germans had hewn goods of all kinds from their trees for centuries and were still teaching their children to love wood. Was I becoming a tree-hugging Romantic German?

I was also struck by the intricacy of design and execution. The dolls and figurines, although small, were extremely detailed and articulated with moving parts, which made them almost sinister. Kings, queens, knaves and jesters, they were figures of pageantry, just like those that appeared on the town hall's clock as it struck noon; cartoon-like yet somehow mystical and symbolic, like the figures in a pack of cards. 'Of course Germany is the land of the cuckoo-clock,' stated Manny proudly. So not Switzerland as Orson Welles had said?

The toys were motorised or clockwork and minutely observed, with carefully painted figures, doors that opened, moving steering wheels and other parts mass-manufacturers would not bother with. Stall upon stall of them, these were toys, yes; but they seemed to have been built with the precision lavished on an Audi. *Vorsprung durch Technik* started early in Germany, I thought. Or maybe Audis, Porsches, BMWs and Mercedes were just big toys for adults who hadn't grown up, evidence of a childish streak in German men. If so, it wasn't confined to cars. What about the miniature railways I had seen on Rügen and on the slopes of the Brocken? Germans loved their little narrow-gauge railways.

When I was a child we had a large Hornby railway set which my brother and I adored. My father had lovingly laid it out on an old table-tennis table and added papier-mâché mountains and other scenery. But my parents had some friends with a train set that was our envy. I wondered if the Germans had one of their compound nouns for it, perhaps *Modeleisenbahnneid* (model railway envy)? For this family had trains made by

Fleischmann, the Rolls-Royce (now German-made) of model railway manufacturers. Fleischmann locomotives were not nostalgic reminders of an age of steam and bygone industrial dominance, they were state-of-the-art replicas of a state-of-the-art railway technology. They stood for the difference between Network Rail and Deutsche Bahn today.

But why recreate this technological excellence in miniature? If this impulse showed a slight Peter Pan complex in Germans, it also betrayed much Romantic *Angst* in its desire to create an absolute replica. This miniature world could be made more perfect than the real one.

One wooden toy that kept on appearing I had never seen before. These painted wooden models of soldiers, knights and kings, like the figures on the town clock, seemed to be from some fairytale court of chivalry and pageantry. They varied in size, from a few inches to two feet high. People appeared to be examining and buying them not just for ornamentation but for some practical purpose and it was only when I saw a lady demonstrating the use of one that I realised I was looking at decorative nutcrackers. Not for Germans the plain metal tool we Britons use.

Nutcrackers like these, I learnt, had been around since at least the fifteenth century, when the first-ever Christmas market was held in Germany, in Dresden. The most famous nutcrackers were made in Sonneberg, just north of Nuremberg in the same forested state of Thuringia, where Froebel came from and where wood-carving was for centuries a main source of income. That the nutcracker had become part of the trappings of the global Christmas was down to the German-Jewish writer E. T. A. Hoffmann, who in 1816 wrote a fantasy tale called 'The Nutcracker and the Mouse King', about a nutcracker soldier, given to a small girl as a Christmas present, who came to life, first defended and then fell for and married his owner. The challenged imaginations of advertising executives would have been lost over the years without the magical, soft Glockenspiel ('play of bells') tingles of the 'Dance of the Sugar Plum Fairy', adapted by Disney from a Tchaikovsky opera, to accompany the twinkles and stars of their Christmas campaigns.

Adjacent to the marketplace was a small square with a children's playground full of ancient wooden carousels and wurlitzers – the invention of German-born Rudolph Wurlitzer, Manny was keen for me to note. The playground had a wooden frame around it as if it were the playroom of a giant Wendy house. In its cornices were fairytale and Christmas scenes depicted by figurines and automata: fairies, elfs and garden gnomes; and wholesome, idealistic and patriarchal scenes such as a gnomish, balding and bespectacled *Biedermeier* father in waistcoat and trousers reading to his two children. This was the perfect nuclear family, imbued with *Gemütlichkeit* and the German values of, not this time FKK, but KKK: *Kinder, Küche und Kirche* (children, kitchen and church).

Speaking of gnomes, I had seen them everywhere: on the lawn of many a *Schrebergarten* on the Baltic coast, in Munich and most recently in Sandhausen. They seemed to be a national symbol of the German child-spirit. In one of those self-examining television debates about their national identity a studio audience of Germans were asked what they would do if guests presented them with a gift of a *Gartenzwerg* (garden gnome). The alternatives were (a) throw it away, (b) politely give it back, saying you had one already, or (c) proudly take it and place next to the others already in your garden. Seventy-five per cent of the audience chose the last option. Never in England, where gnomes were banned from the Chelsea Flower Show!

Like the nutcracker, the garden gnome was born in Thuringia – seemingly the heartland of German *Kinder* – and the prototype was introduced to the world by one Philip Griebel in 1884 at a Leipzig fair, where it was an instant runaway success. Apart from a brief period when they were banned by the

East German government – goodness knows what threat they presented – a personal gnome (or whole garden gnome scene) has been not only a national heirloom for most Germans but a lucrative generator of income. Manny had some in his garden and apparently there was a huge export business to America. And, perhaps not surprisingly, German-made gnomes now came not just in the traditional pose of bearded sage perched on a rock, but in all manner of earthy poses and various states of FKK.

The whole Christkindlmarkt in Nuremberg was conducted with peaceful and discreet festiveness. The aisles were full of children and families gently ambling and perusing, stopping here and there for more sweets and a fillip of hot wine. There was no bustle and no stallholders or street-criers trumpeting their wares. Christmas in Germany did indeed seem to be heavily orientated towards children but also intended to bring out the child in adults. Its childish origins and meaning were not lost in this thoughtful combination of commerce, craftmanship and seasonal cheer. So different from the scrum and fleeting opportunism of Britain at this time of year, Germany was one of the most Christmassy places I had been to in a long while.

I had witnessed the family congeniality of the Baltic coast and how even a huge piss-up like the Oktoberfest was not only geared towards, but probably even dreamt up by children. As Manny had said, a German's love of children wasn't an exuberant, saccharine Latin love of the bambino; it was – no surprise – on a philosophical level. Children were at the core of the German outlook on life.

'How ironic that you have started recreating German markets in your own towns and cities,' Manny had gloated. 'Did you know that Birmingham now has the largest Christkindlmarkt outside the German-speaking world, complete with nutcrackers, *Glühwein*, fine bratwurst and beer?'

But people still weren't prepared to actually go to Germany for the experience, I thought to myself. Any more than I was prepared to go to Birmingham.

Not far from Nuremberg lay the walled medieval cuteness of Rothenburg-ob-der-Tauber, an immaculately well-preserved town of crenellated stone defences, portcullis gates, moats, bridges, turrets and wizard's-hat spires. Rothenburg was a child's ideal of a medieval fortress town. A Camelot. Anyone who has striven to built the ultimate sandcastle on the beach has unconsciously modelled their effort on Rothenburg and it was no surprise to learn it had featured in that one-time children's favourite, *Chitty Chitty Bang Bang*. I found the place something of a museum piece, an introverted town, not producing any more history, just showcasing it. But in a country where so much time was spent 'conquering the past' this was a rare thing. Next Manny's itinerary sent me just north of Nuremberg, to a town profoundly related to Britain and from which Britain imported one of its central Christmas ingredients. Coburg lay in the north of Franconia, in a cul-de-sac on the border with the former East German region of Thuringia. The resulting commercial neglect had rather suited the city's haughty, aristocratic heritage and it remained unblemished by industry.

As we approached from the south the town's imposing medieval fortress was caught in the golden evening light and visible from afar. The fortress belonged to one of Germany's powerful medieval ruling families, the House of Wettin, from Saxony, who in the sixteenth century made Coburg capital of one of their duchies, Saxe-Coburg. Then, in the nineteenth century, they set about the conquest of Europe through self-promotional intermarriage with the royal families of Belgium, Bulgaria and Portugal. The final masterstroke was for Albert of Saxe-Coburg-Gotha to marry his first cousin, who had spent some of her childhood in Coburg's castle and was by now a queen.

'And not just any queen,' said Manny. 'Your very own Queen Victoria, Queen of England!'

During the First World War Mr and Mrs Wettin judiciously decided to de-Germanise their name to 'Windsor'. Manny had included a snippet from *The Times* of Wednesday 18 July 1917 which read: 'Royal House of Windsor – the King's name – All German Titles Dropped.'

Manny was obviously a true American fan of Britain's royal family. But he might as well have been a fan of German royalty.

It was Queen Victoria's consort, Albert the German, who brought the Christmas tree from Germany to Britain. An evergreen tree is thought to have symbolised renewal already among pagans celebrating the Yule festival on which Christmas is based – trust the Romantic Germans, even when they were pagans, to venerate trees – and by the eighteenth century the custom had become widespread in Germany. Gradually the fashion caught on in Russia, Austria, France and eventually England. King George III's German Queen, Charlotte of Mecklenburg-Strelitz (in whose spa resorts I had spent my summer holiday) had insisted on having a tree at the palace. And an 1832 entry in Victoria's childhood journal read: 'After dinner . . . we then went into the drawing room . . . There were two large round tables on which were placed two trees hung with lights and sugar ornaments. All presents being placed round the trees . . .' The custom did not spread outside royal German circles until popularised by Prince Albert, who donated trees to schools and regiments, with the result that images of early tree-hugging royals appeared in Victorian equivalents of *Hello* magazine. The rest is history.

But the Germans were not content to invade Europe with their trees. They also brought the practice of giving presents, a Christmas ham, Carols such as 'Silent Night', the Yule log, holly and mistletoe; this last plant's name coming from the German '*Mist*', or 'dung', on account of its being spread by bird faeces. A parasite, mistletoe had been used since ancient times by German herbalists to cure – guess what – the old *Kreislafstörung*. It took the Romans to turn it into an aid to seduction.

Coburg's huge, untouchable villas, built up the steep slope to the fortress, reminded me of Hampstead in London, and the inhabitants, mostly silver-haired but elegant, oozed a similar air of affluence, culture and sophistication. The Christmas market was as impeccable as a Victorian nursery and a twelve-piece brass band filled the frosty, twilit air with mellifluous tones from the balcony of the town hall. It was the sort of strict town where one's immaculately attired, obedient and old-fashioned only children were generally seen and not heard.

After warming ourselves with a thick and creamy hot chocolate in the inevitable Prince Albert Café we travelled on, following Manny's route map, to Bayreuth (pronounced 'Buy-roit' and not to be confused with the capital of Lebanon).

Neo-classical and appropriately stagy, Bayreuth was linked not with dynastic royalty but with the self-appointed master of Germany's musical heritage. For this town was the spiritual home of Wagner and his four-part opera cycle *Der Ring des Nibelungen*, a marathon of heroic action and emotion that he held to be the ultimate expression of the German soul. With Romantic absolutism Wagner regarded the Ring as the first *Gesamtkunstwerk* (complete work of art) and had a special auditorium built in Bayreuth where it could be performed on the massive, *Grossmannsucht* scale it demanded to achieve its intended Dionysian effect.

The music of Wagner has been compared to Marmite in its capacity to illicit polarised reactions. For some, like the Italian composer Rossini, it was the length: 'Wagner has lovely moments but awful quarters of an hour'; for some its bombast: 'I have been told that Wagner's music is better than it sounds' (Mark Twain). Some are put off by what has become received knowledge about the composer as a man: he was supremely egotistical, sexually manipulative and an anti-Semite whose work is pervaded by an idea of German superiority and was adulated by Hitler.

I was amused by the presence of not one but two Beate Uhse shops in the aristocratic home of the Ring. Then, over a Proustian pretzel and mulled wine at one of the Christmas market stalls, I found myself dipping again into my childhood and reminiscing to my wife.

As children our father used to tell a wondrous yet frightening bedtime story. For some reason I pictured a camping holiday where my brother and I lay in a zipped-off sleeping section of the tent while my father and mother sat silhouetted at a folding table in the main part. The comforting roar of a Calor Gas lamp and the flicker of an insistent moth were the only other sounds as my father's soft but clear voice embarked on its solemn rendition. It was a story of love and greed, a ring lost at the bottom of a river, of dwarves, giants, maidens and a hero called Siegfried, like the vet from *All Creatures Great and Small*. It wasn't until some ten years later that I twigged: my father had been indulging his passion for Wagner by recounting for us the story of the Ring.

Was this more proof of latent German tendencies whose seeds had been sown in my childhood?

Give or take a few details, you could tell a child the same story now and have them accuse you of cribbing from the DVD of *The Lord of the Rings*. Peter Jackson's extremely popular film trilogy based on the novel cycle by Tolkien, whose family originated in German Saxony, was itself Wagnerian in length. It was clear to me that German Romanticism had had a strong influence on children's imagination all around the world.

Returning to Nuremberg, we drove through a part of Germany that might have inspired both Wagner and Tolkien. We were now in the heart of 'Franconian Switzerland', a contorted landscape of towering stalagmites and limestone cliffs with small, higgledy-piggledy, half-timbered cottages perched on top of them or on precarious parapets halfway up, their chimneys gently puffing out the smoke of wood fires; gushing torrents, weirs and cold, still, deep-blue pools; gorges, caves, green valleys, overhanging trees and gnarled, life-like trunks. We stopped briefly in the one-horse-hamlet of Pottenstein. There was an eerie lack of people. Yet there was something in the bizarre limestone protrusions, the rockfaces and the twisted trees that made you think it was alive.

According to Manny, Germany had inspired most of the fairytales I had grown up with. 'You have been back to the cradle of your childhood. Now you must return to the land of your childhood imagination. The city of Frankfurt is the gateway to fairytale land. Just to the . . .'

Hang on. Just run that by me again, Manny. Do you mean the same Frankfurt that is Germany's banking centre, all skyscrapers and trade fairs. How much more unmagical could you get? To me Frankfurt had always resembled a giant kitchen whose white furniture, tiles and surfaces sparkled after a fresh dose of Jif. Could it really be the 'gateway to fairytale land'?

Just twenty miles east of Frankfurt, in the town of Hanau, were born two brothers who would define the landscapes of the imagination for children all around the world. Jakob and Wilhelm Grimm, contemporaries of the Romantics and most of the German educators I had encountered, were the first to collect German folk tales such as 'Little Red Riding Hood', 'Sleeping Beauty' and 'Cinderella'. Hanau was the start of the Deutschemärchenstrasse (German Fairytale Route): six hundred kilometres of fairytale locations and associations that finished in Bremen in the north of the country.

I was in the central-western state of Hessen (from which came the Hessian sackcloth essential to all Romantic wanderers). I knew Frankfurt from so many business trips. But what was the rest of Hessen like? If it had been able to inspire such lasting images and legends, perhaps it was rather beautiful. Could you actually see the castle where the imprisoned Rapunzel hung out her hair? Or the wood where Little Red Riding Hood met her wolf?

I had ordered a hire car through my business-style Frankfurt hotel but was not expecting the garish, blue-and-silver-striped Mercedes Smart car that turned up. Much to the concierge's amusement I had trouble removing us from his forecourt. By the time I got underway I was feeling more like an estate agent than Alice on the verge of Wonderland.

My first port of call was the university town of Marburg, where the Grimms had studied. I arrived with the sun going down, casting a golden light over the tall, thin fortress that is Marburg's icon, as it sat precipitously on a rocky outcrop with the rest of the town tumbling away beneath it. Of Marburg Jacob Grimm once said, 'I believe there are more steps in the streets than in the houses,' and I could well believe him as I strode out that night among the stairs and alleys of the old upper town in search of a bedtime story. Above me the castle loomed in Kafkaesque fashion. Copper light shone from old iron street lamps and cast angular shadows across cobbled streets that shone with a patina of drizzle. Half-timbered houses sat on top of one another on the steep cliff slope, filling every nook and cranny, their beams skewed and heaving from the movement of centuries.

The following morning I set out early in the direction of Schwalmstadt and the wood where Little Red Riding Hood, Rotkäppchen in German, met her wolf. In this sleepy village on the gentle little River Schwalm a few teenagers were kicking a ball about, but otherwise the streets and school playgrounds were deserted, and each bounce of the ball sounded a lonely echo, as of a lost childhood. It didn't seem like the kind of place you'd want to grow up in nowadays.

The meek young woman in the tourist office seemed rather nonplussed by my inquiry as to where I should best go to enter the world of Rotkäppchen. Schwalmstadt clearly did not publicise its association with the fairytale, which I found rather refreshing. The girl had milk-white skin, freckles, Heidi plaits and thick glasses that magnified her eyes. All the better for seeing me with, I thought. And she wore a traditional bodice like the women's folk costumes at the Oktoberfest. I didn't know whether this was out of choice, duty or *Gemütlichkeit*, but I did learn that it was the local costume, as worn by Little Red Riding Hood herself. Since medieval times the womenfolk of Schwalmstadt had worn a then famously beautiful costume containing elements of courtly fashion and military dress from various epochs. Young married women wore green, maidens red. And so it was presumed that Little Red Riding Hood and her distinctive dress had links with Schwalmstadt. The surrounding countryside explained the rest of the story. Like much of Germany, Hessen is densely forested and what towns there are amid this unspoiled landscape have largely intact medieval, half-timbered old centres.

The forest is not just a wellspring of Romantic thought, a German national symbol or, nowadays, a source of ecological *Angst*. It is also a common ingredient of children's stories. The forest is a magical place, suggesting mystery, the unknown, and the seductive presence of evil. From the tales of Little Red Riding Hood and Hansel and Gretel to *The Lord of the Rings* and even *Shrek* (from the German word, '*Schreck*', meaning 'fright') every decent fairytale should contain a wood that is either the source of magic or evil, or the guardian of an ancient knowledge.

The landscape was now one of gently sloping river valleys cloaked in the green, goldening and russet leaves of beeches, oaks and pines that shimmered in the breeze like the iridescent scales of a salmon. This was an array of autumn hues on a scale to rival the fall in Vermont and I could see how the medieval imagination could have conjured up stories of giants, witches, princes and maidens here. In the Grimms' day this would have been a God-fearing land, full of superstition, where the story-teller was king and the popular imagination could be shaped so as to promote good Protestant behaviour. Germany was not yet formed and so this was also still a land of small-minded, feuding duchies where the words 'Once upon a time there was a tyran-nical king' would have been more a statement of fact than the start of a fairytale.

Inspired by the Enlightenment passion for encyclopedias and dictionaries, the Brothers Grimm initially planned simply to cat-alogue, by writing down, tales that had previously only been recounted orally. But the more tales they heard – most of them told to them in a brewery near the city of Kassel by the buxom old Huguenot housewife Dorotea Viehmann, who possessed a formidable memory – the more they realised that these were a sign of something more fundamental. Surrounded by Napoleon's occupying forces, they saw in the fairytales a shared national consciousness which could be exploited to foster a unifying sense of German-ness. For a start, there were plenty of trees, and these could be used to evoke the forest-dwelling Arminius and his nation-defining victory over the Romans. The fairytales also chimed with the sense of a rural, medieval past that the Romantics in Heidelberg had tapped into. And as I had seen, not just in the grand villas of Heidelberg but in the far north, along the Baltic coast, the architecture of Germany's fairytales – cas-tles, towers, moats and portcullises – reflected exactly the architecture of the Romantic imagination. And so when it appeared in 1812 the Grimms' *Kinder- und Hausmärchen* (Children's and Household Tales) was, like the manifestos of Jahn and Schreber, one of the most important books in the German language since Luther's Protestant translation of the Bible; and one that would have an enormous resonance around the world. Disney and indeed Hollywood as a whole has drawn heavily on the work of the Grimms and the mythology of child-hood that sits at the core of the idea of Germany.

Like the Grimms, Manny was inviting me to enter the world of German folklore. And I could see that a crucial period of the country's history itself read rather like a fairytale: 'Once upon a time there were three brothers, Britain, France and Germany. Germany was the last-born and ugliest brother, who was never invited anywhere and always given less than the others, until one day, envious of his elder brothers' wealth, he sought to claim back what he thought was rightly his . . .'

Journeying on through my childhood imagination I reached the fort town of Trendlburg, with its thirty-eight-metre tower from which the imprisoned Rapunzel let her hair down to her waiting prince below. The only sign of her presence was a rather miserable wooden statue that stood mournfully absorbing the drizzle of the autumn afternoon. The castle was now, pre-dictably, a hotel that was a favourite for weddings.

I got caught in a traffic jam outside the old, half-timbered town of Höxter, where Hansel and Gretel came across the witch's house with the marzipan roof. Apparently it was caused by a nearby fire: an apt analogy of the witch's fate.

A few miles further north came Polle, where the ruined castle was reputed to be the one from which Cinderella fled the dance and lost a shoe. And then Hameln, Hamelin in English, famous for its Pied Piper.

So often magic was better left in the imagination. The Märchenstrasse had become gradually more unbelievable and, the countryside apart, I had shattered any illusion that I would capture a sense of the characters and locations of these famous fairytales.

There are places that do try to maintain the illusion of some of these tales. In Hamelin every Sunday between May and September the story of the Pied Piper is re-enacted in front of the suitably named *Rathaus* (town hall), by adults and children in thirteenth-century dress. In Polle the locals stage the Cinderella story – perhaps as some medieval beauty contest? In fact pageants take place throughout the summer all along the Fairytale Route. This was all family-oriented fun and good for tourism but, like the German carnivals whose mythology resembled that of fairytales, the Oktoberfest and the Karl May Wild West festival, it smacked of *Gemütlichkeit*. It was a cosy nostalgia for local traditional costumes – perhaps no more than an excuse for dressing up – and an illusory longing for the elusive trappings of an invented national identity.

So it was appropriate that I should also come across the village of Bodenwerder, birthplace of one Baron Karl Friedrich Hieronymus Freiherr von Munchausen. He actually did exist. He served in the eighteenth century in the Russian military against the Turks and on returning home told outrageous tales about his exploits, including riding cannonballs, travelling to the moon and escaping from a swamp by pulling himself out by his own hair. Munchausen's confabulations became a standard for lying and his name would be attached to the medical condition of creating symptoms of illness in order to attract attention to oneself. Then there was Munchausen's by Proxy, the harming of others to attract attention to oneself. The Poles and French knew all about that.

There were more places that lay beyond my reach: Oberweser, with its Puss in Boots and Snow White connections, and Ebergötzen, where the mill stood that ground to death the naughty brothers, Max and Moritz, who terrorised the poor local farm folk with their pranks. But it was getting late and I needed to reach my final fairytale destination.

It was a cold and windy night when I arrived at the castle of Sababurg in the heart of the Reinhardswald forest. Against a glowering sky the trees drew giants with their silhouettes and the wind strained their branches, occasionally releasing them with a twang that catapulted showers of raindrops and leaves against my windscreen. I parked and unloaded the car, the sound of the door closing stolen immediately by a gust, and looked up at my haven for the night: the forbidding silhouette of the castle with its twin towers like soldiers' helmets and a solitary light at the porch. Between me and the doorway lay a slippery, shining path covered in a pasty pot-pourri of huge fallen leaves. The smell of conkers filled my nostrils. I felt like I was in some parody of a murder-mystery movie. I pulled the bell cord and it jangled. Once.

Sababurg is also known as Dornröschen after the impenetrable thorn bush that is said to have surrounded the castle, the fictional home of Sleeping Beauty. Like Trendlburg, it was now a hotel, having itself been kissed awake in the 1950s, after several decades of neglect, and restored, although a seductive amount of Romantic ruin remained.

A rather camp man opened the door – hardly a prince – and showed me to my room. While my atmospheric arrival had been rather fitting, I found the inside rather disappointing. Sleeping Beauty lived in the days before regulations that stipulated fire doors totally out of keeping with the original architecture. She also lived before the invention of Formica and fitted carpets. The castle was built in 1334, so she would have had to go on sleeping for some 640 years to wake up in the 1970s, where I now found myself. I wasn't too sure about the thematic pumpkins in the reception area, either.

I hadn't booked in advance but, this being tourist-bereft Germany, not only had they been able to offer me a room but that evening the Schloss was empty. I was to be the only guest in Sleeping Beauty's castle. I was hardly a worthy successor.

The room was certainly comfortable enough for a lengthy rest, with the kind of enveloping bed and soft, plunging pillows a castle with this kind of legend had to have. But was it intentional German humour to supply a 'Do Not Disturb' sign? And why, in the castle of Sleeping Beauty, was there a

TV? She hadn't watched endless evenings of *Friends* while waiting for her prince, let alone explored the standard German option of pay-per-view FKK.

But the place was cosy and autumnal, with log fires flickering, and oil paintings and leather furniture you could lose yourself in. And there was an excellent wood-panelled restaurant complete with a spectacular array of antlers and trophies and which, I learnt at breakfast, had spectacular, romantic views of fields and hills. I don't know how long the waitress had slept but she looked like she'd just woken up. Despite this she treated me unassisted to sumptuous German game food, including two inter-course surprises from the chef and all washed down with a bottle of Spätburgunder (German for Pinot Noir) red wine. Perhaps not a hundred years, but I could feel a welcome long sleep coming on. I walked in a sated trance upstairs to find an 'evening poem' on tasteful parchment had been planted on my pillow. Something about the moon, stars, a black, silent forest and a rising white mist . . .

It was the sound of sheep bleating, not a prince, that woke me. From my window was a scene of utter and surprising Englishness: a verdant Jerusalem of pastures glowing in a golden sun, divided by tumble-down stone walls and dotted by gnarled oaks. Obscured by the dark of the previous evening, it was now revealed as a twin to Blake's 'green and pleasant land', untouched and totally isolated in the middle of the German countryside.

After breakfast I went for a walk in the nearby *Urwald* (primeval forest), passing, as I entered, a corny signpost that suggested 'Look behind you!' as I was on the Fairytale Route. I was renewed, inspired and alert to the forces of nature. The forest was no less imposing by day without the mystery of the silhouettes and the *Sturm und Drang* of the previous night's wind and rain, and it was easy to see how, amid its depths, reason succumbed to wild thoughts, and how the trees could be imbued with life, wisdom or whatever you wanted. I sat for a while on a fallen trunk, trying to harness Wordsworth's 'impulse from a vernal wood', and briefly imagined myself as a youthful *Wanderer*, knapsack on back and crook in hand.

By now I had seen enough to realise that Germany, against all expectations, was a place of fantasy as well as science and efficiency. But I'd also begun to have trouble distinguishing between the old and the new, the real and the fake. There had to be more castles here than in any other country in the world, presumably a vestige of the feuding duchies and city states. It was certainly true that along the Rhine valley alone there was a castle every two kilometres; real castles that had survived from the Middle Ages and had become nineteenth-century symbols, icons of a national mythology. But then elsewhere there were also those faux-medieval imitations and footballers' pastiches.

Schloss Neuschwanstein was the epitome of this urge to imitate. It was surely Germany's most photographed, most commercialised and most visited icon, though not obviously by Germans; a paradigm of a castle, so perfect I'm surprised they haven't yet made seaside sand moulds out of it. But it was the castle of Baron Bomburst in *Chitty Chitty Bang Bang* and was adopted as their logo by that ultimate pedlar of children's paradigms, Disneyland.

Was Manny sending me on a pilgrimage to see what most of his compatriots seemed to think was a copy of the real thing back home?

Neuschwanstein sits in the foothills of the Alps, in the far south of Germany, in a place called Füssen. This is the heart of Germany's lake district, as alpine and beautiful as its Italian counterpart across the mountains. The castle occupies a rocky peak, the ideal location for a magic ring or a damsel in distress. Surrounded by a ravine and dense deciduous woodland, it overlooks the lush meadows where Steve McQueen tried to jump the border-crossing on his motorbike in *The Great Escape*.

From afar the castle is a tall, thin, white and elegant complex of intertwined buildings on many layers, mixing Romanesque, Byzantine and Gothic styles with as many invented flourishes. It is piled high with turrets, spires, arches, promontories and interconnecting passageways, and its overall labyrinthine effect resembles a drawing by Escher.

But, close up, this air of mystery doesn't stand up to much scrutiny. Short cuts in the stonework and a lack of age in the pebble-dashed smoothness remind you that it was built in an industrial nineteenth century. It is not debased by simplicity, like Hitler's Nuremberg congress centre, but by a lack of sincerity. And above all it betrays a lack of real purpose. Although now a museum, it was always a plaything. A parody of a castle, Neuschwanstein does perhaps belong in Disneyland.

It was commissioned by Bavaria's beloved King Ludwig II. Not a great name, Ludwig, by all accounts, and I had to keep reminding myself it was simply German for 'Louis'. But this one was saved by dashing, Byronic good looks and was himself the kind of character that might have appeared in a fairytale and once been a frog. He modelled his dreams on the life of Louis XIV of France, calling himself not the 'Sun King' but the 'Moon King', but slowly and Romantically went mad. He retreated into himself, to the Bavarian Alps and into an artistic dreamworld where, with abundant *Grossmannsucht*, he spent the region's coffers on commissioning a stage designer to turn the sandcastles of his dreams into real stone. Neuschwanstein is just the most famous of many such fantasy castles. Ludwig even met a mysterious fairytale end: he was found inexplicably floating in the Starnberger See lake south-west of Munich, together with his doctor, with whom he had gone on his customary evening stroll.

Ludwig sounded to me like a sort of German Don Quixote,

tilting not at windmills but castles in Bavaria. 'Quixotic' was not an adjective I had ever associated with anything German before. Like the idea of carnival, it felt more Latin. But Ludwig seemed to symbolise not just a very German fairytale – that was all very positive and child-friendly – but also a tendency to seek or hide in illusion instead of reality. But, plagiarised, devoid of any original artistic impulse, superficial and hollow, wasn't it all a bit kitsch?

I had often used this word but never thought about its origins. It must be German, I thought to myself. And I discovered that it was. 'Kitsch' originated in the Munich art market of the 1860s, where it was used to describe cheap but marketable pictures that appealed to the emergent bourgeoisie and allowed them to copy the tastes of the cultural elite.

True artists railed at 'the culture industry', which was debasing their métier. Well, wasn't the modern travel industry just an extension of that same culture industry, now debasing not just art but also true travel? My *Weltschmerz*, my lack of *Wanderlust* as a self-styled 'true traveller', were the fault of kitsch. Tourism was a cause, even a tool of kitsch. It took the unique and our most exotic dreams and turned them into recurring patterns and clichés in the form of ad campaigns, postcards and brochures. Any itinerary suggested by another and the whole lexicon of the travel industry – 'hip' this, 'unspoilt' that – was a kitsch, received idea of luxury. As were those holy grails, 'tips for the discerning traveller' who liked to go 'off the beaten track'. Mere displacement versus a journey. EasyJet kitsch versus the foot-bound *Wanderer*. Manny was right!

My own visit to Neuschwanstein was an exercise in kitsch. Yes, it was a windy day in autumn, that ultimate season of Romantic decay, and as I stood on the wooden bridge that allowed you to look back at the castle from slightly above, mist swirled up from the sheer ravine below, mingling with the roaring water. The fog moved imperceptibly, forming screens that seemed to come together and part again fleetingly to reveal the castle in the distance. All around me hung trees wrought into twisted shapes by the wind, their roots spread out and cloven into the rock like tentacles and their serpentine branches laden with cancerous golden-brown leaves. It was a scene of pure *Sturm und Drang*, such as Caspar David Friedrich might have painted it, and surely as Ludwig would have wanted me to see it. And my heart would have been open to wild passion were it not for the Japanese tourists posing for a picture in front of me and in front of a view that, through a thousand digital lenses, became more kitsch with each click.

Nor was I dressed for poetry. Caught short by the weather and betraying a bourgeois need to stay dry that scuppered my chances of ever being a Romantic, I had sought some emergency rainwear and bought a blue plastic cagoule from a tourist shop at the foot of the hill where they were selling miniature Neuschwansteins made of onyx. Already I'd been confronted by the huge queue for tickets, which filled a cattle-ranch kraal of metal-gated channels. I had declined a ride on one of the ponies that were meant to recreate the ascent to the castle in a medieval manner. (The only thing medieval was the smell they left in their wake. But the Germans had thought about that and a man was employed to drive a poop-scoop car up and down the path, cleaning the way.) And now I stood on Ludwig's favourite bridge looking like a blue plastic diamond, feeling sweaty and claustrophobic and with drops of rain dripping down my collar. Surely not even Goethe could have composed any verses dressed like that. The modern world was poetry-resistant.

'Now, now, you are regressing,' pleaded Manny when, back in London, I attacked the country that had invented, and ever since indulged in, kitsch.

But, ironically, I realised it was Romanticism that begat kitsch. The *Angst* of unrequited love, suicide, longing and so on were instinctively appealing to the masses. Like the truncated life of

Goethe's Werther, the lifespan of the genuine Romantic movement was depressingly short. And surely that was why a travel
destination began to pall when the hordes arrived. Goethe himself said, 'There is nothing worse than imagination without taste.'
As a withering indictment of the modern travel industry it was a
great dinner-party line.

I now found myself evaluating my whole journey through the
German child spirit in terms of its kitschness. Christmas these
days was kitsch. Despite being wooden and individually crafted,
the model trains, the whole paradise of toys and the nutcrackers
of Nuremberg were kitsch; the gnomes were kitsch and even
the Grimms' fairytales. But not because they had no artistic
merit, for this they had, but because, in evoking a miniature,
more perfect world, they shut out and denied what was unpleas-
ant in life.

And now that I thought about it, the same was true of the
pastiche architecture and narrow-gauge railways of the Baltic
coast, the childish gigantism and outsize automata at the
Oktoberfest, the *Gemütlichkeit* of *Lederhosen* and the Bavarian
hunting mythology. The kitsch instinct to suspend reality was
evident in the costumed pageants along the Fairytale Route, in
the medieval dress of fiercely traditional carnivals in small
Swabian villages and in the polished beams of Germany's
immaculate medieval half-timbered houses. Wagner had massive
kitsch potential and Hitler surely recognised this. Like any dic-
tator, he was a master of popularising every emotion, idea or
impulse and turning it into the opium of 'a better world'. And in
the German people he had perhaps had a peculiarly susceptible
audience.

But surely every culture and people had its idea of a perfect
world? Utopia, Eldorado and Shangri-La were all conceptual
paradises, though from different cultures. But maybe Germans
had an exaggerated sense of the Ideal that stemmed from their

Romantic soul and the child within them. In Voltaire's story *Candide* the eponymous protagonist who is disabused of the belief that 'all is for the best in this best of all possible worlds' is a German.

Then I discovered that the Germans had their own unique utopia. It was called Schlaraffenland and was based on a folk tale that spoke of a land where everything was abundant – just like at the Oktoberfest. Milk and honey flowed in the rivers, there was wine instead of water, all creatures flew through the sky, the houses were made from cakes and, bizarrely, instead of stone there was cheese. Enjoyment was the greatest talent of the inhabitants and work and industry were treated as sin (this was clearly before Luther). When your wife grew old and ugly you could trade her in for a new one (like at a *Puff* in Cologne) and the old ones got dipped in a youth-bath (something like the Müllersches Volksbad) and came out young and nubile again.

Schlaraffenland lay at the confluence of Romantic longing and a kitsch desire to bury one's head in the sand. 'Once upon a time' was a phrase that opened the door to an easier somewhere-else. And with its neat villages of simplistic, plastic-looking, white, red-roofed houses Germany often looked like Schlaraffenland: a giant, supremely intricate and perfected model train set like the ones on sale in the Christmas markets. It was a perverse kind of *Grossmannsucht* of the miniature. (And of course, a German firm, Miniatur Wunderland, holds the world record for the longest model railway.) It was a sure sign that the child and the systemising Romantic philosopher were alive and well in the soul of your average German – an idealised world that nevertheless perfectly represented the complexity of the real world so that it could better be understood. You could even say that wonder is the beginning of philosophy.

But a model world represented a world that could be controlled and where a human being could play God, and this was an illusory world that suspended reality and allowed no fault or flaw. And we all knew what that meant. Battling with layers of illusion like this, no wonder Germans found conquering their past so difficult.

But that was probably going too deep. With its forests, lakes, mountains, gingerbread and half-timbered houses, castles and Gothic church spires, Germany's landscape was without doubt the original landscape of a collective global childhood imagination, at different times homely and comforting or wild, dark and mysterious. From a child's first building blocks via the *Kindergarten* to the first toys, first Christmas and first book of fairytales, Germany was responsible for the common heritage of so many children all over the world. Indeed it seemed to me that in the Western world the child's imagination was essentially a German creation. In Germany I'd had my child's eyes reopened and if I could always see the world through German eyes, then by implication I would always see it like a child, with fresh, wide eyes and curiosity. And at least when it came to *Wanderlust,* that was a good thing.

9

Delikatessen

nn, *delicate eating*

'In your insatiable appetite for new conquests you consumers don't seem to be able to enjoy a place unless you enjoy its cuisine. A country has to deliver good food, which in turn becomes part of its fashion status; witness the new balsamic vinegar to be found at every dinner party where you sip your Chablis, or should that be Chavlis?'

Until Manny put it to me I'd never really considered the relationship between palate and passport. Even so, I had difficulty thinking sauerkraut could ever be cool.

'And so you now have "delis" all over the place with their trendy faux-rustic décors and overpriced goods. But do you know what the word "deli" actually means and where it came from?'

No, I didn't. Something to do with India? Or a faddish use of the word 'deli-cious'?

'"Deli" is in fact a short form of the German word *"Delikatessen"*, a combination of *"delikat"* and *"Essen"*, basically meaning "good eating" and imported and anglicised to "delicatessen" by German immigrants to America.'

A German term that was a byword for good food? Surely German food was all sausages, potatoes and dumplings – anything but delicate. Germans were great at making cars, but not to be trusted in the kitchen.

'How much do you actually know about German cuisine?' Manny asked.

Well, the adjective 'German' didn't fit cooking any more than it did fashion or humour. My experience of Asterix-sized portions of pork knuckle, tripe, veal lung and sausages at the Oktoberfest, itself one monstrous stomach, had not dispelled any prejudice that Germans were devout carnivores. And now I remembered an amusing story that had hit the international headlines in 2003.

A German by the name of Armin Meiwes (perhaps related to the original Arminius?) admitted to having eaten a forty-three-year-old man (also a German) with the latter's consent. He had advertised on a website, inviting someone to come and be eaten – something along the lines of 'Single white cannibal seeks partner in crime' – and was probably amazed to have a taker. It didn't take long for the police to come looking and, having traced the website to its owner, they found a freezer full of human flesh. Armin recounted how he had filmed the ritual – and it did indeed appear that the other guy appeared to be consenting – and how he had sliced off his penis and, having fried it, the two of them had sat down to eat it. Perhaps it tasted a little like bratwurst. At one point it wasn't clear if it was pre- or post-emasculation when the victim had decided he was no longer up for it, had a brief change of heart (almost literally) and gone home, only to come back having decided to go through with it. He must have had some pretty incurable *Angst*. It was a truly extraordinary story and between shades of FKK, fetishism and sausage references it did appear curiously German in nature. Most extraordinary of all, however, was the fact that Meiwes could not be convicted because cannibalism, in the rolled-back state of Germany, is not a crime.

'But surely you of all people, as an Englishman, can appreciate a German breakfast!'

When travelling there were few things better than a country that appreciated a good breakfast. And it was true. In Germany there was none of this 'nibble on a croissant, a quick fix of overstrong coffee and it's all over' nonsense. No. Germans seemed to understand that breakfast should be a feast to gorge on slowly over multiple helpings of as wide a variety of fare as possible. I remembered a full monty I'd treated myself to in Nuremberg and how eventually, after the sweat-bath, I had restored myself in Munich's Viktualienmarkt on proper bacon, *Bratkartoffel* (basically hash browns) and mustard.

'Ah yes. The German breakfast understands what it is like to overdo it on the Pils! And there is even a sort of black pudding you English should like: *Blutwurst*, blood sausage. Have you ever tried curing a hangover on an Italian breakfast?'

It was true. Custard-filled brioches or *penne al pesto* didn't quite cut the mustard. The Italians didn't even have a proper word for a hangover so couldn't really be expected to understand the value of grease, excessive salt and starch.

'In Germany they may not have your "greasy spoons", but they do have a word for hangover, a *Kater*, and you can order a decent *Katerfrühstück* (hangover breakfast) in almost any pub in the country.'

Nevertheless, it was with some surprise and suspicion that I found in my therapy pack an invitation to the German Embassy to be regaled by an evening of Michelin-starred cuisine from a region called Baden-Württemberg. Manny was obviously well connected. More to the point, I had never associated Michelin stars with Germany. Michelin-sized men maybe, but not stars.

But now, in the company of the Ambassador (who, from a brief conversation with His Excellency, I gathered was a keen

German walker) and food critics from the British journalistic establishment, I was being told by the formidable Frau Süss (sweet by name, sweet by nature) of the Baden-Württemberg marketing department that in the 2006 Michelin Guide Germany had more stars than any country after France and was second only to France in the number of three-star restaurants, of which there were seven. They were all over Germany, many in Berlin and Munich, but most of them were in her south-western state, which was near France.

Germany and France spent most of the Middle Ages beating each other up over religion and territory, with Germany largely on the receiving end. France, according to Manny, was Germany's *Erbfeind,* or 'hereditary enemy', and the root of all evil suffered by any German citizen. What a great word! And one that seemed equally suited to English attitudes towards Germany, at least in the twentieth century. Was Germany in fact Britain's *Erbfeind*?

'But remember,' said Manny, displaying an un-American knowledge of 'old Yurrup', 'Germany was previously a country you admired for its culture. Look at Anglo-French history down the centuries and your mutual political and cultural superiority complexes. Surely France, not Germany, is Britain's real *Erbfeind*!'

Touché. Yes, it was a lovely place, France. Great for holidays, good food and wine and complete with corners that would be *toujours* Chelsea. Just a shame it was full of the French!

When it came to the kitchen Germany put aside its Francophobia and welcomed French influence on its dining-room table. In the eighteenth century the German royal court ate exclusively French food and French influences around Germany's borders percolated into many German culinary traditions. The Huguenots, French Protestant refugees, then added their gourmet traditions, until the nationalist and militarist Kaiser Willy (the Second – it was easy to confuse your Fritzes and Willies) decreed that only German food should be consumed in Germany. And then came the two wars and food for Germans became a matter of survival, not art.

After the Second World War the *Wirtschaftswunder* coincided with the *Fresswelle*, a wave of guzzling as Germans once again found Marshall Plan-assisted food on their plates. Quantity, wholesomeness and heartiness were the peasant-like qualities that defined the cuisine of this time. Known as *Gutbürgerliche Küche*, citizenly cooking, it was light on vegetables and side dishes were virtually non-existent. *Gutbürgerliche Küche* lived on in the thick soups, ample meat cuts and dumplings that I had found many times on German menus. It seemed like the culinary expression of *Gemütlichkeit* and much like British steak-and-kidney pie comfort food.

But now, at the German Embassy, I was being spoilt by a terrine of vegetables and goose liver with a confit of figs followed by a fried fillet of pikeperch with cinnamon on pumpkin and sauce verveine, followed by a ragout of oxtail with mashed potatoes, truffle sauce and sautéed crêpes and finished off with a composition of orange and caramel with toasted almonds. Delicious. And German!

The meal was created by a consommé of German chefs from the gourmet restaurants and resort hotels in the Black Forest, including the village of Baiersbronn, population sixteen thousand, which alone had three of the aforementioned three-star restaurants.

According to Germany's youngest three-star cook, Christian Bau, 'Germans take food very seriously, but not necessarily as gourmets. German cuisine is a rustic cuisine that is down-to-earth (a culinary equivalent of FKK?), which is not something that is practised in *haute cuisine*.' But he supported the view generally held around my table that German cuisine was being rediscovered by Germans, polished up and plumped up like Hansel, ready for export. 'Germany is definitely not a gourmet country but we are well on the way.' If Christian Bau was to be believed Germany would soon reign supreme in the kitchen. 'Cooking is like a sport. If you want to win Olympic gold you train hard for years so that when it comes to the crunch you are top fit.' I had visions of German chefs training on their local *Trimmdichpfad* for a touch of the old *Gesundheit*, and of typical German competitiveness.

'It's not as if the British have a culinary reputation to be smug about. Sauerkraut and sausage is your fish and chips.'

'And hot dogs and onions is the US's, for that matter!' I countered.

'How often have you seen a British restaurant outside the UK?'

Unless you counted the all-day breakfast café-pubs on the Costa del Sol, probably never. But how many German restaurants were their outside Germany? Equally few, I reckoned.

The Italians, the French, the Belgians, the Spanish and the Greeks had all successfully exported their cuisines around the world. But when it came to German and British food other people typically found them inedible. But I did remember once going to an Austrian restaurant in London where the owner and waiters were all kitted up in full-on *Sound of Music* garb and Johann Strauss was piping through the stereo. It wasn't until after I'd finished my Wienerschnitzel and chocolate Viennoise that I got talking to the head waiter. The reason he didn't understand my German was not because it was so bad. It was because he, like all his colleagues, was from Naples.

The British meanwhile never emigrated. We merely colonised and in so doing invented afternoon tea and after-hours curry nights. The Germans had also never been economic migrants. They were usually the educated and skilled white-collar organisers wherever they went, invited for their industrial expertise. Other people cooked their food.

But now the recent trend for gastropubs had resuscitated

the Sunday roast and things like home-made pies and Gower cockles, turning home-spun recipes into a British 'cuisine'. Maybe the Germans had lots of equivalents of these dishes, equally unknown beyond their borders?

Manny had asked me to consider German food and look out for certain specialities throughout my therapy as I visited various parts of the country. 'The basis of every good cuisine is to be found in its regions,' he had said, 'but can you name the German regions as you can Provence, Tuscany or Andalusia?'

Beyond Bavaria and now a few recent additions, like Hessen and Mecklenburg, I confessed I couldn't. But regional difference was not something I'd associated with Germany. It had always seemed to me a vague but homogenous whole.

'Did you know Germany has borders with no fewer than ten other countries – more than any other country in Europe?'

So many neighbours! No wonder so many people had so much to say about the Germans.

'All these contiguous countries have had their lasting influences on German cuisine. And remember, for centuries Germany was just a collection of German tribes. You could even say there is no such thing as a German. And you will see in your visits and in the dishes you sample a great regionalism and localism that still exists to this day.'

To convince me, Manny had enclosed a cookbook written by a friend who was clearly a nostalgic American of German decent. No naked chef, his friend would nonetheless have me believe it would take a lifetime to sample the variety of German cuisine. I didn't have that long but the book gave me some insights into what was put in front of me at each visit.

I learnt that the Germans of the north were often referred to by other Germans as '*Fischköpfe*' (fish heads) and the northern port city of Bremen nicknamed '*Fischstadt*' because of their predilection for delicacies such as the *Labskaus* (lobscouse) and *Aalsuppe* (eel soup) I had tasted in Hamburg. The local

Matjehering herring was apparently venerated by all Prussians after Bismarck was prescribed it for the good of his *Gesundheit*. Lübeck meanwhile claimed to be the home of marzipan but, as with many of the exotic ingredients, such as ginger, which pepper the local dishes, this was courtesy of Hanseatic trading with faraway lands. By far the greatest proof of north-German culinary skill had been in the puddings. On the Baltic coast I'd enjoyed *Rote Grütze*, or red-berry pudding, which was as much of a symbol of the area as cream teas were of Devon; the delightfully named *Verschleiertes Mädchen* ('veiled farm girl'), an apple and pumpernickel crunch much like apple crumble; and *Qualle auf Sand*, a nutty meringue whose name meant 'jellyfish on sand'. They were dishes with delicate tastes and figurative names I had previously scarcely associated with German cuisine.

When Germany was reunited it was also reunited with half of its cuisine. This meant lots of eastern influences from Poland and Czech cuisine, such as dumplings, patties and lots of duck, venison and other game. It was a heartier, more filling cuisine, and one ideally suited to the East German socialist regime. They clearly didn't believe in delicacies and used prosaic names such as *Sattigungsbeilage* (filling side dishes), placing the emphasis on keeping the population full rather than telling them what was actually on their plate. Some of these dishes had apparently had a revival as part of a wave of '*Ostalgie*', or nostalgia for the East, that followed the drubbing of everything from the Eastern Block. Chief among these were the *Spreewaldgurken*, gherkins from the flooded woodland area south-east of Berlin, which played a starring role in the hit German film *Goodbye Lenin*, and the *Teltower Rübchen*, a unique turnip that would grow only in the sandy soil around the town of Teltow. Well, German cuisine faced an uphill struggle if gherkins and turnips were its flagship, I thought. Yet Pope Pius IX apparently once ordered these turnips be imported to him in Rome, the French court treated them as a delicacy and they frequently ended up on the plates of the

Russian Tsars. Berlin was also very strong on puddings, be it the *Berliner Luft*, which had nothing to do with the airlift but was a delicious apple mousse with berry coulis, the enormous *Baumkuchen* (tree cakes), which could be up to three metres in height, and the famous *Berliner Pfannkuchen* doughnuts. Apocryphally, when Kennedy delivered his famous '*Ich bin ein Berliner*', one newspaper thought the US President was displaying an intimate knowledge of Berlin cuisine and mistranslated his phrase as 'I am a jelly donut'. But this was not as bad as Clinton, who, trying to emulate his Democrat predecessor, found himself in Cologne saying, '*Ich bin ein Kölsch*'. But a Kölner is the name for a person from Cologne and *Kölsch* is the local beer. East German cuisine had also played a huge part in Germany's Christmas culture: Dresden was the home of the sweet yeast loaf called *Stollen* and *Berliner Brot* were delectable cinnamon-flavoured biscuits I had tasted at German Christmas markets.

'The *Stollen* is a classic example of food as a travel brand,' said Manny. 'Over the past ten years you have sought out Italy's *pandoro* and *panettone* and sugared almonds and *turrón* from Spain. But you will soon see the German *Stollen* become an essential for your trendy Condé Nast dinner parties at Christmas.'

The west of Germany was the most influenced by France, with dishes like *Saumagen* that were reminiscent of Lyon's haggis-like *andouilette*. And around Heidelberg, where we used to live, and generally the whole south-west, I now learnt, was home to the delicious German white asparagus.

Meanwhile, as a regular visitor to Munich and the Austrian Alps, I found the south-German cuisine was the one I felt most familiar with: *Käsespätzle* ('little cheese sparrows'), cheese-dribbled macaroni-cum-gnocchi; *Schweinebraten*, roast pork medallions; a predilection for veal, dumplings and *Rotkohl* (red cabbage) and a strange camembert spread called *Obatza*. It was also the home of the sour-milk cheese called *Quark*,

Lebkuchen (gingerbread biscuits) from Nuremberg and, of course, *Schwarzwalder Kirschtorte* otherwise known as Black Forest gateau. Apparently invented in 1927 by a baker called Josef Keller, the dish that had given me so much joy but also so many migraines through excess as a child, in fact originated in Bonn, not the Black Forest. The forest is just where the cherries come from. And if the thought of all this food gave me indigestion I was reminded that it was the Bavarians who had invented all manner of medicinal schnapps to give the stomach a helping hand. Numerous occasions came to mind of waking up with regrets about ill-advised late-night Alpine rounds of Jägermeister.

The book pulled together two hundred uniquely German recipes and made a pretty good fist of presenting Germany as a country with a little-suspected diverse cuisine. But honestly, when it came to German food I could still only think of four essential ingredients: cabbage, sausage, potato and bread.

'Ah, but remember the trick!' Manny said. 'The trick is to be able to romanticise these commonplace ingredients.'

What, like 'Give the potato the appearance of the unfamiliar? Or the sausage an impressive aspect?' That sounded a bit FKK to me.

Well, Manny, I tried.

Germany is, not surprisingly, the world home of the sausage, and eastern Germany is its epicentre. There are more types of *Wurst* in your average German butcher than you can shake a frankfurter at. A butcher in Frankfurt got out all his sausages for me to prove it and proceeded to boast that Germany had some fifteen hundred kinds of sausage. I shouldn't have been surprised; thinking back to the Oktoberfest menu, I knew that Germans were past masters at using every piece of an animal's body. Of course, if you're Herr Meiwe, you probably start with a bull's pizzle.

I learnt too that the word '*Wurst*' plays a huge role in both the German psyche and the German language. There are lots of expressions and proverbs that revolve around sausage: '*In der Not isst man die Wurst ohne Brot*', or 'As a last resort one eats sausage without bread' – whatever that means; '*Alles hat ein Ende, nur die Wurst hat zwei*' ('Everything has an ending, only the sausage has two'); '*Das ist mir Wurst*' ('It's all the same to me'); '*Es geht um die Wurst*' (It's time to talk turkey'). '*Ein Kleines Würstchen*' means 'small-fry', a '*Wurstblatt*' is a tabloid rag, '*Wursstig*' is 'trifling' and '*Wurst wider Wurst*' means 'tit for tat'. Even the south of Germany, I learnt, is sometimes defined by a culinary border, the '*Weisswurstäquator*', north of which no *Weisswurst*, the regional sausage speciality, is served. Germans take purity in their *Wurst* very seriously indeed, and German law dictates that only meat, bacon, offal, salt and spices may be used.

Thuringia and Nuremberg fight over which is the home of the original bratwurst. I once heard the owner of a Nuremberg bratwurst restaurant interviewed on the radio about the local delicacy, the interviewer noting that 'people come from all over the world to see your sausage' and asking, 'Why is your sausage so small?' and whether it had a skin on it. Needless to say, the double entendres went over the poor restaurateur's head and instead he offered an earnest historical explanation/excuse for the size of his sausage: apparently they used to be slipped through the keyholes of the prison doors by the wives of Nuremberg's male convicts.

Then there was the boundary-defining Bavarian *Weisswurst* I had enjoyed with a Bavarian *Dunkelbier* (dark beer) at the foot of Neuschwanstein, beloved of mad King Ludwig II, a delicious blend of pork, veal, parsley, lemon peel and spice; *Berliner Bockwurst* pickled in beer sauce; and, most famously of all, the *Currywurst* held up by Berliners as a sign of *haute cuisine* and which had featured in that little yellow book of *Fifty Great*

German Inventors. It was clearly a proud German story; the story of Berliner Frau Herta Heuwel, who in 1949 was bored and had no customers at her *Imbissstube* (snack bar) in the city's Stuttgarter Platz and started playing around with ketchup and spices to create new toppings. Her invention was so popular that in 1959 she decided to patent it, only to find herself involved in a legal dispute with a sausage maker in Hamburg who claimed he had 'invented' it. Berlin won and the *Currywurst* now has its very own museum there.

I was amazed to discover that many German sausages, for example, the frankfurter, were protected from imitation by European law, as if they were Parma ham or cheese. Only frankfurters made in Frankfurt have the right to that much sought-after appellation. Moreover this glass city of banking is not only the home of an EU-protected sausage but is also the Taunton of Germany, and home of local *Appewoi* (*Apfelwein*, or cider), usually quaffed out of ceramic jugs to down mouthfuls of *Handkäse mit Musik*, hand-sized lumps of cheese, or Jurassic portions of *Frankfurter Rippchen*, salted pork ribs.

Perhaps not romanticise it, but I would never look at a German sausage in the same way again.

But what about those Krauts (by which I mean the humble cabbage, not the people)? You are what you eat, we are consistently told. And if this is so, the Germans are justly called 'Krauts'. More of a cult in the north, *Kraut*, I found, is nevertheless ubiquitous in Germany. But I never knew that cabbage came in so many varieties or that Germans had so many words for it: *Kohl* (as in Helmut), *Grünkohl*, or simply *Kraut*, to name a few, and this suggested the vegetable played a large role in German life. Well, they really did eat an awful lot of *Kraut*, particularly of the *Sauer* variety, cured in vats of salt. German families went on *Kohlfahren*, excursions into the countryside to collect cabbages, as the Russians collect mushrooms and the Piemontese truffles. *Kohlfahrt*! My puerile humour thought it a suitable name, given the gastric side-effects of overdosing on cabbage.

So, Germany, not just sausage capital of the world but cabbage capital of Europe, with the northern town of Dithmarschen producing a smelly eighty million a year.

And as for the humble *Kartoffel*, or potato, it was King Frederick who brought it back from the Andes to Germany, which had since become the potato capital of the world. There were festivals held in its honour in Jerichower Land, and in Odenwald they even had a potato week. Even for the less potato-headed Germans the national cuisine served up the potato in all its forms for daily consumption, be it *Bratkartoffeln* (roast potatoes), potato dumplings or potato pancakes. On Rügen I had tasted the local *Kartoffelbuletten* (potato patties) and on the Baltic coast a delicious dish from Cologne called *Himmel und Erde* (Heaven and Earth), a soft and light purée of mashed potatoes and apple topped with onions and bacon.

'And now for the king of German foods,' declared Manny. 'Bread!'

Sausage. Gherkins. Turnips. And now bread! How much more Romantic could it get?

'Yes. In recent years you have allowed the Italians to bang on about the varieties and subtleties of something so simple as pasta. It's time the huge variety and healthiness of German bread is recognised. German rye bread is a supermodel's dream!'

For Manny, '*das tägliche Brot*' (daily bread) was as much a German religion as beer and *Wurst*. And for him it was the best in the world and certainly the best thing since British white sliced Sunblest.

The way Manny went on about German bread was strange. He talked of missing it as if he had some *Heimweh* of his own for German bread. I had read how in the lead-up to the 2006 World Cup a German perfume manufacturer had come up with the idea of a 'smells tour' meant to evoke each participating country. For

Germany it recreated the smell of freshly baked bread. And for England? Not cut grass or Earl Grey, but, bizarrely, the smell of the After-Eight mint (produced in Switzerland since 1988).

'For a German being a baker is a very serious thing. There are still some sixteen hundred independent bakeries in Germany whereas in the UK the number is in the tens. In Germany becoming a baker is still a matter of vocation and real apprenticeship that takes time, handed-down wisdom and experience.'

Jürgen Klinsmann apparently passed his baker's apprenticeship before pursuing an alternative career as a diver-cum-footballer. In a pre-World Cup interview he recalled how he had had to work fourteen to sixteen hours a day and how in comparison football training was, well, a piece of cake. You can still pop in for a pretzel at the Bäckerei Klinsmann, run by his family in the Stuttgart suburb of Botnang.

It was a romantic view but its central tenet was sound: a reliance on fresh ingredients and pure recipes with no artificial additives. Celebrity chefs had recently taken up the cause of the demise of the British loaf. By contrast, Germany with its localism had never stopped producing a huge range of breads that fitted perfectly with our diet-conscious, post-Atkins lives. Could it be that, like becoming green, steam baths and allotments, German bread was on the verge of cool, in line to become the new balsamic vinegar?

Along with Westphalian pumpernickel, a dark rye bread, and *Schwarzbrot*, 'black bread', from Oldenburg, there were over three hundred types of bread in Germany, and over twelve hundred types of biscuit and cake, each containing an abundance of vitamins, carbohydrates, proteins and mineral salts (for, needless to say, purity in German bread was a matter of law). The morning snack of *Brotzeit* (bread time) was an important feature of German rural life, like elevenses. And instead of the British cup of tea at four o'clock the Germans had *Kaffee und Kuchen* (coffee and cakes). The icon of the German bakery, the symbol on the German Bakers' Guild's coat of arms, was the pretzel, originally from Speyer near Heidelberg, whose distinctive taste came from its golden-brown lacquer of caustic soda, which, as someone presumably found out the hard way, is poisonous unless baked.

It was true now I thought of it: German bakeries were nostril-teasing and satisfying places, particularly at stations and any other place where I had been seized by hunger. Germany has its fair share of golden arches and supersized human beings, but I had never once had to suffer an overpriced vacuum-packed sandwich and instead had been treated to ham and cheese beautifully sandwiched between fresh, varied and delicious bread. And the bread would always be served with such attention to detail in the name of the bread, it being a local speciality, and handed over in paper bags with bread-related, healthy family poetry on it: '*Mit Herz für Familie und Natürlichkeit*' ('With the heart, for family and being natural'); 'A lost day is a day when you have not laughed' (on that basis, what was German life expectancy?); 'Where there are children there is bread'; and 'When only one person dreams it is a dream, but when lots of people dream it is the beginning of reality.' Tell that to the Poles!

So where did ex-pat Germans and nostalgics like Manny get their daily bread. Well, he told me there was, against the odds, a German *Delikatessen* in London. And, appropriately enough for a cuisine so legendary for its meat, it was located in Ham, near Richmond, which, with its German School, was as near as London got to having a *Klein Deutschland*, or Little Germany. But sadly Das Backhaus did not do justice to the yeasty warmth of bakeries back in Germany. There was nothing wrong with the produce but sadly it wasn't the fragrant hanging garden of Wurst and breads it should have been and unlike Italian delis it definitely didn't market its food as oral sex. Instead it was neuter, bare and Protestant, as if therein lay some Catholic–Protestant

divide and an explanation for Germany's inability to sell itself as
a tourist destination over the years.

My communion with German food was halfway accomplished.
That was that for 'the body of Germany'. Now for 'the blood of
Germany'.

'Where would you be without Becks?' asked Manny, smiling
knowingly.

I looked blank.

'Well, not in the World Cup final, that's for sure!'

Aha! Was this the famed American sense of humour?

Of course Manny was not talking about the erstwhile England
'soccer'-celebrity with the curving free-kicks but about the beer
with the aid of which tens of thousands of England fans went on
a different sort of bender throughout Germany during the World
Cup.

And, Manny added, what about that German word that even
the most resolute anti-German, *Sun*-reading English hooligan
used every day? An object of worship, the ultimate reliever of
Angst, which in excess could lead to involuntary and unsightly
FKK and which, the morning after, left a throbbing *Weltschmerz*
in the head. Lager.

'Lager louts', getting 'lagered' or simply ordering 'a pint of
lager' were all expressions that had passed effortlessly into the
English language. But they came from the German word *lagern*,
meaning 'to store', after the practice of German brewers before
the dawn of the fridge, who laid their bottom-fermenting beer
down in the winter months to let it self-filter. The word '*Lager*'
itself is not actually used in German to describe beer or to order
a pint. It is the German for 'a camp'.

A brief overview taught me that Germany was without doubt
the world capital of beer production. The Germans might have
been surpassed by the Czechs in annual per capita beer consumption but they still produced more of it, with more care and

more variety than any other nation on the planet. And, as Defoe wrote, long before the Czechs claimed this title, 'Drunkenness the darling favourite of Hell/Chose Germany to rule and rules it well.'

Beer has for millennia been central to human existence. It was first brewed in 5600 BC by the ancient Egyptians, who wisely used it as currency, calling it '*kash*', from which English gets the word 'cash'. This cloudy liquid containing the husks of the grain wouldn't have borne much resemblance to modern beer but, as Benjamin Franklin said, it was still 'proof that God loves us and wants us to be happy'.

It is principally the Bavarians we have to thank for perfecting the art of beer – the word comes from the old High German '*Bior*' – and for turning it into the drink the world enjoys today. Back in the fifth century AD they were a pagan Germanic tribe with brewing central to their creed. Christian missionaries found they could not tame the Bavarians' love of beer so they decided to incorporate it and encourage its production among monks for their own good and sustenance. Liquid nourishment was not deemed a breaking of the fast and so beer came in particularly handy for Lent. The world's first brewery was established in 1040 in Friesing near Munich and it is said that the medieval monk would consume up to five litres of beer a day, putting most lager louts to shame. Such was the strength of beer's hold on the populace of Bavaria that it became the subject of a power struggle between the Church and the feudal lords, with both sides trying to gain control over its brewing. Finally the merchant classes got hold of beer and turned it from a brew that had bits in it and of which no two pints were the same to the beverage we know and love.

As I had seen in their spas and saunas, sausage and bread, the Germans set standards for freshness and purity in their food and drink long before the word 'organic' was invented. And in another piece of Romantic systemisation the Bavarians invented the *Reinheitsgebot*, or 'purity law', enshrining the regulations under which all beer should be brewed and in particular the stipulation that it should contain nothing but barley, hops and water (yeast came later). Applied first locally in 1487 by Duke Albrecht IV but then across the whole of Bavaria in 1516 (around the time Luther was inventing Protestantism), the *Reinheitsgebot* is the world's oldest written food law.

'Naturally, in their homogenising wisdom the European Commission declared it illegal in 1987 on the grounds that it prevented the free trade of chemically enhanced beer within the EU,' said Manny bitterly. 'Although the purity law is still observed by most German brewers, it's thanks to the EU that cat's piss is now allowed to be served in certain German bars.'

Beer is still something of a religion in Germany. It is the subject of veneration, a piece of the country's culture, and its powers are long revered by eminent German cultural figures. 'Beer gives us pleasure, books only frustration,' said the poet-philosopher-scientist Goethe, and 'a glass of lager makes me feel comfortable in my armchair' was the view of Thomas Mann. While Kaiser Wilhelm once stated, 'Give me a woman who loves beer and I will conquer the world.' Whoever she was she has a lot to answer for.

Mark Twain once said, 'German beers are as different as hens in a farmyard.' A Twain remark is rarely 100 per cent pure. But, although he was implying there was only so much that could separate one beer from another, he was conceding that in Germany beer came in a huge number of varieties: over five thousand today, far more than in any other country in the world. I reflected that in Britain the monopoly of a few breweries on all pubs apart from a few 'free houses' had ensured that the taps served a limited selection of real ales and the rest were imported lagers. In Germany the Campaign for Real Ale would never have to exist. You didn't find imported lagers on tap and every region, almost every city and every town in Germany, had its own distinct beer.

The variety of German beer was both regional and seasonal. I had never really considered the manufacture of beer in seasonal terms. But while a can of Stella was available from a supermarket all year round, I now learnt that a genuine, fresh and pure lager beer '*vom Fass*' (from the tap) was ready in early spring, having started brewing at the end of September. At the Oktoberfest I had overdosed on *Märzenbier*, which was a March brew. It was strange. The idea of a harvest, even different vintages of barley and types of water seemed more applicable to grapes and wine. But that is exactly what, I discovered, the Germans do: they consider beer-making every bit as much an art form as making wine (what that said about their wine-making was another matter) and herein lay an interesting culinary and cultural phenomenon.

As I now knew, the Romans never really figured out their wood-dwelling Germanic neighbours and beer was a part of that mystery. In his *Germania*, the first travel book about Germany, the poet Tacitus wrote disdainfully of their drinking habits, 'for their drink, they draw a liquor from barley or other grain; and ferment the same so as to make it resemble wine'. He wrote from a Latin, wine-making perspective as if wine were the only drink worth drinking. Beer and wine symbolised the clash of the Saxon and the Roman worlds and the same snobbery of Roman times still exists now. Was the Rhine in fact more than a river: a cultural frontier between the wine-tasting and the beer-swilling worlds?

Before Louis Pasteur and the invention of the fridge, a cool place was needed to store the brew and this led to the invention of that German institution, the *Biergarten*. No ordinary pub garden, a true *Biergarten* had to have a cloister-like quality about it, was usually outside the town or city and often in the hills, and usually contained aged chestnut trees whose leaves were once supposed to provide shade and keep the beer cold. Bavaria, and in particular Munich, were home to the *Biergarten* and the summer country headquarters of Oktoberfest *Gemütlichkeit*. Indeed a good

Biergarten was an Eden of *Gemütlichkeit* and all that is earthy, peasant-like, traditional and nostalgic about Germany.

King Ludwig I of Bavaria initially prohibited the consumption of food on the premises. But Münchners disregarded this decree and brought along everything they needed from their farms and spread it all out on communal benches in the middle of the garden, thus establishing the blueprint for the convivial picnic I had seen Germans all over the country eat in the summer.

The longer a beer was left to ferment and the later it was tapped the stronger it grew. That much was obvious to me. But I learnt the Germans made a whole range of different-strength beers with this process. A Bock was stronger than a *Märzen*; after that came *Superbock* and a *Jubiläumsbock* was an especially strong beer usually made to commemorate something. Imagine being a monk on the brink of Lent trying to devise the best way to get through months of abstinence from food. You'd do what every right-thinking monk would do and brew some extra-strong brew to knock you out and help you sleep through the torture. This is why in April Munich held a hard-core alternative to the Oktoberfest, the Starkbierfest, or Strong Beer Festival, to celebrate the super-strong pre-Lenten beers brewed by the city's medieval monks, all christened with prize-fighting names meant to conjure their strength and defy all but the most daring drinker to consume them: Triumphator, Maximator and Salvator. But, as yet, no Gladiator or Terminator.

In my various visits to Germany I would have the opportunity to enjoy much of the spectrum of German beer. Beyond *Märzen* and Bavarian *Dunkelbier* I had enjoyed several *Stangen* of *Kölsch*, which was the alternative eau de cologne, signifying not only a local beer but a local dialect and a local way of life. It was served in test-tube-sized glasses lined up on long, thin trays like a chemistry experiment and meant to be drunk and refilled tapas-style. In Berlin, I would discover, they liked a *Weissbier* (a pale wheat beer) but with a shot of refreshing fruit syrup, usually raspberry or lemon. It sounded a bit like a beer with a parasol, but as a summer drink it was truly refreshing. In Leipzig there was the revived *Leipziger Gose*, a pint tinged with coriander and salt. And in Lübeck, Hamburg and on the Baltic coast I had enjoyed light, crisp and dry Holstein and Pils beers.

I discovered that the town of Plzen in what was now the Czech Republic was once a part of Germany and there was a large German cultural history in Bohemia. Not only was the first German university in Prague but the seemingly Czech origins of Pils were in fact German. In 1842 a Bavarian brewer, Josef Groll, wanted to experiment with a different malt and the water in Plzen, which was softer than that in Munich. The golden nectar that resulted was an instant hit and called Pilsener after the town where it was brewed.

Manny was on a role with his jokes now, showing me how in Germany beer was the subject of great inter-regional rivalry and mockery. Kölners apparently laugh that the beer drunk in Düsseldorf is made from Rhine water recycled from Kölsch that has been drunk and then pissed out upstream. And then there was the one about the guy from Cologne, the guy from Hamburg and the guy from Bremen who meet in a bar for a drink. The first one orders a Kölsch, the second a Holstein and the third a Coke. The first two look at the third and ask why he doesn't order a beer, perhaps a Becks from his home town. He looks at them and responds that if the other two aren't going to drink a proper drink, then why should he? Hilarious.

But the most extraordinary beer I sampled at Manny's behest lay away from the limelight of Cologne and Munich in a city north of Nuremberg called Bamberg that regarded itself as the year-round capital of beer and where the locals consumed double the German average.

Bamberg was an elegant, Parisian-style town of avenues and a river embankment lined with neo-classical residences. As I

crossed the river I saw a mini Venice of sunken, wonky half-timbered fishermen's houses and old mill houses assaulted on both
sides by weirs and rushing water full of lilies and reeds; and a
frescoed half-timbered town hall eccentrically perched in the
middle of the river and joined by two bridges. Then, up on the
hill, rising haughtily above the town centre, like Prague or
Edinburgh castle, an upper town of baroque church squares,
crowned by the spires of a Romanesque cathedral.

Bamberg had fifty-eight local speciality brews and ten remaining independent and family-run breweries that were popular
pub restaurants and in many cases also had rooms. So as to
have the shortest possible journey to bed after a night of beer-
tasting, I had booked one such room in the crooked,
dark-timbered Spezial brewery.

The German saying 'Drink beer and be fat, drink water and
die' shows that for many Germans beer is still not just a method
of refreshment or intoxication, but also, if not primarily, a
source of nourishment. Time was when mothers gave their new-
borns beer and it was a staple of the manual labourer's
lunchpack. But I'd never seen people drink beer for breakfast.
English football fans, yes. But people, no.

In the morning I came down the rickety wooden backstairs
and was directed to *Frühstück* in a small wood-panelled room
like the snug in a pub adjoined to the main room. This was also
wood-panelled and with varnished and hardened tables and
benches, simply decorated like an old working men's club. And
already at eight in the morning it was half-full of men, some old,
some not so old, sitting at their *Stammtisch* – German pubs
have a table for locals and regulars – leaning into their first
ceramic *Krug* of beer by way of cornflakes. But they weren't
drunkards or old soaks. They read the papers and chatted away
in a civilised fashion, chewing over the themes of the day with
the owner and waitress.

Bamberg's founder, the eleventh-century Emperor Heinrich II, apparently had ambitions to make it a northern alternative to Rome. So I thought, 'When in Rome . . .' and ordered a pint with my scrambled egg and bacon. At first I thought it was the after-taste of my breakfast but it didn't take long to realise that the taste of peppery smoked bacon in my mouth was in fact the aftertaste of the beer. I had ordered not just any old beer, but a *Rauchbier*, Bamberg's distinctive brew made from pre-smoked malt.

Rauchbier comes in many strengths and varieties and epito-mises both the German approach to beer as a form of food and the German dedication, almost Romantic, to the maintenance of tradition, unique flavours and old methods of production in beer, as well as the preservation of original, down-to-earth places in which to enjoy it.

One evening I went out for last orders at another of the town's family-brewery pubs, the Schlenkerla. The seating was arranged in booths where the idea was that you simply found a free spot, squeezed in, ordered a beer from the waitress and then got chatting to your neighbour. By the time I'd said '*Prost!*' for the fourth time, after yet another *Rauchbier* had arrived and been marked up on my beer mat like the days in a very agreeable prison, I had been given a whole lesson on beer-brewing and the finer distinctions of local and regional varieties. My tutors were two locals – strangers to each other but you wouldn't have known it – who were real German-beer enthusiasts; beer-tasters if there was such a thing.

Despite thinking I had got a degree in beer-drinking at uni-versity I felt a complete novice. I had never considered that there was so much to beer. These men were talking about it as if it were wine, looking at its colour, its consistency, the fluid it left on the glass when swilled about, sniffing its bouquet and swill-ing it about in their mouths before finally swallowing. This was not beer as food or route to intoxication, but beer as an element of gourmet cuisine. Not quite 'south-facing Bavarian barley with a hint of Franconian lemon and a strong finish' – but almost.

I found myself asking why, with beer, there seemed to be so little in the way of critical writing, or even widespread critical appreciation, in the same way as there is for wine and whisky. Beer will probably never bridge the social or religious divide. It is the drink of the north, the working class, the farmer and the Protestant versus the southern chalice of the chateau. No matter how distinct they may be to the connoisseur, beers will always be 'as different as hens in a farmyard'. And meanwhile the vine, with its perceived art and culture, was what seduced the tourist.

And so what of German wine? Well, typically, Mark Twain had a view: 'The Germans are exceedingly fond of Rhine wines; they are put in small, slender bottles, and are considered pleasant beverage. One tells them from vinegar by the label.' My own earliest memories of wine was the hock they served at Sunday lunches at school. It was the cheapest thing available and just right for using up on ignorant sixth-formers. It was particularly disgusting. And German.

Two wines, Blue Nun and Liebfraumilch, had always stood for everything that was bad about Germany, the wine equivalent of German humour and *Lederhosen*. But was that really the case? If *Sideways* was anything to go by, Riesling, that most German of grapes, was undergoing a bit of a renaissance. Was that true of German wine itself?

According to Manny, yes. But I had not got off to a good start. On that celebratory first evening in Lübeck with my wife I had enthusiastically ordered the local red wine, *Rotspon*, even though to me the concept of German red wine was about as foreign as Portuguese cricket. But I'd been trying to immerse myself. 'Spawn' just about summed it up and one glass left me with an awful headache the next day. No wonder! *Rotspon* was not produced in the Lübeck region. There were in fact no vines in the Holstein area and Pils was by far the favourite local tipple. *Rotspon* was an old claret shipped in from Bordeaux decades ago, decanted into local barrels and allowed to age further. Lübeckers do not hide its origins and clearly think the wine is improved by this process. As far as I was concerned, it was an example of Mark Twain's vinegar and best used on my salad. But luckily Lübeck's vintners no longer ship in claret, so it is set to disappear.

The image of rolling hills raked with neat rows of undulating vines, baked in golden sun and leading up to a grandiose chateau was something I associated with France, Italy and Spain. And yet I discovered this received image could equally be German. Directed by Manny's itinerary, I followed the *Deutsche Weinstrasse*, German wine route, west from Frankfurt to Wiesbaden and Mainz and then west and north up the Rhine valley, through the picturesque groomed towns of Rudesheim, Bockenheim and Deidesheim to Geisenheim, which is the Beaune of the German wine-making world. It was not the endless lush winescape interspersed with lavender fields, olive groves and cypresses of Mediterranean countries. It was an altogether more rugged and dramatic landscape but an equally titillating and saliva-tickling one. German vineyards were steep, small and probably hard and expensive to harvest: an intricate affair rather like a German Christmas toy. And in its backyard German wine-making still felt local, unsnobbish and uncommercialised, and each *Weingut* (chateau) generally had a *Probierenstube* and was only too happy to let me in for a taste. Maybe they always kept the good stuff for themselves. After I got back to London, Manny, giving further proof of unspoken political connections, got me invited to a wine-tasting of Rhine wines at the German Embassy. And no ordinary wine-tasting; we were to be honoured by the presence of the German Wine Queen. Who was she?

After the Ambassador had bade us 'wery velcome' we sat down to some Rhineland specialities. But, before we were allowed to eat, a pretty girl with long, dark hair stood up, glass in hand, as if to give a toast. She wore a sparkling tiara on her head and a nineteenth-century-style corseted purple frilly dress. She introduced herself as Katja Schweder and explained who she was.

Every year young women from all thirteen (yes, there are thirteen!) wine-growing regions of Germany – each the Queen of their own region – compete in a Miss World-style wine-tasting pageant for the title of Wine Queen of Germany. A jury of seventy-three wine professionals, from producers and merchants to restaurateurs and journalists, quiz the candidates, in German and English, on all matters relating to German wine production and consumption and also tourism. The winner becomes a global ambassador for German wine, attending some three hundred functions worldwide in the service of German viticulture's rehabilitation, with two German Wine Princesses at her side. She is supposed to be not only knowledgeable but also charming. And whether it was *Grauburgunder*, Germany's Pinot Grigio, or *Spätburgunder*, Germany's Pinot Noir, this sparkling twenty-six-year-old was quite alcoholic in her charm and I didn't need to drink a sip to lap up every word she said. She could have even made Liebfraumilch taste like wine.

Yet I couldn't help mocking the pageantry that underlay it all, and which was about to get a whole lot worse. It was a Rhineland wine-tasting and Katja was from that region, so the German Tourist Board didn't want to lose an opportunity to remind everyone that the Rhineland was the home of Romanticism. To think I'd done all that hard work in Heidelberg, only to have to see two Germans dressed up in full nineteenth-century garb as the writer Mary Shelley and the painter Turner act out a fictitious meeting of two English cultural icons in thrall to Germany, and in stilted, totally unenthralling Victorian English with a German accent! *Frankenstein* meets *The Guns of Navarone*.

The trinity of wine royalty was straight out of a German carnival. And the whole thing was further proof of the German love of costume and pageantry, but also of childish play-acting and kitsch.

'There is nothing better than a good German Riesling,' said Manny, pouring me a midday glass back at Infinity, 'perfect for a pre-lunch tipple or to go with an afternoon plate of raspberries and cream.'

'Did you know that at the end of the nineteenth century German wine was the most expensive and coveted in the world?' he continued.

I found that hard to believe. It was all so saccharine, like a kitsch castle, and obvious and unsubtle as a *Puff*. Then there was the illegible Gothic script and a complicated grading system that was Romantic, to say the least. And the names themselves. I looked at the bottle Manny had opened and rested my case. It read, 'Schlossböckelheimer Küpfergrube Spütlese, Dönnhoff'. Far from a delicate wine, it sounded like a rank in the German army.

'Did you know there would be no Australian wine industry without the Germans who emigrated to the Barossa valley in South Australia? And that many chateaux in South Africa and North America were founded by German immigrants?'

But the most astounding revelation was that some of the great champagne chateaux, producers of high-society bubbles, were originally German, from when that part of the world lay within Germany's borders: Heidsieck, Bollinger, Moët, Krug.

'To say nothing of Riedel glasses, generally acknowledged by wine experts and Michelin-starred restaurants as the best glasses to taste wine from.'

As always, Germany had the technology and delivery side sewn up. It could also claim the heritage. But not the modern-day and couldn't sell itself off the back of that success.

'The Wine Society's 2005 guide speaks of "one of the best vintages of Riesling in modern times, ranking alongside 1975, 1976 and 1990".'

Were they World Cup years?

'German wine is something that needs to be discovered but once discovered is intensely satisfying and rewarding. Like Germany itself – a wine, a destination, for connoisseurs, not tourists.'

This was an attempt to clear Liebfraumilch's name and a viticultural metaphor for my *Wanderlust*. Previously the ugly duckling of European cuisine, Germany was now apparently a nation on the brink of discovery. Low-hanging fruit, definitely not sour grapes but plenty of sauerkraut, and Manny was convinced that Germany could be the envy of my fellow dinner-party guests. But, however beautiful the Germans thought they were, I still needed convincing that a sausage could be grounds for food envy; or, as the Germans, well used to it, would say, *Futterneid*.

10

Schadenfreude

nm, *joy at someone else's misfortune*

(lit. misfortune joy)

'What is the head of the Beijing Traffic Police called?' asked Manny, a glint in his eye.

I looked blank.

'*Um-lei-tung*!'

Silence.

'*Um-lei-tung*,' he repeated. 'It's the German word for "traffic diversion". Geddit?'

So this was the fabled German sense of humour! But surely to the Germans irony was a branch of metallurgy or something you did with your shirts. And as for sarcasm? Well, try it on the Germans and the effect was surely more likely to be 'sarchasm': the vast gulf of understanding between we hilarious English humour-mongers and a collection of helpless and baffled Krauts.

'The perceived wit and spirit of a people is an essential value sought by tourists,' wrote Manny. 'You make judgements about the likeability of nations based on ideas you have about their people.'

Well, if so, in the international league of humourlessness

weren't Germans serial champions? And a particularly Germanic type of American, like Manny, came a close second.

'But probably you know little of the German spirit.'

Surely the only purpose of humour the Germans served was as whipping boys for their past and also for their incomprehension of our proudly elusive humour. There could be few more enjoyable sights than that of a double entendre sailing unnoticed over a German *Dummkopf*. I recalled the Nuremberger talking earnestly about his little sausage.

'Ah yes, the enjoyment of someone else's misfortune. Such a fundamental part of British humour. So you will surely find it ironic that it is the Germans who have a neat word-concept for this. They call it *Schadenfreude*.'

I had never really known what this word meant but had always taken great pleasure in others misusing it.

But just because they knew a lot about the suffering of others, that surely didn't mean the Germans had a sense of humour.

'Well, did you know that the actor who played Manuel in *Fawlty Towers* was a German by birth?'

So there was a spy in our midst!

Manny went on to say that the Germans had tried to make a German version of the show. But it was a flop. And they had also imported *'Allo 'Allo*, in some bizarre masochistic mix of comic *Selbstwahrnehmung*.

Before the Second World War the British authorities had actually outlawed anti-German jokes. Britain was friends with Germany and it was considered bad manners to makes jokes at another nation's expense, and especially against Adolf Hitler as he was a Head of State. But during the war humour became an important weapon in both sides' armoury. We had Noël Coward and Charlie Chaplin and they had Joseph Goebbels. It wasn't really a fair contest. Goebbels was the nearest thing Nazi Germany had to a head of tourism and he set up a jazz orchestra led by a man called Karl 'Charlie' Schwedler, a misfit plumber and some-time crooner, that did spoof versions of US songs such as 'Stormy Weather': 'Don't know why, I can't look into the sky, stormy weather/Since the Germans got their planes and ships together'; and 'Making Whoopee', aimed at fleeing German Jews: 'Another war, another profit, another business trick [. . .] we're in the money thanks to Frankie [. . .] we throw our German names away.'

Well, the Wettins had changed their name to Windsor, too. And now Manny sang these songs to me almost boastfully. Given his bizarre enthusiasm for Germany verging on patriotism, I could have been forgiven for thinking Heimway was an anglicised German name!

As for after the war, Manny assured me that the German tabloids had given as good as they'd got whenever it was England versus Germany. Apparently they referred to the British as *Inselaffen* (island apes) and tried to hurt us with such jabs as 'Why can't you pull a decent pint of beer?' Not exactly mortifying but now I knew a bit more of what they meant. And 'Why do you wear trunks in the sauna?' No comment.

'But don't take my word for it!' Manny said, just like the MC in *Cabaret*. 'See for yourself!'

Clearly you had to be there. In Germany. I needed to meet some new Germans to see if the Fatherland had made any comic *Vorsprung* beyond jokes that were as obvious as an FKK bather. I recalled a 1990s Audi advert where a German stand-up performed his wittiest '*Waiter, es gibt eine Fliege in meiner Suppe*' to a silent and near-empty theatre. This was going to be a short module!

But wait a minute. Wasn't Boris Becker the new host of the comedy quiz show *They Think It's All Over*? Or maybe he was just there to guarantee a supply of jokes about marching in *Lederhosen* and two minutes of FKK in the broom cupboard of a Japanese restaurant.

Manny suggested I tap into the German community in London. Did such a thing exist? If so, where were they hiding?

Curiously, having mentioned my assignment to friends, many of them, after all these years, had revealed they had what they called 'my German friend' as if German acquaintances were an embarrassment best kept secret. Though that hardly constituted a community. But now Manny told me about a monthly gathering he sometimes attended in Soho called the Towel Club. Good name. And possibly the spark of a German sense of humour. But just in case it wasn't I thought I'd better get there early.

It was a very pleasant evening, almost *gemütlich* if not fun. And proof that any humorous Germans had to have been anglicised. I walked away with a list as long as my arm of German comedians, comedy shows and films that apparently had members of the Towel Club in stitches. But I wasn't about to sit through hours and hours of German comedy on DVD. What were the highlights?

Well, one show was apparently a national institution in Germany. It had been broadcast every year on New Year's Eve since 1963 and could be found in *The Guinness Book of Records* under 'world's most broadcast television programme'. It had been exported to tens of countries. But not yet to Britain. It was called *Dinner for One* and, ironically, this bastion of German humour was in English with English actors.

'Go to Germany. See for yourself!' Manny urged me.

And so, not wanting to miss out on this cultural milestone, I went with my wife and young son to celebrate Silvester, New Year's Eve, among the Germans, so called not because of endless reruns of *Rocky* on television but after the patron saint, among other things, of fireworks.

Berchtesgaden and its surrounding area, in remotest south-eastern Germany, used to be an independent state and was a favourite retreat for Germans for both summer and winter sporting holidays. It lies in the foothills of the dividing wall of the German Alps, as far as you can get in Germany without being in Austria.

Dominated by the sheer face of the Watzmann mountain and its surrounding peaks, this was without doubt one of the most beautiful corners of Europe I had ever visited. Legend has it that the Watzmann was a tyrannical king who was punished by God who turned the king, along with his family of seven children, into the surrounding peaks of stone. The crystalline, blue-green Königssee, or King's Lake, that stretched like a fjord at their feet, was named after him. It is the highest and purest lake in Germany and at its mid-point stood the isolated postcard water-front church of Sankt Bartholomei and the former hunting lodge it was attached to.

We were there on a calm, snowy day. The church had light-yellow walls and a baroque red onion dome, and, with the lake's surface lightly freezing over to catch slow-falling sacramental snowflakes, it felt like we had been transported to Russia and my wife was Lara from *Dr Zhivago*. Or to Narnia. There was even a herd of docile Bambi-like deer to watch us as we pulled our bundled-up one-year-old around the surrounding woods on a traditional 'Rosebud' wooden sleigh.

Already there was an all-German fairytale atmosphere as we set out on the boat, the only means of reaching the church. I dreaded the prospect of a kitsch boat trip in some juggernaut with a guide stating the obvious. But we were in Germany and no such thing was allowed to pollute the waters of the Königssee. A limited number of private boats were allowed on the lake, moored in stylish wooden boathouses, and they all had to be electric. The sleek, polished wooden launch that purred us imperceptibly up the long, thin lake was straight out of Henley Royal Regatta.

Nor was the boatman a paid-by-the-hour tourist guide. A local of about forty, he was dressed in the simple blue overalls of a mechanic. He was also a fine trumpeter. On a clear day a note sounded at a certain point on the lake could apparently be heard to echo up to seven times off the many-angled mountain walls.

The boatman stopped the engine and we drifted into the right spot. He pulled out a trumpet case from under one of the benches and produced from it a worn old cornet. Then, clearing his own tubes, he stood up in the middle of the boat and sounded a beautiful clear and mellow note that Buddy Bolden of New Orleans would have been proud of. In the snow-filled silence we could hear a muffled echo rebound back and forth across the lake. He then lapsed into the melodic line of a lilting waltz – the music form that originated in this corner of the world – with a cheeky chromatic, almost bluesy twiddle at the end. Each note could be heard clearly and individually, with a staggered delay, before lingering above the water with the others to create the trace of a chord. The fjord filled with this music like the marble hallway of a fairytale palace where a brass band was playing in a distant ballroom. The hills were indeed alive with the sound of music.

On our return to the bustle of the shore we found preparations underway for a municipal family fireworks display. A bandstand was being set up and stalls with *Stehbars* (standing bars) selling the usual array of sausages but also fish from the lake, beer and *Glühwein*, and emitting that delicious German festive smell of cinnamon and ginger. Again, as on the Baltic, in the Christmas markets and at the Oktoberfest, I witnessed how the Germans celebrate so well for all the family.

We returned to our family-run *Gasthof* and, having put our son to bed, settled down for our own New Year's Eve 'Dinner for Two'. We then watched the show with our hosts and fellow guests, who were all German.

Dinner for One was a black-and-white short film about a New Year's Eve dinner party in a Victorian manor. The lady of the house, Miss Sophie, has, as in previous years, invited her four friends, Sir Toby, Admiral von Schneider, Lord Pomeroy and Mr Winterbottom. Except Miss Sophie's guests are not there, never have been and in fact are most likely deceased. The butler is already a little tipsy by the time Miss Sophie arrives and with every course he serves gets still drunker, having to toast her on behalf of each of the imaginary guests. At the start of every course the butler turns to Miss Sophie and asks in his posh, slurred voice, 'Same procedure as last year, Miss Sophie?' to which she replies haughtily, in the tones of the Queen, 'Same procedure as every year, James!' And so it is first sherry with the soup, wine with fish, champagne with the chicken and then port with the cheese. The butler's toasts – each guest has their own refrain – become more and more slurred and exaggerated, and his pouring of the drinks and circuit around the table ever more hazardous. All but once he manages to avoid tripping on the head of a tiger that one of Miss Sophie's ancestors obviously shot and had turned into a carpet. And each time she appears to be taken aback. At the end of the meal she announces, 'I think I shall retire now.' The butler sees her out of her chair and asks her one final time, 'Same procedure as last year, Miss Sophie?' to which she replies, 'Same procedure as every year, James!' The camera then closes in on a winking James, Miss Sophie on his arm as they exit, who says, 'I shall do my best, Miss Sophie!' And then, to camera, 'Good night!'

And with these lines the Germans next to me and all around the country chuckled with *Gemütlichkeit* and a sense of the comfort of routine. Only now had an old year finished and a new one could begin.

Dinner for One was a comedy of manners that parodied the eccentricity and Victorian etiquette of a bygone English aristocracy that still believed in its own existence and lived in its own delusional world. Was that what the Germans with *Schadenfreude* thought about the English? Or was there also nostalgia, affection and some patriotic envy mixed in?

The whole film was shot in Hamburg, took place on a single interior set and was filmed with minimal camerawork. It was theatrical and its humour basically farcical and visual but I had to admit I rather liked it. For its simplicity and understatement, as well as its content. And it was full of tiny quotable details of the kind that could understandably lead to a cult.

And so it was, having tobogganed down the snowy slopes of Berchtesgaden in the afternoon, that we slid into a German New Year. '*Guten Rutsch*' was what Germans said to wish one another a Happy New Year. Often thought to derive from '*rutschen*', meaning 'to slide', as if the New Year were some physical, not just temporal, border crossing, the phrase apparently came from a Yiddish word, '*Rosh*' for 'head' or 'beginning'. I had not previously considered the German-Yiddish link, surely a good example of irony.

German seemed generally such a heavy, prickly-sounding language and its love of concepts made it more suited to philosophical probing than light-hearted banter and sleight of mind. To my knowledge Schopenhauer and Nietzsche were not known for their spontaneity or sense of humour.

And yet it was precisely this stereotype of the over-analytical German treating humour like an Audi car engine that one German comedian, I discovered, had turned to his advantage. Enter the words 'German', 'stand-up', and 'comedian' into Google and you might expect the message 'No search results have been found' or 'Did you (really) mean German stand-up comedian?' I was presented with more results than I expected for this rare species I had summoned. Among these was a German stand-up who lived in London, performed in English and had won the Hackney Empire New Act for the best new comedian of 2005. There was definitely a fly in the soup, if not in the ointment! I had to investigate. What was more, I might not have to go to Germany to find a stand-up comedian after all.

His name was Henning Wehn (pronounced 'vain') and he billed himself as 'The German Comedy Ambassador'. The first time I saw him he was one of ten acts performing that evening as the penultimate round of a BBC New Talent knock-out contest in the Ginglik club, a transformed former public toilet. Henning came on last, dressed in a spoddy C&A-style cardigan and a stopwatch around his neck. His act was a meticulous, over-analytical German who timed each joke on his stopwatch and then after telling it, no matter how unfunny, proceeded to explain and analyse it to the audience, whether they had got it or not (Germans after all put the 'anal' in 'analysis'). The comedy was in the manner of the explanations: full of pedantic vocabulary and details, and long, tortuous sentences full of suspended subordinate clauses. It almost qualified as understatement.

There were also some bold *Selbstwahrnehmung* gags. 'Why did my grandfather cross the road? Answer: To invade France'; and 'The big news was England qualifying comfortably for the World Cup ahead of Poland and Austria. Our two main provinces really aren't the forces they were in the past.' Was this German *Schadenfreude*? Wehn was clearly of the Manny school of thought that it was time for the British to move on and he did in fact get a lot of laughs that indicated perhaps attitudes were changing. Throughout the World Cup he went on to tour Britain with a one-hour act of German humour called 'Three World Cups and One World Pope', which contained more risqué war gags such as one about the logical German who, uncomfortable with the asymmetry of the number of world wars Germany had caused as against the number of Reichs that had caused them, proposed that now Germany was a Republic it should start a third war to achieve symmetry.

I approached Wehn afterwards to ask him about being German and the business of humour. He came from around Dortmund in the Ruhrgebiet, or 'dour-gebiet', Germany's grey mid-west industrial heartland, the equivalent of the UK's West Midlands. After arriving in England in 2002 he had worked in a company that sold corporate hospitality and had really enjoyed the office jokes at his expense: 'Shall we go to the Polish restaurant? Oh no, better not. We'll never get Henning to leave.' Wehn liked these and other stereotypes and didn't see why people should be forced to give them up. Far better to be a country with lots of stereotypes than none. He sounded like Manny.

As for his own burgeoning career as a comedian, Wehn told me that after a number of years working in London he'd gone one evening to a gig in Greenwich and (with typical German *Grossmannsucht*) thought, I can do better than that! With Teutonic doggedness he had analysed magazines like *Viz* and studied them for hours on the loo (I had visions of cries of 'Eureka!' as the philosopher 'got' each joke). *Viz* as a TEFL aid? Why not?

Sadly Wehn didn't make the final of the BBC New Talent contest. This was not because he had lost on the comic equivalent of penalties (surely England would win every time if there was such a thing) but because apparently in one of his gags – something about how women should stay at home and do the washing up instead of trying to understand football – he had been sexist and the BBC had disqualified him. Honestly, what would improv night at the Comedy Store turn into if you couldn't get away with things like that?

Henning Wehn excepted, the Ruhr valley was not conspicuous for its humour. But then Germans have conflicting views on where the centre of their country's comic universe resides. Some say Cologne, some Hamburg and some Berlin. The very fact that there had to be one place said it all. In the UK we recognised the differing humour of Geordies, Scousers, cockneys, the Cornish and, latterly, of the Hindu and Asian communities. They all slagged each other off and they all slagged off Brummies. Maybe Germany's post-war exaggerated sense of tolerance didn't allow jokes at others' expense. But in Britain these sparring enclaves were part of a delicious, multi-faceted whole, not one that excluded others.

In Hamburg and Munich Manny encouraged me to try various examples of *Kabarett-Theater* but these were routines involving music, dance, magic and the odd comic quip that represented old German comedy; to be watched, soaked up and applauded and yes laughed at but not viciously. It was the very opposite of *Schadenfreude*. In fact it was feel-good comedy. In other words *Gemütlichkeit*.

What I saw in Hamburg and Munich was a modern take on the cabaret of the Bob Fosse film of that name. In 1930s Berlin stand-up hadn't yet been invented and cabaret was the perfect, if sinister, way of sending up the prevailing political climate. Berlin then was also unique with its climate of licentiousness that permitted such unheard-of political lampooning and frank public representations of polygamy, lesbianism and cross-dressing. But it didn't really suit the fast-moving, twenty-four-hour information world of nowadays, where a bit of flesh and more openly blue material were the order of the day. German modern *Kabarett* belonged with the circus and was further proof of the German love of dressing up. Life might be a cabaret in much of Germany, but in terms of a developed sense of humour that was precisely the problem. The clown was the comic equivalent of the German garden gnome. And if Hamburg was the most British of German cities, that didn't extend to its sense of humour.

Manny had already sent me to Cologne in search of its party spirit. Now he touted it as a centre of German excellence when it came to a love of satire and laid-back approach to life. All things being relative. Cologne's most famous asset, aside from its citrus perfume, is its *Dom*, or cathedral, whose neo-Gothic spires dominate the city's skyline. Apparently Kölners quip that they have never seen the whole of their cathedral as it is so big there's always one part under scaffolding being restored. This was a good sign that they didn't take themselves or their city too seriously. And they could ill afford to. Modern Cologne was not a pretty place, having been flattened in the war and hastily rebuilt as a featureless amalgam of grey, medium-rise blocks surrounded by a one-way motorway system and the trundle of efficient trams. Maybe a city's humour was in inverse proportion to its superficial beauty and Kölners had a wit that did not need architectural splendour and was all the stronger for its absence.

According to Manny, there was a man, beloved of all Kölners, who could be held up as symbol of the German capacity for wit and satire. He is, along with Konrad Adenauer, Cologne's most famous son: the Nobel Prize-winning twentieth-century novelist and humorist Heinrich Böll. And as good as unobtainable in the English language.

In the 1950s Böll relished sending up the work ethic of the *Wirtschaftswunder* that rebuilt post-war Germany. He adopted the voice of misfits and marginalised loners engaged in pointless and invisible jobs despite their obvious superior intelligence: the station platform announcer at a one-horse town with a small tourist attraction; the time-and-motion surveyor who doesn't want to make a statistic of his lover; a prescient 'green' parable of a man whose job it is simply to throw away all the superfluous packaging in department stores; and the intellectual who wins a job in a factory where staff have been hired on the basis they can answer ten phones at a time, type simultaneously with both fingers and toes while suitably employing any other limb or moving part. What the factory makes is never mentioned.

Böll's observations seemed valid for a twenty-first century of 'human resources' departments and patronising, American-style euphemisms for menial jobs.

Böll also enjoyed the humour in Germany's collective desire to conquer their past, caught between obsession, illusion and a desire to wipe the slate clean: the story of a radio technician forced to listen to a former Nazi sympathiser wanting to re-record certain things he might have said that could be misinterpreted. So much rubbish does the narrator-technician have to listen to all day, he takes the silent bits that end up on the cutting-room floor home with him at night and listens to them to in order to shut himself off from the world of hot air. Böll's Christmas story 'Nicht nur zur Weihnachtszeit' ('Not only at Christmastime') tells of a family that has to keep up the pretence that it is Christmas every day lest the ageing grandmother go mad. They think the charade is going to last just a few days but it goes on for weeks, months and years. Every evening, summer or winter, they have to sit down to the same meal, sing the same carols and go through the same routine, even stealing out-of-season Christmas trees in summer, just to satisfy the old woman. In the end they replace the children with gnomes and get actors to stand in for the adults.

'You see, while there is common ground and international humour, every nation has its own particular circumstances that create a universe of humour all of its own,' Manny affirmed. 'You cannot hope to understand German humour unless you understand Germany. This is essential to your *Wanderlust*.'

We had war jokes about Germans but in true masochistic style they also had war jokes about themselves. What would that be in German? *Selbstschadenfreude*? Enjoyment at your own suffering!

Illusion was a common theme. *Goodbye Lenin*, one of few German film hits in Britain in recent years, seemed to be a modern take on Böll's Christmas story. It was a comedy about a family of East Berliners who have to maintain the illusion that the German Democratic Republic is still up and running even after the Wall has come down in case the mother, an ardent comrade, who went into a coma the night the Wall fell, wakes up and dies from the shock of learning her beloved GDR no longer exists. The film *Cabaret*, although not German-produced, showed how the cabaret venue was used as a place where Berliners could go 'to leave zer trubbles outzide' and watch caricatured camp National Socialists while the real ones were

setting fire to the city and beating up Jews and gays outside. And
Dinner for One itself: wasn't this also a tale of hiding from reality or being obsessed by the past? And as the Germans were
serial viewers of it, wasn't their very love of it further evidence of
a love of illusion and its sinister overtones?

I had seen it in the *Gemütlichkeit* that replaced reality at the
Oktoberfest, in the systemic idealism that was the essence of
the German Romantic mind and in how the whole of the
German nation had been built on an ideal of the past. It was in
the clownishness of German *Kabarett*, which was the opposite
of reality, in the gnomes and kitsch of Neuschwanstein, in the
fairytales of Baron Munchausen and the idea of Schlaraffenland,
and in the prevalence children's fantasy in German life. And
now I saw it in German popular culture, in its television and literature. It was hard not to think there was a national character
trait in here: something not only simple, childish and idealist but
prone to being duped. It didn't require great wit to amuse a
German, so how could Germans be prone to producing wit?

So was it just Rhinelanders with their Roman legacy that gener-
ated and appreciated German satire while the rest of Germany
drank beer and guffawed at banana-skin jokes? Wine was good
for lifting the German spirit while beer dulled it and was only
good for putting monks to sleep? So what about the vaunted
Latin spirit of the Bavarians and their love of beer? Well, Bavaria
was Catholic. From the moment the first Münchner had greeted
me with the words '*Gruss Gott*' instead of '*Guten Tag*' I had
been in a Catholic region of the country. And although
Cologne's Gothic landmark was finished by the Prussians from
Berlin as a sign of the supremacy of Protestantism in a united
Germany, the city is a predominantly Catholic city of the Holy
Roman Empire. German humour was a religious and culinary
thing and the Rhine not only a religious and culinary border but
the Rubicon of Europe's sense of humour. On one side there

was sun, wine, olive oil, artfulness, corruption and humour; on the other brooding weather, beer, butter, earnestness, efficiency and banana skins. Protestants from the land where the break-away religion was born, and places north, took life too seriously. Humour was too fluffy and intangible, and the product of unplanned flights of spirit and fancy neither forthcoming nor well received. How many comedies came out of Scandinavia? And the kind of Americans that look blank when you cracked a remotely subtle joke were of the George W. Bush Protestant 'Bible-belt' variety. It was the importance of being naked again.

The Jews also had a part to play, no doubt, with the Yiddish tradition of subverting language and an aggressive mocking of both themselves and others. Yiddish and German had strong links but the German-Jewish sense of humour had apparently also emigrated, changed its name and propped up decades of American showbiz humour.

Comic self-awareness about its past, I now learnt, was just one example of a humour that was unique to Germany and its history.

Berlin was a Prussian city that was synonymous in my mind with humourless militarism and the discipline of Protestantism and personal responsibility born in nearby Wittenberg. And yet I would discover that Berlin's inhabitants pride themselves on a great sense of humour. How could this be?

As I'd learnt from its progressive attitude to nudism, Prussia before Kaiser Wilhelm I, 'the Soldier-King', was a Prussia of the arts that looked to France; the Prussia of the beautiful Sans Souci (No Worries) landscaped French gardens at Potsdam; and the Prussia that provided a haven, not a ghetto, for the religious refugees of Europe, including thousands of Huguenots and Jews. Quite the opposite of the same city in the 1930s and 1940s. And therein lay the answer; perhaps an answer to the secret of any nation's humour: immigration.

Berlin was again on the front line of immigration when the Wall came down in November 1989, letting in millions of East Germans, who, after three decades of division and five of living under different ideologies, were basically 'foreigners'. Initially there was euphoria at the prospect of reuniting both families and this divided country. But the economic strain of this reunification, combined with a slowing down of the German economy, led to resentment, estrangement and a form of strange, internal racism. One of the biggest beneficiaries of this outlook was Germany's sense of humour. At last they had understood: for humour you needed to have an enemy!

Henning Wehn had slagged off the 'ungrateful and lazy East Germans' who had voted for the Communists in the recent German general elections. And in fact the reunification of Germany had sparked a sub-genre of *Ossi–Wessi* humour between the *Jammer Ossis* (whingeing easterners) and the *Besser Wessis*, a play on '*besser*' ('better') and '*wissen*' ('to know'): 'know-it-all westerners'. There were jibes at *Ossis* unable to control BMWs because they weren't used to driving cars that went over 40 mph, and *Wessis* who crashed their Beamers on pot-holed *Ossi* roads. The Trabant was substituted for the Skoda or Lada in the cheap-car jokes circulating during the early 1990s. And the Trabant itself assumed iconic, retro-trendy status. In Berlin you could buy, apart from endless bits of Wall, model Trabants, blocks of monopoly Ostmarks, as worthless now as they were on 10 November 1989 and little blue notebooks mocking the rules and regulations of the former East Germany.

Created mostly by West Berliners, this phenomenon of looking back to the supposed golden days of the DDR became known as '*Ostalgie*': a cross between *Ost* (East) and *Nostalgie* (nostalgia). It described an ironic state of *Sehnsucht* (longing) for a lost yet newly beloved country and all its trappings. This longing was not limited to Trabants, but extended to anything, including Communist comestibles, that used to be available in East Germany but had now been lost, or nearly lost, with the arrival of McDonald's. *Goodbye Lenin* made hay with *Ostalgie* and had the family running around looking for *Rotkäppchen* (Little Red Riding Hood) champagne and jars of gherkins from the Spreewald forest just outside Berlin. In the 1990s Berliners held *Ostalgie* parties (no entry without a visa, I presume) and at one time there were even plans for an *Ostalgie* theme park near Berlin where all the strictures and Cold War atmosphere of life in the DDR would be recreated. The *über*-trendy Cologne-based publisher Taschen published books celebrating DDR design. And someone even tried to patent DDR as a brand.

Now, you couldn't do all that unless you had a sense of humour. In fact where else would you find this? I didn't see the French rushing to set up Vichyland outside Lyon.

Ostalgie was by now a hollow business for tourists and of little other than economic interest to Berliners who had moved on. But in its heyday it served a secondary cultural purpose of repudiating the idea that everything in the West was better. Bizarrely, the most heated debate centred on traffic lights.

In West Germany the *Ampelmann* ('green or red man') that told you when it was safe to cross the road was a no-frills stationary and anodyne icon. In East Germany he wore a coat and hat like an electronic *Wanderer* and 'walked' with the thoughtful gait of a *Fahrradmann*. When the Wall came down they started changing all the traffic lights to the West Berlin model. But after a debate that reached the Bundestag and made national headlines it was agreed that East Berliners and East German cities could retain their own beloved *Ampelmann*, and in some cases have them put back. That he could become a hero of national debate seemed to affirm the national disposition to fantasy. The imaginary *Ampelmann* was like a *Gartenzwerg* (garden gnome). Reminded of the disappearance of red phone boxes and hop-on hop-off double-decker buses from my own city, I wished that at times the British were more of a nation of gnome-lovers.

After the fall of the Wall Berliners had made a virtue of Berlin's schizophrenia and anomalous status as a former island-city, divided by the most significant fault line of Europe's twentieth century into two cities, whose rubbing together was a rich source of humour and creativity. It was certainly light years from the cabaret tradition which had, via Bob Fosse's film, been the prism through which I had always seen the city. Berlin had left that behind, in Hamburg, Munich and elsewhere in Germany.

So for humour immigration was important. But *Ossis* were not the only foreigners in Berlin. However international in outlook, Germany had always seemed a monocultural country to me. Germans after all liked purity in their beer, sausage and personal hygiene and had form for wanting purity also in their blood. But now I learnt that there had been a Turkish population in Germany ever since Turks were invited as *Gastarbeiter* (guest-workers) to help rebuild the country after the war. And that the largest Turkish community in Germany was in Berlin.

Now I encountered the language of *Kanaksprach* ('Turk-speak', from the German slang for a Turk, '*Kanak*'). This subterranean language was the nearest German thing to the 'bling' language of Britain's Asian and West Indian rappers and R&B musicians. There were compendiums of *Kanak* culture published by mainstream publishers. The Turkish-German MP Cem Ozdemir, Germany's first, wrote a satirical account of his experiences as both a Turkish immigrant and a member of Germany's parliament entitled *Ich bin Inländer*, meaning 'I am an Insider' (and a pun on Kennedy's '*Ich bin ein Berliner*'). There was a comedy sketch show by a Turkish-German double act called Erkan und Stefan and a sitcom entitled *Türkisch für Anfänger* ('Turkish for Beginners') that was a bit like *The Kumars at No. 42*. The German media had begun to adopt the country's immigrant population and make them part of the pop culture. In Berlin at least, '*multikulti*' was now a hip word and after three or four generations of Turkish presence this most unlikely of rainbow nations' sense of humour had benefited from outside blood.

So Berlin had a special place in Germany's pantheon of comedy. And to such an extent that, when the row broke out in 2006 over supposedly anti-Muslim cartoons published in Denmark and Teheran briefly eclipsed even the *Sun* in its anti-German xenophobia (Iran's Foreign Minister recommended Israel be transplanted to Schleswig-Holstein because its creation was Germany's fault and suggested that Merkel was just another Führer), the *Berliner Tageszeitung* responded by printing a daring cartoon of its own. With Germany set to meet Iran in the early stages of the World Cup the paper ran a cartoon picturing the German squad as soldiers (Berlin had just announced that soldiers would be available to help sort out any hooliganism) lined up against the Iranians dressed, beards and all, as suicide bombers.

German TV comedy shows had apparently even won International Emmys – and in the category they had actually been entered for. One, *Berlin Berlin*, had even been sold to twelve other countries. But, notably, not to Britain or any English-speaking nation. I looked at the daunting and consequently untouched stack of DVDs of German comedy shows Manny had given me. From what I understood from the cover notes I couldn't see any of them, not even *Traumschiff Surprise,* a gay spoof on *Star Trek,* taking over the British TV schedules or high-street stores. Not just because they might not have been funny, but because you had to speak German to understand them and, given the number of people nowadays sitting GCSE German, they might as well have been in Latin.

'You British have a basic import-export problem when it

comes to any piece of culture that does not grow from within,' Manny insisted. And this from an American, albeit one with German sympathies!

'It comes from the false pride of having had a disproportionately large empire. You have developed a snobbishness about the worthwhileness of other cultures and it's a wonder you bother to travel at all.'

Well, had not Cecil Rhodes declared that every man born an Englishman had won first prize in the lottery of life?

'*Wanderlust* and the Romance of true travel will always be beyond people with this attitude.'

It was time to stop being condescending, an attitude that for some reason was ingrained in me. It didn't help that satire had proven a perfect tool for dressing down German *Grossmannsucht*. But perhaps the import restrictions on Germany were a bit fierce. Who had ever raved about the Polish or Portuguese sense of humour? And with our obsession with our New Labour political correctness – the antithesis of Cecil Rhodes – could we any more be sure of our comic pre-eminence?

'Thankfully humour is not owned by any one nation. Nor is there a standard of humour the world over, like Starbucks or McDonald's. Give German humour a chance,' urged Manny.

Well, I had discovered and respected Germany's unique Turkish and *Ossi–Wessi* strands of humour. I had seen humour in German advertising: an optician's on the Fairytale Route used the tag line, 'All the better for seeing you.' On the subway on my way back from the Müllersches Volksbad I'd seen a young man from a group of Münchners go up to some drunken Italians and pretend to be a ticket inspector. The Italians didn't have tickets and were terrified until they realised the locals were having them on. I had been assured of a German love of word-play: a new law had been introduced in Baden-Württemberg, bordering on the Rhineland, which stipulated that all immigrants would have to pass a citizenship test and a man had joked to me in a pub that he hoped it was a case of '*Ausländer 'rein, Rheinländer 'raus!*' ('Foreigners in, Rhinelanders out!'). OK, so you had to be there.

I had scoured the bookshops and purchased German joke books which confirmed that Germans had the same attitude as the British to blondes, regional differences (the Bavarians were our Irish), politicians and general comic sexual discrimination. And on the same bookshelves I noted that German publishers had translated and published books like the spoof guidebook, *Molvania*. I found the Germans to be big fans of *Monty Python* and they had even made a successful German version of *The Office* called *Stromberg*, after Germany's David Brent equivalent. Could Germany one day make a local version of *Little Britain*? It could be called *Klein Deutschland* (a neat pun on how Bismarck referred to his vision of a united German nation that excluded Austria) and feature nudists, gnomes, saunas, *Puffs*, sausages, bicycles and lots of leather; and maybe Henning Wehn saying, 'I'm the only comedian in the country.'

'With so much material I don't understand why Germany has not been able to discard its comically challenged stereotype?' Manny challenged me.

Well, why fix something that worked. By now Europe's nations had been assigned their attributes and they were fixed, just like national borders. Sorry, guys! Germany would for ever be not only humourless but a primary source of *Schadenfreude* for others. Not for nothing had former Chancellor Helmut Kohl once said he wished he came from 'an easier fatherland' where the past didn't resurface everywhere he looked. Well, thank God for the 'difficult fatherland of Germany'. British humour would be lost without it.

I also remembered my business dealings with Germans where rigid professional etiquette did not permit any deviation, undermining or superficial joking and what humour there was was rather contrived. Contrast this with the British businessman, who was usually the first to start a PowerPoint presentation with a joke, aware of how boring it might be. Whether or not this was again the responsible Protestant work ethic or the Romantic spirit wanting to turn the work environment into a system, there was a clear dividing line between a German's public life and his private life, and between the attitude and things he permitted himself in his job and his life outside work.

In Britain humour might start in the comedy clubs but before long it pervaded pubs, dinner parties and the whole workplace. It was even part of the British parliamentary tradition of heckling and an aggressive 'shoot down or be shot down' *Schadenfreude*. That required a strong sense of identity. But the strength of their own identity, as I'd discovered, was something Germans were both very aware of and afraid of. The British took pleasure in, and at times even lived off, the misfortunes of others. For a post-war German to be seen doing that was too frightening a prospect, and so they had castrated their own humour.

Against that background, according to Manny, German comedy had not been an industry for as long and was simply less developed. Wit came from the German word '*Witz*', meaning 'joke', but for decades, as their own Helmut Kohl said, they'd been 'so afraid to laugh that they would hide in the basement to do it'. Perhaps at last the new generation felt more able to laugh for laughter's sake and no logical reason at all.

But British humour was surely also a symptom of British nervousness, the need to break the ice, not wanting to say what we mean and generally preferring to retain a distance without appearing unfriendly. Such characteristics did not come naturally to a land of direct, FKK sausage-fillers intent on being Mr Big. I wasn't sure it could all be blamed on the war.

The idea of a German comedy industry tickled me. Yes, the Germans would wish humour was something that could be fathomed, forecast and systemised; an object to perfect, like a car. I pictured German would-be stand-ups working on a production line in lab coats putting car jokes through wind-tunnels to ascertain their efficiency.

So I couldn't believe my eyes (and luck) when I read that the television station Sat Eins had been sponsoring university courses in stand-up comedianship. Could you study stand-up? And that a professor in Munich called Heiner Uber had founded a successful (in Germany) chain of Laughing Schools. He was making a bid to be the Schreber/Jahn/Kneipp of German humour. Classes started with exercises to get the old comic *Kreislauf* going and then pupils were told to march round a room chanting 'ho-ha-ha-ha-ha' and staring into one another's eyes. Students were then walked through a variety of laughs, from lion's guffaw to giggle, and asked to flap their arms like chickens, before being asked to lie down on the floor and imagine a funny scene from their childhood. Apparently groups never failed to end up splitting their sides in unison. At the age of five Herr Uber had been told by his father that only stupid people laughed. Now, with Germans paying 260 euros for a two-day session dancing 'The Birdie Song' and his courses over-subscribed all over Germany, he was laughing all the way to the bank.

I rest my case, I told Manny. As long as this was the attitude, in Germany clownish cabaret would continue to prevail over stand-up comedy and impede any *Vorsprung* of German comedy into something more natural, spontaneous and all-pervasive. For centuries Germans had been depressing themselves (and others) with dark philosophy. Now they were trying to turn comedy and laughter into an MBA-style business philosophy. Too much 'sinking' again. Romantic perfection and spontaneous humour were surely chalk and cheese! Comedy was a Trabant, not an Audi, and the Germans didn't so much need computerised fuel injection as a cataclysmic comic conversion.

11

Zeitgeist

nm, *the spirit of the times*

(lit. time spirit)

'You are almost at the end of your course of therapy,' announced Manny.

That was a relief.

'Remember what I said. Travel is the new high street, where every nation is a brand. When you are buying a German car, seeing an Italian opera or holidaying in the south of France you are responding to brand images – just like shopping for your latest pair of Pumas, which are, of course, German. Governments, companies and hoteliers invest millions of pounds lining the pockets of marketing quangos, image consultants and so-called "futurists", who they task with seducing ever more potential consumers.'

Why did Manny suddenly have it in for his vocational brethren?

'Nowhere is this more true than in the realm of popular culture, which determines whether or not a brand registers on your Condé Nast radar. But what do you know of German popular culture, of modern German music, film and art?'

A land of deep-thinking *Fahrradmänner* with their heads in the clouds, Germany had made a huge contribution to European *Hochkultur* (high culture) across classical music, the visual arts, drama, literature and philosophy. But what about low culture? The post-war world was a lo-fi, superficial world of ephemeral news and celebrity and relative values. How did the German mindset cope with this? Could Germany indeed lack shallowness? In brand-speak Germany would surely be 'classic not contemporary' and indeed Manny's statistics showed that a huge 46 per cent of non-business visitors to Germany were middle-aged or older, drawn by Bayreuth's Wagnerian operathon. Quangos examining 'the case of Germany' had identified the country as 'lacking in feminine attributes'. Well, was it surprising if their *Puffs* were an insight into their attitude to women? Also, high culture was strong, resilient and male; Doric and ancient. But the comfortable, modern consumer-entertainment world was probably a more touchy-feely and female world. And consequently Germany had a particular problem attracting the world's young.

No surprise. Apart from Pumas and Birkenstocks, Germany's contribution to global pop culture seemed to me to be pretty minimal. Unless you counted the Turner Prize, surely culture at its lowest, recently won by German Tomma Abst for a bunch of overblown geometric doodles in oils that she herself admitted she started not knowing how they would end up. Germany's sports stars were famous largely for relentless superiority, not flair. Germany's models were low-key, unflamboyant types of no interest to the gossip columns. And, despite Boss, Lagerfeld and Sander, Germany could hardly be called a fashion hotspot. And where were the German globally best-selling books, the successful German films and, most of all, the German chart-toppers? You'd think the Romantic spirit would be supremely adapted to our sentimental pop age. But no. Lying naked on the beach or in a *Puff*, this land of Protestants didn't appear to do either superficial or sentimental.

What was German cinema if not porn films and *The Great*

Escape? For me Germans on the screen all looked like Anton Diffring, the German actor with piercing blue eyes and clipped diction who played the Nazi officer or camp *Kommandant* in just about every memorable war film. I also had black-and-white visions of Wim Wenders' guardian angels, a bit like Manny, roaming around Berlin on people's shoulders reciting torrents of philosophical poetry. Goethe didn't belong in the cinema. And lastly *Heimat*, the three-part epic about the modern German soul, just the latest instalment of which lasted 677 minutes: a *Gesamtkunstwerk* that required Wagnerian endurance. Germans had the same approach to cinema as they did to philosophy. A story got lost in the obsession with its own meaning. Cinema, like humour, was unsuited to the German predilection for ideas and serious analysis. They forgot halfway through that they were supposed to be telling a story.

And as for German music, could I name any German songs or bands? Apart from the Nazi pop anthem, 'Horst Wessel Lied', there was Nena of the 'ZZ Top-in-a-headlock' armpits and '99 Red Balloons'. I also remembered a German act called Nicole winning the Eurovision Song Contest one year. But Eurovision just about summed it up. What else was there apart from DJs Paul van Dyk and Sven Vath, the DJ Ötzi alpine anthem 'I Wanna Know If You'll Be My Girl' and a model singing about guys with '*Zwanzig Zentimeter*' between their legs?

And as for Germans' taste in other people's music just two words came to mind: the Hoff. The man the rest of the world knew as a ham actor who spoke to his car, or as Mitch Buchannon, the coastguard from *Baywatch* with ZZ Top road-kill on his chest, the Germans seemed to think could sing and turned into one of their biggest rock stars.

David Hasselhoff had to have German roots. He had released ten albums in Germany. You'd be lucky if you could find one among 'World Music' in Virgin Megastores. And the song he was most remembered for in Germany, including by himself, was his fortuitous cover of a 1970s German hit called '*Auf der Strasse nach Suden*', which was given English lyrics and the title 'Looking for Freedom'. The song hit the charts just as tension was rising the other side of the Berlin Wall in 1989 and throughout eight heady weeks of November that year, when the Wall came down, it stayed at number one in the German charts. It became the unwitting hymn to the fall of the Wall. The then Chancellor, Helmut Kohl, subsequently invited Hasselhoff back for a New Year's Eve concert of kitsch soft rock to celebrate the reunited city. And the Hoff would later claim he was partly responsible for the fall of the Wall: 'I find it a bit sad that there is no photo of me hanging on the walls in the Berlin museum at Checkpoint Charlie. After my appearance I hacked away at pieces of the wall that had the black, red and yellow colours of the German flag on it, I kept the big piece for myself and gave the smaller pieces to colleagues at *Baywatch*.' Very kind of you, David.

Ever modest, the Hoff also had a go at playing ambassador not just for Germany but for Europe: 'Many Americans joke about my popularity in Germany. But they have no idea how beautiful Europe is and how rich it is in culture and fun and warmth and children. In Germany children have brought me thousands of flowers.' Who needed a tourist board when you had that kind of endorsement?

Greeted in German with headlines like, 'Hasselhoff: not since the Beatles', the Hoff struggled to make the UK charts, crawling in 1993 to number 35 with the single 'If I Could Only Say Goodbye'. If only! But now, in 2006, he was back peddling his soft-rock Liebfraumilch with the single 'Jump into My Car', belatedly adulated in the UK like a Trabant. Had the British finally seen a talent long lauded by the Krauts?

'You must go to Berlin,' exhorted Manny. 'There you will

have your eyes and ears opened to the sights and sounds of a new, young Germany.'

Ber-lin. They were two syllables that had resonated throughout the twentieth century and my childhood with multiple layers of meaning. Berlin meant Hitler, the Second World War, *Funeral in Berlin* and a mysterious Pink Floyd-type Wall that hid a sad, forbidden land. Thanks to the Cold War, Germany carried on being a land of soldiers, checkpoints, *Achtung* and barbed wire. And Berlin its disturbingly magnetic, cinematic face of mystery, menace, danger and evil. It was a feeling I recognised from standing in front of the Prora on Rügen and on the old parade grounds in Nuremberg. Surely with their love of concepts and compound nouns the Germans had a word for it. No? Then how about *Teufelszauber*, the magic of evil?

'Before the outbreak of the Second World War,' Manny said, 'Berlin rivalled Paris as the centre of the cultural universe. Like a kind of Hollywood the city attracted misfits, refugees, chancers, investors and swindlers; and girls, "each and every vun of zem a wergin", looking to be talent-spotted and who worked the cabaret dance floors and "bumpsed" with their male clientele to get on in the world, much in the way Sally Bowles is portrayed in Isherwood's Berlin novels. It was a city of music, film, design and architectural innovation. In the words of one of its greatest musical daughters, Marlene Dietrich, it was the *"ewig junge Stadt"*, 'the eternally young city.'

Hitler apparently hated Berlin for its licentiousness and liberal attitudes and for being an exception and the opposite of his beloved, *gemütlich* München. But during the heady, apocalyptic years of the Weimar Republic, Manny said, Berlin had had that something that underpinned all pop culture.

'Berlin was in tune with the "spirit of the times", or in German, with the *Zeitgeist*.'

But what about after the war? Well, Manny had strong support here too. In the 1980s David Bowie lived in the Schöneberg district of West Berlin and the city was clearly an influence on him: 'It was a city of extremes. It vacillated between the absurd – the whole drag, transvestite nightclub type of thing – and real radical, Marxist political thought. This really was the focus of the new Europe. It was right here. There's something about Berlin. Throughout the twentieth century it's been the cultural crossroads of Europe. There's an artistic tension in Berlin that I've never come across the like of anywhere else. Paris? Forget it. Berlin has it.'

This was high praise indeed. Could it be, as Manny would have it, that 'post 1945 a country whose culture until 1930s was every bit as vibrant, magnetic and central to Europe as France's had simply been all but brushed under the carpet'? In my search for German humour I had seen that, in Berlin at least, life was no longer a cabaret and the city had moved on. What would Bowie find here in the early twenty-first century? As the song by the eponymous band went, could Berlin 'take my breath away?'

I had left a packed Heathrow on a Monday morning with businessmen rushing off to all corners of Europe on commuter flights. In the airport lounge I'd been surrounded by suits but on the plane to Berlin I found only scruffy, non-business types: long hair, leather, trainers and nondescript holdalls. And, while planes to Munich, Düsseldorf, Frankfurt and Cologne were full, here was the first flight of the week to Germany's capital city half empty.

It was February and snow had been falling across Germany for many weeks. The plane had approached from the east and we had circled over the *Plattenbauten*, identical breeze-block apartment buildings, mostly grey but occasionally garish orange or yellow in a fake attempt at cheerfulness, that were the legacy of DDR urban planning. Berlin-Tegel airport was a tiny affair, like something you would only now see in the movies: 1950s-style plastic capsule gangways with rounded-corner windows, and when you left the plane you were straight away at Customs, behind which were the baggage carousels and then immediately the exit. There used to be four airports, one for each of the powers that had a slice of Cold War Berlin, including Tempelhof, an icon of Nazi architecture and the one used for the airlift that broke the Soviet blockade of the city after the war. And for now Berlin continued to use an airport that made me feel more like I was arriving in, say, Bristol.

It was proper *Ostblock* weather outside. Snow and black ice on the pavements, Berliners wrapped up in overcoats, hats and scarves, and there was an alienating muffledness to the city's noises. Above was a big, open northern sky full of an eerie, winter glow cast from surrounding lakes such as Wannsee, where once the top Nazis met to dream up genocide but now modern Berliners went boating and bathing at weekends.

As the taxi made its way into Berlin I had the sense of a centre-less city. The suburbs seemed to go on and on, grey and mournful in the snow. And then suddenly, without a sense of approach, there was the Reichstag parliament building with its postcard dome, and the Brandenburg Gate, smaller than in its own mythology.

The city was a building site. It seemed you were nobody in architecture unless you had a building commission in Berlin. Renzo Piano, Daniel Liebeskind, Norman Foster and others were all at it, ripping up the city's bombed-out core. Never mind Kennedy's '*Ich bin ein Berliner*'. It seemed everyone wanted to be one. They were giving a facelift to the whole of Unter den Linden, the impressive avenue that was once and will one day again be Berlin's Champs Elysées. And they were just about to put explosives under the Palast der Republik. The ugly former headquarters of the DDR government had passed its *Ostalgie* sell-by date. But apparently it was ever thus. In 1906 the *Berliner Morgenpost* reported: 'Berlin stands under the sign of the pick-axe. In every nook and cranny of downtown, clouds of dust, ramparts of wheelbarrows, and placard-covered construction-site barricades proclaim that one structure is disappearing from the spot to make room for another. It is a never-ending process of rise and fall in modern Berlin. One could even speak of dem-olition mania . . .'

And there were the hawkers selling bits of the Wall to those who wanted to grab a bit of history. Somewhere in a cupboard I had an orange-painted shard of concrete that someone once gave me. But whether it belonged to the Berlin Wall or was just picked up on a building site and painted by a hawker, I'll never know. I'm sure that if you stuck together all the chunks of con-crete that have been sold to tourists since November 1989 they would form a wall at least twice as long or high as the original Wall.

Apparently, long before the Wall, Berlin had started life as two separate cities, Berlin and Cölln, and after these were merged Berlin, like London, grew up as an agglomeration of villages. It underwent a rapid expansion at the close of the nineteenth cen-tury as the Kaisers injected money into the city they had chosen as the flagship of their recently formed nation. And so quickly did it grow that a local anecdote told of how it was possible to be born in the village of Charlottenburg and die in Berlin without moving; Charlottenburg now being one of the chic, leafy quarters of the central western part of the city. Even in its 1920s Weimar heyday Berlin was a divided city, with the Kurfürstendamm, then as now, representing the rich West End and the east being where the wind blew coldest and where the polluting factories and their poor workers therefore were. It was not because they had advanced from the east that the Russians got the eastern part of the city in 1945. They wanted it because they knew that their ideas would be better received by its poorer population.

Central Berlin was the opposite of Paris with its grand sym-metry and consistent lines. It seemed quiet, indecipherable and vaguely anti-climactic, and certainly not a pretty place. The efforts of the global architectural elite hadn't managed to create an identifiable whole and the city had no distinctive icons on its skyline save the Fernsehturm, the radio tower the East German government had built to symbolise the Eastern bloc's technological supremacy. Despite all this, Berlin was the only city I had come across in Germany that felt truly metropolitan. Baroque Munich, for all its laptops and *Lederhosen*, seemed provincial alongside Berlin. Frankfurt, devoid of its financiers and bankers, was empty at the weekends. Cologne and Hamburg, with their strong local identities, didn't feel global either. Berlin had that something else. Whether it was the Blues Brothers rumble of the trams going past the window or the slack-jawed accent and couldn't-care-less attitude of its cab drivers (Berliners are known for their '*Schnauzer*', best translated as 'Berlin lip') or the endless graffiti or the juxtaposition of the run-down and haphazard with the ephemeral trendiness of experimental bars, Berlin seemed to me the epitome of urban. And although no Berlin street had a consistent style and at every juncture there were scruffy yards, some of these surprising open spaces and vacant tarmack-ed lots reminded me of parts of New York or Hackney. Even the ruins seemed part of the city.

I had booked into a hotel in the inner-city area of Kreuzberg, which contained Checkpoint Charlie, the famous security post on the boundary between the former American and Russian sectors. Why 'Charlie'? I had always wondered. I now learnt that this was the third of three checkpoints which followed the military alphabet. The first one stood between Potsdam, a royal Prussian satellite city of Berlin, and Berlin itself and was called Checkpoint Alpha, while the second one was Checkpoint Bravo.

Kreuzberg was in the former West Berlin but its former factory buildings and its working-class housing made it indistinguishable from the east. In the sixties and seventies Kreuzberg's buildings had been saved from demolition by activist students and a veneer of politics still oozed from the streets, betrayed here and there by the odd sign of gentrification in the form of chic bars and shops.

My hotel was one such regenerated building. This former telephone factory was called die Fabrik. Brick-built and set back from the street, it offered large, loft-style rooms complete with industrial iron columns and girders. Each room overlooked the enclosed courtyard that is a distinctive feature of many old Berlin properties. It was the kind of zeitgeist post-industrial space that cities killed for nowadays.

It was more of a hostel than a hotel and had that distinct German sense of community, shared space and respect for others that epitomised the *Wohngemeinschaft* and *Komune* movements. The bathrooms were shared but kept meticulously clean and tidy by the inhabitants. The heating was supplied by solar panels and the foyer was awash with flyers advertising clubs, activities and meeting places to suit every persuasion or creed.

Die Fabrik was staffed by friendly, hip young people whose heads were usually deeper in some book than in the concept of hospitality and who were trying to sustain their student lifestyle with a bit of not-very-hard-earned cash. They rotated between shifts at the reception desk and shifts at the out-front bar, which, rather like an extension of their home, was a place where they could play their own music, drink, smoke and hang out with their mates.

With snow falling outside and the flickering lights of filmic trams passing by the window in the late afternoon light, I had no trouble settling into my own Jim Jarmusch film. Berlin was a middle-European café city *par excellence*, full of inspirational locales for people who, as the Austrian writer Alfred Polgar put it, 'want to be alone, but need other people to do it'. They were the kind of places where even people who didn't smoke were convinced to and where, like the male protagonist of *Cabaret*, 'everyone is a writer' or an artist and where just being is almost a profession. I settled down to read the local Berliner-format paper and, like those around me, occasionally scribbled down unique thoughts that fitted the moment but would have no sense when I next came to read them.

Manny's pack contained a slim paperback by the German author Sven Regener entitled *Berlin Blues* that, unusually, had been translated and published in English. It told the story of a couple of days in the life of a likeable loafer nicknamed Herr Lehmann and a bunch of his bartender friends, in the days preceding the fall of the Wall. It made no attempt to describe Berlin or to make any grandiose statement of history or emotion surrounding this momentous occasion. If anything, it portrayed a rather inert relationship with the Wall, so that when, at the novel's end, it fell, it was a non-event. Here were a bunch of guys just having fun, meeting in this or that pub, discussing such existential things as whether the sand of time flows faster or slower when you are drunk and it is 'drunk sand', and making unconvincing attempts at enterprise and art. '*Denk an die Elektrolyten!*' ('Think about the electrolytes') was the affectionate mantra repeated by the anti-hero's best friend Karl throughout, reminding him to eat lots of salt and starch to counterbalance the beer. Not surprisingly Berlin was the German city that best understood the *Katerfrühstück*.

Berlin Blues was anti history and, like Heinrich Böll, anti the work ethic of the rest of Germany. Early on, Herr Lehmann is challenged by a girl he quite likes as to whether bartending is a fulfilling job. 'Is that what life is in fact – just a container for something else?' he rebuffs her. 'A barrel, maybe, or a sick-bag?' The novel took the mellow and existential view that whatever you did or didn't do was worthwhile, as long you were basically humble and a nice guy.

Although initially rather thrown by the book's inertia, I understood Berlin all the better for it. Amid the verbose intensity of drunkards and the philosophical musings there was a sense of real time, the companionship of friends and the art of wistful conversation that I saw all around me now in cafés and bars.

As in London, incomers seemed to outnumber natives of the city. Mostly they were students like Herr Lehmann, attracted to the place not least by incredibly low rents and huge high-ceilinged old apartments, but also by the metropolitan anonymity of a city where you could be anyone and anything without the judgement of others. Lots of young Berliners were, like Lehmann, refugees from parental *Gemütlichkeit* and Germany's traditions and work ethic. In past decades they would have been also refugees from the German draft. In West Germany West Berlin was an autonomous *Land* and, as an island in a sea of Communism, had no use for an army. So residents of Berlin were excused the draft into the German Bundeswehr, and not surprisingly, much of the country's post-war activist youth tried, like Kennedy, to say they were Berliners.

Berlin had remained true to the 'live and let live' tolerance portrayed in *Cabaret* but which, I now knew, went back to the early Prussian Kaisers. Unlike in the rest of Germany, there was no *Sperrstunde* restricting the time and noise of nightlife on the streets. Berlin was, uniquely in Germany, '24/7'. This went back to the early years of the Cold War, when the US and the Russian sectors were embroiled in a case of one-upmanship, each wanting to show the people that they provided a better ideology and place to live.

The city's gay mayor liked to be seen turning a blind eye to the impromptu and illicit raves that periodically took place among the city's demi-monde. And the androgyny, transvestism and open homosexuality of Berlin's nightlife was still as unique to the city as when Isherwood went to live there in 1929.

It was a German scientist, Magnus Hirschfeld, who invented the term 'transvestite', and through his research on the whole spectrum of human sexual and erotic urges earned himself the epithet 'the Einstein of Sex'. Throughout his life he campaigned to have the laws that criminalised homosexuality repealed and his legacy was to drive the gay subculture of Germany, particularly in

Berlin, where it kept the city very much in tune with the spirit of the twenty-first century.

The Love Parade, Berlin's yearly orgy of PVC *Polizei*-chic phallic adoration and transvestism, began in July 1989 as a birthday party for a resident DJ with just a few hundred people marching through the streets towards the Siegesäule victory column under banners declaring: *'Friede, Freude, Eierkuchen'* ('Peace, Joy, Pancakes'). Nowadays the Love Parade attracted a million and a half ravers and was the largest free assembly on the planet (typical German gigantism), with several millennia of civilisation rolled back to allow the momentary acceptance of widespread sex between strangers outdoors and in daylight. Only in Germany. During the Cold War Krushchev once apparently said, 'Berlin is the testicles of Germany. When I want the West to scream I squeeze on Berlin.' Nowadays it more accurately described the actions and noises emanating from the bushes of the aptly named Tiergarten (animal garden) park during the Love Parade.

Incredibly, and perhaps symptomatic of Berlin and German post-war tolerance, the Love Parade was officially a demonstration rather than a festival. And this meant that the city's council footed the bill for the Glastonbury-style Augean detritus of mud, drink cans, condoms, food and polystyrene packaging left in its wake.

So, in Berlin it would still be possible to hole up like Isherwood for months, paying little rent to share a decadent, wood-panelled apartment with a drunk lesbian prostitute-cum-nightclub singer. The city of Helmut Newton seemed sexually charged. But not in the gawping, neon-and-prostitution way of Hamburg.

And yes, there was a left-wing dissidence about the young people I met and saw. But how genuine was it? How necessary even? Was it not just an imitation, in more stable, consumerist times, of an attitude more genuinely felt by their parents, the protestors of 1968, when the spectre of the Second World War was still much closer in the rear-view mirror? It was easy to see these 'artists' and 'writers' in their cafés with their iBooks as acting out some gentrified idea of what an artist or writer should be. Even the streets of former East Berlin working-class districts such as Prenzlauer Berg were beginning to fill up with mothers and their prams and rich media types who wanted to grunge down and catch a bit of working-class scruffiness. It was hard to tell where the line fell between genuine student indigence and phoney poverty. Berlin was a hive of artistic activity but also stylised inactivity. Was it finally becoming gentrified? Or would some future impetus arise to keep it revolutionary and avant-garde?

Now, as in the days of Isherwood, there appeared to be little or no middle class in Berlin. In the 1930s they were either killed or fled. When Bowie was here he too remarked on the scarcity of middle-aged people. For artists this was perfect, since the artist usually has no greater enemy than the bourgeoisie who turn his ideas into kitsch. But, by the admission of some Berliners, it was a problem. However rich a creative seedbed, Berlin was also a bankrupt city whose creativity and high-profile architecture were all financed from outside. And even though it was now the capital of a reunited Germany, investors and companies were leaving or still shunned Berlin. Deutsche Bahn, Germany's national rail company and the country's largest employer, threatened to follow many others and decamp from Berlin in early 2006 and many of the fancy new designer-label office blocks in the city's revamped centre stood empty. This situation was reflected in the city's social life. The papers were full of stories about the opening of Berlin's first yuppie-type lounge bar-nightclub, Goya, in a former theatre. It had undergone a million-euro refit and was touted as a flagship of the city's initiation into the world of hip hotels and flâneur, dandy nightspots. But early signs suggested it was going to be a flop. Berlin wasn't ready, and perhaps would never be, for a club that didn't have a feeling of underground edginess. Even if the city's comfortable youth was becoming bourgeois it wasn't going to admit it.

I knew the feeling, and Manny had identified it as central to my *Weltschmerz*.

In a more unstable world Berlin would be living on borrowed time, on the edge of a fatal crash like that of 1929, when the US, whose loans propped it up, suffered the Wall Street Crash and effectively called in the debt. To me modern Berlin felt like nothing other than a flimsy stage.

In fact, with its nineteenth-century tenements, its yellow *Strassenbahn* subway and its *Cabaret*-cum-Jim Jarmusch existentialism, and despite its occasionally contrived dilapidation, Berlin had cinematic style in abundance. The city, I learnt, was the spiritual home of Germany's film industry and keen to flag up the slightest tie to the popular film world they could, even dragging up the German lineage of one Leonardo Wilhelm DiCaprio – he has a German *Oma* (grandmother) – whose talent was apparently first unearthed in a 1980s German TV series.

Fittingly I had walked on to Berlin's set during the Berlin Film Festival, where the city's film critics were full of Teutonic self-analysis over the state of German cinema.

Germany in fact excelled in the early years of the cinema and laid the foundations for much of today's screen language. Berlin's Ufa film studios were once Europe's equivalent of Hollywood – Berlin and LA are indeed twinned – and the ideas and styles pioneered there underpinned much of the cinema that followed and triumphed in California and then the rest of the world.

The expressionist horror classic *Das Cabinet des Dr Caligari*, about a murderous travelling magician, distorted perspective, invented suspense and made exaggerated use of shadows in a way that was to become familiar in film noir and the work of

Hitchcock, the Austrian émigré Billy Wilder and Orson Welles. Hitchcock, who learnt his trade at UfA, would later say that the Germans were his greatest influence. German cinema set the template for the pulp-fiction, Chandleresque world of detectives, paranoid loners and deceptively angelic women.

Fritz Lang's *Metropolis*, a parable of man's dehumanisation by machines, was the world's first and much-purloined sci-fi film, not least by that cone-breasted Überwoman-machine, Madonna, for her David Fincher-directed *Vogue* video.

And Murnau's 1922 account of the Dracula myth in *Nosferatu* gave birth to the horror film. Max Schreck (the original Shrek) portrayed the pasty-faced Count Orlok with pointed ears, shifty eyes, pincer-like fingers and crab-like movements that passed into popular culture as the paradigm of a vampire. Similarly, the backdrop of jagged, brooding mountains and of a city of tall houses, shadowy streets, arches and stairways to stalk and hide in was the epitome of the nightmarish landscape on which so many later horror films were based. Just as the Grimms created the landscape of fairytales, so the Germans created the equally sylvan landscape of nightmares.

That was all very well but I was struggling to think if any German film had bridged the gap into the frivolous post-war world of pop culture, where ideas, at least outside Germany, were less in demand than fun. I couldn't think of much that was German that had made it at the Oscars, but then Manny set me a challenge. Could I name all the actors in *The Magnificent Seven*? Of course! There was Yul Brynner, Steve McQueen, Charles Bronson, Eli Wallach, Robert Vaughn, Brad Dexter and, and . . . oh, what was his name? Horst Buchholz. A German, naturally!

Who was the lord of the jungle? There seemed to be as many Tarzans as Doctor Whos. But there was one actor who played the loin-clothed crusader and became associated with the role more than any other: the shy, one-time Olympic swimmer

Austrian-born Johnny Weissmuller. A David Hasselhoff for the black-and-white era. His leathers were surely the forerunner of *Lederhosen* and the *Tarzan* movies had more than a touch of the Karl May myths about them. It seemed somehow appropriate that the incarnation of the jungle *Übermensch*, in tune with the forests and a clear fan of physical education, swinging his daily *Trimmdichpfad* through the trees, should be of Germanic origin.

And did I know that *The Sound of Music* was originally a German film entitled *Die Trapp Familie* and directed by Max Reinhardt long before Rodgers and Hammerstein (and Hammerstein had German roots) got hold of the stage rights and decades before TV talent contests.

There was more!

Behind American blockbusters like *The Perfect Storm*, *Poseidon*, *Independence Day* and *The Day after Tomorrow* were German directors, Wolfgang Petersen, he of *Das Boot* fame, and the so-called 'Swabian Spielberg', Roland Emmerich.

This was German *Grossmannsucht* meets German Romantic sense of the universe and myth.

Then, after baffling all but the Cannes jury in 1987 with *Wings of Desire* the German director Wim Wenders not only tapped into the *Zeitgeist* with *The Buena Vista Social Club* but bankrolled the Cuban tourist industry.

And it wasn't just the images. It was their soundtracks too. Where would *Gone with the Wind* be without 'Tara's Theme' by Max Steiner? Or *Gladiator* without Hans Zimmer's soundtrack to Romans beating up his ancestors, including the haunting theme which in true German style elevated the action to the realms of something more universal and eternal about human will. Cinema provided the perfect theatre for the Romantic symphonic musical ambition.

Latterly Britain had become more accepting of 'art-house cinema' and recently some German films had made it through

HM Customs. There was *Lola Rennt* (*Run Lola Run*), a high-octane but arty kidnapping thriller with three endings, set in Berlin and directed by Tom Tykwer, since drafted in by Spielberg to film the supposedly unfilmable olfactory murder-mystery novel *Perfume*, a rare global best-seller by German author Patrick Süskind. Then there was *79 Quadratmeter DDR* (*Goodbye Lenin*) with its subtle and understated humour and *Ostalgie* for the bygone East Germany; *Der Schuh des Manitu*, the all-but-untranslatable parody of Germany's Romantic obsession with the Wild West; and *Der Untergang* (Downfall), about the last days in Hitler's Berlin bunker, which had marked a watershed in German film-financing and post-war *Selbstwahrnehmung* and was justly Oscar-nominated.

But perhaps the most significant of recent breakthroughs was *Gegen die Wand* (Head-On), remarkable because it was written and directed by a German of Turkish origin, Fatih Akin. *Head-On* told the story of a raw and bloody relationship between two second-generation German Turks who meet in a clinic having both half-heartedly tried to commit suicide to escape from their respective personal tragedies (in the man's case a death and in the woman's the tyranny of a stiflingly traditional family). The two decide to embark on a marriage of convenience so that the woman can evade her father's clutches, but in the end, despite a large age gap and totally different lifestyles, they fall in love. *Head-On* won the Golden Bear top prize at the 2002 Berlin Film Festival and achieved limited release in the UK.

As in German comedy, Germany's new multiculturalism had begun to bear cultural fruit. And multiculturalism itself, like Berlin's liberal attitude to homosexuality, was a sign that Germany was catching up with the international *Zeitgeist*.

Did that extend to German music too?

As someone brought up in a musical family, Germany and music had always been synonymous. My mother taught the piano and the house was full of volumes of German sonatas, preludes and other sheet music. My father played bassoon in the school orchestra, was an avid Wagner fan and had miles of reel-to-reel tapes and acres of vinyl recordings of the great German composers and conductors. Long holiday journeys by car through the continent were accompanied by a medley of classical music on cassettes. My brother and I had one or two we quite liked, such as Holst's *The Planets* and that famous bit from Prokofiev's ballet *Romeo and Juliet* depicting the clash of the Montagues and Capulets. But the rest of it, for a long time, was generally painful and meaningless noise to our petulant pre-teen ears.

I played the piano, although I was not taught by my mother as she feared altercations between us, and was forced to get up at seven in the morning and practise my scales. I also played the French horn and acquainted myself with Beethoven and Mozart in particular. Eventually, after years of adolescent rebellion I found I quite enjoyed and was comfortable with a lot of classical music.

My brother, on the other hand, had an on-off relationship with a violin which was cut short by a distressing experience he had with his German language-exchange partner, Sebastian.

Sebastian was the youngest son of a large Austrian family, the Crispers, who were distant friends of our wider family. The Crispers were also a very musical and competitive family. When Sebastian came to stay in the summer we initially enjoyed each other's company. Needless to say, he spoke excellent English, so much so that he didn't seem to think he needed to be there. The more tennis we played the more competitive he became, almost to the point of racket-breaking and protracted, McEnroe's-style 'Ze ball voz in!' line disputes. And he even managed to make a contest out of an afternoon of fruit picking at the local farm.

It was then my brother's turn to visit Sebastian at his family's summer house in the Austrian mountains. And it was here that he was subjected to a German musical humiliation. After supper one evening the whole family got out their violins, violas and cellos and began to play *Eine Kleine Nachtmusik* as if they were performing for the Viennese Court. My brother didn't have his fiddle with him and so was lent one, only to be told after a few strained bars that he was spoiling the soirée and was banished to the audience. Mozart had apparently not written a part for a slowly expiring cat.

So I had been brought up on a diet of Beethoven, Brahms, Schumann, Schubert, Haydn, Handel and all three Bachs, and knew that Germany was the *Heimat* of classical music. *Peeps at Germany* had confirmed this back in 1911 with the words: 'You probably know that the greatest musical composers have all been German, and that anyone who wishes to be a musician goes to Germany, if he can, at some point in his career.' And nowadays there were apparently more registered professional orchestras, choirs, opera and chamber groups in Germany than in any other country, each of them places where the Corinthian spirit of the amateur's hobby was scarcely admitted. As my brother had found out to his cost, the German people treated the practice and performance of music with Romantic intensity.

Was it the mathematics underpinning musical harmony that appealed to them? Harmony was a metaphor for the laws of nature and of the universe, which therefore made music the most Romantic of arts. More than any other medium, music enabled the Romantics to explore the realm of feeling and the absolutes of existence. Beethoven's symphonies were pure expressions of human *Wille* (willpower) and the 'Ode to Joy' that concluded his Ninth and final symphony was a virtual anthem to the human spirit.

But Johann Sebastian Bach was the real mathematician behind classical music, making exercise routines out of musical forms as if they were multiplication tables or perhaps a musical *Trimmdichpfad*. Just the mention of him brought back painful memories of my early-morning piano practice sessions. And whereas most people would be content to compose a prelude or fugue in just one or two keys, Bach had to go and do one in the major and minor of every single key from Do to Si; presumably lest the concept remain too relative. But perhaps his favourite form was the fugue, characterised by an insistent, motor-like rhythm of see-sawing notes that propelled the music smoothly forwards. Like a finely tuned engine (unless played by me), the fugue was the epitome of *Vorsprung durch Musik*. Musical science.

Through his work Bach created a Protestant musical standard, as Luther had done for the German language. In the first half of the eighteenth century he was Germany's great musical educator, in the way that Jahn, Schreber, Kneipp and the others would become educators in their fields during the early nineteenth. His studies and compositions had a pedagogic value, allowing the pupil to practise with the building blocks of music rather like children using Froebel's *Kindergarten* play blocks. Mozart studied Bach endlessly and is reported to have exclaimed, on first hearing his music, 'Now, here is something we can learn from!' Beethoven called Bach '*der Urvater der Harmonie*' ('the original father of harmony') and punned on his name to express Bach's universal influence: '*nicht Bach sondern Meer*' ('not a brook but a sea'). And Goethe, when listening to Bach's music, described it as 'eternal harmony in dialogue with itself'.

Why was this relevant? This was all the high culture the silver surfers came to Germany for. I was hardly the target audience.

But Bach was not just classical music. According to Manny, the structures of his music underpinned all jazz and pop music, from the so-called 'Air on a G String', itself a piece of pop music thanks to the ad for Hamlet cigars, to the organ riff on Procol Harum's hit single 'A Whiter Shade of Pale'. Memorable cars ads had featured the opening hellfire-and-damnation chorus of Carl Orff's *Carmina Burana* (a work that is actually about the rather filthy thoughts of a bunch of German monks). And the 1990s group the Farm were just one in a long line of bands to plagiarise Pachelbel's interminable Canon for their hit single 'All Together Now'.

So German influence was apparently at the root of both cinema and popular music. But, like good German wine, you had to look pretty hard for it.

Still, I thought, in terms of what young people listened to on their iPods, Germans hadn't bridged the gap between classical and pop music. It was like looking at the achievements of the Ancient Greeks and comparing them with their modern-day compatriots. So why this gulf, given the country's enormous musical heritage? After 1945, where had it all gone wrong? Or was there German music out there I should know, love and be able to sing along to and which reflected the *Zeitgeist*?

For young Germans the end of the Second World War was, I now learned, a kind of ground zero, or as they called it, '*Stunde Nul*' (zero hour). They rejected everything their parents and grandparents were widely deemed to have done, and rejected their country's past. So while their parents listened to nostalgic crooning, or *Schlagermusik* (the German equivalent of Sacha Distel), Germany's youth refused to write or listen to anything sung in German and instead avidly sought out music from abroad and in particular from America and the UK. There were *Schlager* German translations of great Elvis songs, just as during the war jazz songs like 'Lili Marlene' had been translated and migrated across cultures. But young Germans, as I knew from Hamburg, wanted the Beatles and, most importantly, the English language. It was not acceptable to sing about love, loss and longing in German. These themes no longer represented the rebellious new young German teenager and were old, Romantic notions from a tainted past. Tainted love. Tainted *Gemütlichkeit*.

Not surprisingly, music sung in German had to have an

Anspruch, a message: it had to demand something politically and socially, just as the '68ers had demanded things with their nudity and communes and the Baader-Meinhof gang with their bombs.

The breakthrough came with the *Neue Deutsche Welle* (meaning 'German new wave' and not a hairstyling cream). This was German punk rock, left-wing and highly political. Nena's '99 Red Balloons' were not for some birthday party but the barrage balloons of an anti-war song. She was railing against Vietnam and all the world's injustices. No wonder she wasn't concentrating on what was under her armpits.

Around the same time, Krautrock was born. Nothing to do with cabbages but fronted by groups like Tangerine Dream who put educated lyrics of socio-political parody to electronic music that presaged the synthesiser rock of the 1980s. Maybe. But I was pretty sure it was the same racket we used to wake one another up from hangovers for a joke at university.

But the ultimate German electronic band was surely Kraftwerk (meaning Powerstation), made up of four bicycle-loving recluses based in Düsseldorf. Kraftwerk put the programming into pop music. Wired up to sonic circuitry, they played music on laptops as if they were mechanics fixing a Merc. Their robotic approach made them more like lab technicians making sonic cars or Hugo Boss audible suits. This really was *Vorsprung durch Musik*, with a fugue-like pulse that you could almost – but only almost – dance to. At last, here was a link back to Bach and Germany's great musical ancestry.

But even Kraftwerk, according to Manny, were engaged in an ironic statement on the flawed utopia of a technology-obsessed and dehumanised world. It was the 1980s musical equivalent of Fritz Lang's *Metropolis*. But was there really anything ironic about four deadpan men in Boss suits claiming to play live music?

Remembering my own record collection, the eighties was in

fact quite a German decade, all angular and metallic and dominated by synths, samplers and sequencers. Then Germany was the land of *Technik*, technology, and the German language briefly became a cipher for the sonic right angles of electronic music. Bands even started calling themselves Spandau Ballet and Bauhaus. Germany had paved the way for the New Romantics – the likes of the Human League, New Order, Depeche Mode and OMD – and the decade that style forgot.

Then, in the mid-1990s, a revolution happened. German bands started to compose and sing in their mother tongue again, and this said something significant not just about German music but about German society. Its youth deemed that enough time had now passed, enough history had been created since the war for it to be acceptable to sing again in German and about old-fashioned stuff like love.

In Berlin I discovered the coquettish voice of Annett Louisan, Germany's answer to Nora Jones or Katie Melua, bringing the German Lieder tradition up to date in a wistful jazz-folk style whose global renaissance had started with Diana Krall. Louisan could sound commonplace to an ear spoilt by a plethora of female jazz-folk vocalists from around the world. But as far as Germany and German pop music was concerned she was a first. And I heard Zweiraumwohnung (Two-bed Flat), that unlikeliest of things, a German bossa nova band, seamlessly melding German melancholy with Brazilian rhythm and harmony.

For the first time it was permissible for someone to go back into Germany's past and sing about love, loss and normal human things without an *Anspruch*. Like Germany's comedy, its cinema, its food and its sense of humour, German music had lost fifty years.

There were others, like German rappers Die Fantastischen Vier (The Fantastic Four) and Wir Sind Helden (We Are Heroes), with the drained heroin-chic of their female lead, who'd done a one-off gig in London that was a sell-out. And maybe the borderless digital world meant this music from outwith their parochial Anglophile sensibility would soon be found in the ears of the British iPod generation.

But the real soundtrack to Berlin and so to the German *Zeitgeist* was once again the voice of Sven Regener – this time not as novelist but multitasking as the lead and singer-song-writer of the German band Element of Crime. Here were mellow and melodic songs, predominantly played on acoustic guitar and with wistful trumpet and harmonica filling out the choruses. Not over-produced, they were reminiscent of French film music from the sixties and seventies, or Kurt Weill's Weimar-period songs mixed with shades of Lou Reed, Dylan and Gainsbourg's melancholy philosophising. They sounded like rediscovered songs but they were all original. And, sung in a gruff voice that didn't always mind whether it was in tune, they collectively evoked a picaresque, after-hours, closing-time world of indolent friends like his Herr Lehmann alter ego; the romantic beauty of urban solitude and the sense of community on the last tram home; puddles, drizzle and the white sun of winter mornings. This was the Berlin I had lived in for a week.

As in Regener's book, the message was positive: 'Don't let things get you down, make grandiose plans or quarrel with fate. Simply enjoy the present and if that means having more in common with old tramps standing on a street corner and sharing a cigarette with them, so be it.' For Element of Crime it was not about '*Du bist Deutschland*' and what people could become, but what they already were. Being with the *Zeitgeist* meant not chasing grand designs, solutions and systems and trying to be the biggest, but standing still: '*Wo deine Füsse stehen/ist der Mittelpunkt der Welt*' ('Wherever you are standing/is the centre of the world'). It was a humble, simple and admirable message – an antidote to German *Angst* – and again it hinted that the Berlin of grand history, be it the Wall, *Ostalgie* or the Second

World War, was the Berlin of tourists and not of real Berliners. Once again elusive, Berlin had moved on, with the times.

I had almost finished my journey through German pop culture. But Manny's itinerary stated I had to go to the small town of Dessau, south-west of Berlin. What could be *Zeitgeist* about a provincial town in Saxony? Well, here, apparently, I would understand Germany's fundamental role in shaping today's modern culture, not understood just as the arts but in the very wallpaper of our life.

Like Isherwood, I said goodbye to Berlin and made the short journey, passing the home of Luther in nearby Wittenberg.

Dessau was where the Bauhaus came from. Not the eighties rock band from Northampton but the Bauhaus school of thought and art academy whose exponents, chief among them the German architect Walter Gropius, came up with another radical German proposal. This time not an idea that would redefine the spiritual world as Luther had done, but one that would shape the physical post-war world. The Bauhaus was the beginning of design.

Until the Bauhaus aesthetics had been something applied only to fine art. The Bauhaus changed this by marrying form and function and turning everyday objects into designed objects. It was the essence of giving the familiar the Romantic impressiveness of the unfamiliar. For the first time, thanks to the Bauhaus, art no longer hung just on the wall or stood on a plinth. It was in everything you held in your hand, sat on or used in daily life. Starting with architecture, its members focused on the human living space right down to the fork you ate with or the cup you drank from.

But it wasn't all Romantic. The overriding dictate of the Bauhaus and its legacy was that form should only follow function and that objects should first be pared down to what they were supposed to do. Thus, a Birkenstock shoe for walking, a

Mercedes to drive or a Löwe television to watch football. How Protestant, bare, clinical and typically German! What about frills and decoration and beauty for beauty's sake?

But, whichever way you leant, the Bauhaus world was now the world we all now lived in. Frills are now kitsch and since the passing of Ludwig II and the similarly tasteless Victorians we simply don't want, or have the time or the space, to build capricious castles or to imitate bygone styles. Not even if we are German. We have passed from a baroque German child's fantasy-scape to the *Kindergarten* simplicity of the Froebel tower blocks that are said to have inspired the great American architect Frank Lloyd Wright.

The iPod world was one created and first imagined by the Bauhaus: be it the skyscrapers inspired by the ideas of Mies van der Rohe, the white goods of Siemens, Bosch and Braun that surrounded us at home, or any one of numerous German brands of car we may have driven. Hugo Boss suits started as hard-wearing workers' clothes and Jil Sander trained as a 'textile engineer'. Birkenstocks were the summer sandal-wear equivalent of the skyscraper.

I had never given this any thought. But now I seemed to be drawing the conclusion that unwittingly, since the war, the Western world has been drawing on an originally German vision that put Germany right at the heart of the global *Zeitgeist*. Pop culture was no longer just music, film and teen culture. The whole world was an interactive, boundary-less entertainment space where even travel and destinations, as Manny had pointed out, took their place as retail experiences and objects. A pared-down approach to function and form throughout was the current trend and would be for as long as we went on living in cities where space was at a premium and we needed to unclutter our lives and spirit. The urban world was, I now knew, a German world.

12

Lebensraum

nm, *living space*

'And so to the last module and the Eldorado of your travel aspirations!'

I would soon be free!

'Owning a property abroad is an Englishman's obsession. It's like some birthright that harks back to your Empire and a belief that some corner of a foreign field should be for ever English. *Lebensraum*. That's what it is. British *Lebensraum*.'

I knew that word. And the old joke: whenever you stay in a German's house and want to know where the living room is, remember, don't ask for the *Lebensraum*! The correct word is *das Wohnzimmer*.

I tried to look blank.

'Let me explain,' said Manny.

The term *Lebensraum*, another in my expanding vocabulary of compound nouns expressing concepts, was apparently coined in 1897 by a German geographer and ethnographer named Friedrich Ratzel, who, looking at Darwinian models of natural selection, reckoned that the development and success of a people depended on their ability to occupy and fill available space. It was adopted as a slogan for the creation of the single German state and very much caught the imagination of a people for so long invaded and divided. But Ratzel's new word coincided with the German expansionism that led to the First World War and came to be synonymous with Germany's attitude to annexing territories, especially in Eastern Europe, that it was forced to hand back under the treaty of Versailles. *Lebensraum* became a cornerstone of Hitler's vision as he tried to get it all back. Except he forgot the bit about '*available* space' and just marched in regardless. Since then the Germans' famed approach to sun-loungers had made them easy targets for jibes about a continued, post-war need for *Lebensraum*.

But now Manny was equating a passion for overseas real estate with British popular neo-imperialism. How dare he?

'Twenty-four billion pounds you have collectively spent on homes abroad, you know! No wonder. You have whole magazines and property sections of your newspapers dedicated to the acquisition of foreign real estate, sometimes to just one country. British estate agents have branches all over Europe touting each new property hotspot. And there's a whole raft of television programmes through which you live vicariously the dream of escaping abroad.'

OK, so, like the Germans, the British were generally a pretty well-travelled lot. In fact we seemed to spend about the same amount of time not in our own country. But surely Britons' attitude to having a home abroad was no different from any other race's.

'In fact there is no other European country where there is such an appetite and tradition for this. And what's more you don't seem to buy just as an investment or holiday home. This I could understand. But you British seem to aspire to a complete change in your life. You'd rather jack it all in for a ruin in the back of beyond, and a life without electricity spent toiling, in pidgin French or Italian, against failing water generators and bemused local tradesmen. This is most strange, I find. Is that what years of

Angst pent up on the Northern Line does to you? Or are you deep down a nation of frustrated peasants; of accountants-cum-olive-growers and bankers-cum-winemakers in waiting?'

Well, why not? Ruins were romantic. Heidelberg had proved that. If you wanted to escape the rat race why not seek out some utopia, a British Schlaraffenland of lost agrarian innocence?

'And all the while everyone else going in the other direction can't wait to buy an overpriced urban shoebox in London and get their hands on all the designer modernity you would reject. Funny, isn't it?'

Manny was right. You didn't hear of many Italians coming to refurbish an abandoned brewery in Yorkshire, or Spaniards coming to run a Fawlty Towers in idyllic Torquay. But such was the dual carriageway of life.

'But, you know, the British won't restore just any old country's rural ruins.'

Absolutely not. We were selective about where we thought rural innocence resided.

'You British can only envisage your idyll in certain parts of the world: British Chiantishire and Chelsea-sur-Loire in France. The Costas Brava and del Sol have long been foreign outposts of suburban Britain while Andalusia is now twinned with Holland Park.'

It was a list of destinations unchanged since the Victorian Grand Tour and which undoubtedly had something to do with climate. But people looking for a change of scene also sought out chaos in a sanitised and ordered world; the perceived *disinvoltura* and spontaneity of southern Europe versus the rigidity of the north. I recalled the organisation and toytown perfection of the Baltic coast. There was no *disinvoltura* there.

'But what about Germany?' Manny resumed the attack.

Here we go . . .

'Why not a villa on the Baltic or a *Fachwerkhaus* (note, not a *Kraftwerkhaus*) in the Black Forest?'

There were places I had found beautiful during my therapy, including the Baltic hinterland, the fairytale land of Hessen, Thuringia, Germany's *Kindergarten*, and the Königsee in Berchtesgaden. But I hadn't for a moment considered moving there.

'And never mind those constant eulogies to *la dolce vita* and building castles in Spain. On the bookshelves, where are the romantic paeans to the German way of life?'

Well, people might want to go back to nature. But there were limits.

There was no 'Under the Rhineland Sun' or equivalent of 'Toujours Bayern'. 'Immer Bayern' sounded more like something you'd hear on the terraces at a Munich football match. No 'Eighty-three Million Germans Can't Be Wrong'. God forbid! They would never admit it even if they were (which they were. Twice). Equally no one had hitched around Germany attached to a Siemens dishwasher or taken the German football team on at tennis. They were surely far too good. Nor had anyone taken it upon themselves to buy a ruined barn in Bavaria and write an account of doing it up entitled *Driving over Bratwurst*. Always assuming that anything in Germany had been allowed to become dilapidated.

So what books on Germany would be lying on bedside tables in the Home Counties? As far as I could see, none. The bookshops were bereft of Teutophile texts to sink into the holiday sun-lounger with – always assuming the Germans hadn't beaten you to it. Germany was some way off being a name to conjure dreams of an alternative life. It was more like *A Year in the Sauerkraut*.

Prodded by Manny's passionate advocacy, I scoured the property sections for mentions of the Fatherland. But despite the reams of newspaper and magazine space devoted to foreign real estate I couldn't find one mention of Germany. Arranged in alphabetical order, they would always leap from France to

Greece as if there was nothing in between. Nor had I ever seen Germany feature on *A Place in the Sun*. Bulgaria made it on to their radar and Albania would probably be next. But as for, 'You know, my husband and I have just bought a rambling old Hessischer manor house outside Frankfurt. Needs a lot of work but we're going to do it up and make our own *Apfelwein* . . .', that was simply a phrase you never heard. I even visited my local overseas property brokers to see their reaction when I asked about properties in their German portfolio. Their faces were predictably blank.

The land of the Protestant work ethic obviously sounded too much like hard work. If people moved abroad they wanted to dematerialise and downshift their lives – the very opposite of *Vorsprung*: regress not progress.

By now I'd been to Germany and learnt about many aspects of the German way of life. But here, according to Manny, leaving aside accusations of neo-colonialism, was the key test of the *Wanderer*. Could Germany be my *Heimat*? Could Germany be my dream 'elsewhere'?

Now that I thought about it, German streets both in towns and in the country had been curiously devoid of estate agents' signs. Nothing seemed to be for sale. And this was because apparently the vast majority of Germans rented, and did so more than most other Europeans. Was this the Romantic fear of credit and a built-in Protestant aversion to the concept of a mortgage? Could this people so famous for the annexation of sun-loungers possibly not have a well-oiled land-grabbing industry?

I thought about the wonderful, high-ceilinged flats I'd seen in Berlin. It'd be nice to own one of those. Or maybe a pad among the Rhineland vineyards or a private nudist retreat in the mystic wilds of Rügen?

'An apartment. A holiday home! Where is your imagination and romance? How about a ruined castle? All the better for releasing the German child in you again!'

I'd be lucky if I could afford a beach basket! But perhaps it was worth investigating. Castles weren't only in Spain. In fact there were hundreds more of them in Germany, and there had to be a few going spare. Yes! Monetary realities aside, I quite fancied a *Schloss* of my own.

It was Internet time again. But this time Manny directed me to a website he seemed to know called Living_Space.com. It was a high-end travel company based not in Germany but in California.

Living Space sold themselves as organisers of expensive and unusually themed holidays around the world worthy of the Condé Nast poker table: fly-fishing in Patagonia, golf in China and – only in America – dentistry tours. *Wanderlust* could mean so many things these days.

But there was also a distinct German theme. Here was that unusual beast in the travel world: a site peddling Germany. Living Space offered tours of Europe in a Porsche, and visits to Germany's historic castles and Christmas markets. I half-expected to see German 'wellness' weeks and FKK tours to the Baltic with a free night in a *Puff*. But staring back at me was a link saying, 'Investing in Castles'. My fingers twitching I clicked and the message came up: 'CASTLE FOR SALE – Have you ever dreamt of owning a castle? It is not as difficult as you think to make that dream come true.'

It went on to explain that there were many castles and manor houses in what used to be East Germany that for various reasons had been neglected and needed renovating. On the following pages were lots of mouth-watering photographs of *Schlösser* with evocative, fantastical names like Purschenstein, Pudelwitz and Fürstenberg that were crying out for a role in a Grimm fairytale. Was it any wonder that Mary Shelley named Dr Frankenstein, the creator of her monster, after a German castle?

A *Schloss* meant many things, from full-blown castle, complete with towers, crenellations and other extravagant excrescences, to simpler manor houses. They were also mostly in an appalling state of disrepair and needed a lot of imagination. Taking on one of these properties was clearly not a job for Mr and Mrs Quaint from Guildford with dreams of a bijou German B&B. But one thing these places all had in common was that they had land, sometimes great swaths of park land with woods and their own lakes. No matter how much work was involved, it all seemed unbelievable.

There was a contact address and I decided email to find out more. But what should I say? I felt the need to come across as a serious investor otherwise I'd never get a reply. I would have to make it up. So I wrote some catch-all but experienced-sounding crap about being a member of a consortium that had identified Germany as a target for the expansion of its portfolio of operations. Could I please be sent more information on the process, some photos, prices and a map locating the properties advertised?

For a few days I didn't hear a thing and assumed that my email must have betrayed my lack of serious intent. But one afternoon I plucked up the courage to call and demand a response.

A cheerful middle-aged woman called Martine answered the phone in typical 'howdy' style and proceeded to be very friendly and helpful, blurring the line in that American way between positive and gullible. Maintaining my investor persona, I spoke with her at some length. I was curious about this distant embassy of Germany in California. It turned out that she and her husband had both been born in Germany but their families had emigrated to America after the war. They obviously had a touch of *Heimweh*.

Martine apologised for her inefficiency and promised to send me the information I had asked for. She also recommended that if we (my consortium, that is) was serious we should organise a week of visits to some of the properties that were of interest.

About a week later a large pack of floor plans, photographs and other details arrived in the post. Included was a commentary with suggestions of what each of some twenty properties would be suited for when renovated: a spa, a hotel, a B&B. I did a double take. There were some amazing and beautiful places here, albeit in a state of decay or outright ruin. In Britain they would have been long since bought up by developers or the National Trust. Was I completely out of my depth? Surely these castles would cost a bomb just to purchase, let alone do up. But then my jaw dropped again. Even if the renovation costs were north of seven figures – they were talking about fancy hotels and spas – to simply purchase some of these castles and their land cost a relative pittance. It wasn't as if I had that kind of cash to spare but for a fairytale castle it seemed incredibly cheap. Surely that couldn't be right. I was verging on excited.

With the pack were details of proposed travel arrangements should I 'and my associates' wish to organise some viewings. It seemed as if Living Space had some form of fixer on the ground in Germany called Herr Ortlieb. And he was expensive. Martine had laid out a presumptuous itinerary for a week. It included a daily consultancy fee for viewing the properties, covering the costs of Herr Ortlieb's food, drink and petrol and – it came across as obligatory – overnighting in his own renovated castle. Just the pleasure of viewing ten or so properties over a week involved an outlay of about a grand. Could Germany afford to be so exclusive? I decided to send a robust but aloof response in the voice of my new-found property developer *Doppelgänger*. I referred to an impending business visit during which I would have some time for some viewings, but added that I would have many other business engagements and so it would be better for me to be flexible.

It so happened that I was due to be in Berlin again within the month and might be able to wing it for little or no outlay and without losing face.

The trouble was, even I was now beginning to take myself seriously. I had begun to kid myself I could really own one of these castles. It had gone beyond the joke of whether anyone would ever want to own a piece of Germany to an idea which was taking on a frightening reality. I was at that stage in life when I felt I ought to be doing something different, entrepreneurial and fun. 'Enough nine-to-five and drawing a salary from someone else,' my new Romantic side said to me. 'Do something different for and by yourself.' Clearly I couldn't afford it on my own but running a bar or club was the kind of thing I'd often talked about with friends. Why not a castle instead?

I mentioned my plan to a few of them and it was met first with derision, then amusement and finally a measure of intrigue. On some level, like me, they were struck by the idea, especially after a few beers. So they all wanted me to go and have a look and report back. But they also asked, 'What do you want the castle for? Are you planning on moving to Germany or is this some kind of holiday operation or second home? What's the proposition?' Damn the proposition, I thought. That was that USP, target-market brand-speak Manny had tried to drum out of me. I was letting myself be carried away by the idea. Where was their romance? But they had a point. I was bound to be asked at some stage, so I'd better have a story prepared.

Living Space came back with Herr Ortlieb's direct details. They had contacted him and he had confirmed he was available to take me round various properties in the Berlin–Leipzig–Dresden triangle over five days in February. He was now expecting confirmation from me.

Five days looking at ruined castles! I wasn't a serious developer and had no idea what I was talking about. I wouldn't know what clever questions to ask or anything about one castle's structural suitability for one use as against another.

I wrote to Herr Ortlieb and explained that the week I was

coming I was 'exceedingly booked up with important engagements' but that I would have an afternoon and a morning. I
would have a car to drive us around in, so there was no need to
concern himself with transport for me, but I would be delighted
to stay one night in his *Schloss*. '*Alles klar*,' came the response
and we arranged to speak once I was in Berlin.

Köpenick was once a beautiful lakeside village full of bridges,
spires and elegant old civic and residential buildings. Nowadays
it was a beautiful suburb in the south-east of Berlin but it had
retained its villagey, slow-paced atmosphere and was a favourite
waterside weekend retreat of metropolitan Berliners, a little like
Richmond in London. But Köpenick also held a special place in
German folklore as the home of the legend of Der Hauptmann
von Köpenick, the Captain from Koepenick.

   Once upon a time, or more precisely in 1906, there was an
old cobbler from Berlin named Wilhelm Voigt who committed a
crime and was sent to prison. On his release and in order to get
a job he needed a passport. But without a job he couldn't get a
passport. Voigt persisted but his attempts were in vain and he
was expelled from Berlin for his efforts. One day Voigt found a
discarded Prussian captain's uniform in a second-hand shop, put
it on and, having done so, assumed the rank of *Hauptmann* in
the eyes of his fellow Prussians. Somehow he managed to take
command of a detail of soldiers and with them he marched into
Köpenick and stormed the town hall in search of the passport
office and a passport. There he created a forged warrant for the
mayor's arrest and had the soldiers seize him, and, to cap it all,
there being no passport office in the town hall, he made off with
four thousand marks from the town treasury. Voigt was soon
arrested and after a two-day trial sentenced to four years in
prison. But it was too late. He had already become a folk hero
and even the Kaiser (Willy II) was munificent enough to halve
his jail term.

In 1931 the tale of Voigt was made into a stage play by Carl Zuckmayer – he described it as *'ein deutsches Märchen'*, 'a German fairytale' – and in 1956 it was made into a film. Thus it passed into German popular culture.

Why was this important? Because Voigt's tomfoolery exposed a tendency among Prussians to elevate respect for a man's uniform above the man himself. *'Kleider machen Leute'*, 'clothes make the man', was a German saying (although where that left the nudists was not clear). Der Hauptmann von Köpenick was a very German case of 'the cobbler's new clothes'. Wilhelm II was the Kaiser who made Prussia synonymous with the military state (whereas his predecessors, all of them Freddies and Willies, were liberal and patrons of the arts) and who took Germany into the Great War.

It did not take long, especially as another war followed some two decades later, for this story of a love of uniform to be known globally and for it to be widely assumed that this propensity was endemic in the German people. I had always carried around a notion about Germans and uniform, whether in the office or the bedroom. And travelling around Germany recently I had seen numerous examples. *Lederhosen* were a type of uniform designed to perpetuate a Bavarian myth of nationhood; the fairytale pageants and carnival costumes were uniforms designed to incarnate the origins of German nationhood; and uniform was an illusion just like one of the fairytales, and could be childish, escapist and kitsch too, like a child in fancy dress. Uniform was also figurative in Germany. It applied to the verbal dress code that restrained a sense of humour in the workplace despite the private funny man within. And even FKK reduced humans to their most uniform.

Here I was in Berlin about to meet a businessman whose business was the trading and multi-million-euro restoration of castles, and who thought I was a serious and experienced property developer. I had been deemed a good use of his time. And so, mindful of the Captain from Köpenick's ability to command undeserved respect through uniform, I was wearing a suit.

It was a cold and snowy Tuesday morning when I met Herr Ortlieb outside the offices of his Berlin solicitor. We had spoken twice briefly by phone and he had been short and to the point. I was expecting someone tall, quick and busy, like the frenetic factory boss from a Heinrich Böll short story. Eastern Europe was full of gold-digging entrepreneurs, sitting pretty since the tide had changed. Siegfried Ortlieb would probably be one of these or at the very least a man in a snappy, square-cut, very German suit.

Instead the man who got into my Golf and shook my hand warmly was a diminutive, fit but ageing man in his late fifties, balding and greying, with slightly watery eyes, and a Prussian down-turned white moustache that conveyed the impression that he was always sad and reflective. There was no briefcase, just a leather satchel stuffed with rather chaotic papers. And no suit, just a simple shirt and jumper under a rather bulky overcoat. To judge by his clothes, as Voigt was judged, he was more schoolmaster than property tycoon.

We greeted each other and agreed we should get out of the city and on to the right road before getting down to business. We were running late and someone was already waiting for us at the first property. Siegfried directed me this way and that but otherwise we drove more or less in silence until we were in the suburbs of East Berlin, where the border between city and countryside blurred and apartment blocks and shops were separated by huge fields, expanses of *Schrebergarten* and patches of untended grassland.

Stopping for a roadside sausage, we got talking and I was about to unleash my whole spiel. I had rehearsed it many times, thinking I was going to be grilled. But Siegfried seemed like a gentle rural soul, almost bumbling, and so I took a more informal and friendly tack.

I told Siegfried that I was one of a group of five people who had various interests outside their work and were looking to invest together in a significant commercial venture. We had identified Germany as an untapped property market. Not only that, Germany and in particular East Germany was an unexploited leisure market, unknown to most British people and yet our research told us it was also a dynamic, young place. Using my new-found knowledge of the German *Zeitgeist*, I discussed the example of Berlin. I added that, given the British tradition of city breaks, long weekends and multiple annual holidays, we had decided German castles represented a commercial opportunity.

But what exactly? Well, this was where I summoned the disparate fruits of my therapy to date. We were not looking to run some form of B&B or hip hotel, I said. That was boring and had been done before, even if not necessarily in this area. I had been doing a lot of research into Germany and the German way of life and had seen that the country would meet perfectly the needs of a travel-jaded public forever seeking new, unique and trendy destinations.

Listen to that! Manny would be overjoyed. I spoke of how in particular I had come across a number of traditions we felt would appeal to British visitors and German locals alike. I spoke of the German tradition of the spa and exercise that I had witnessed first-hand with such pleasure and how spas and wellness weekends were a big thing in the UK. I mentioned fine German cuisine that was as yet little known, and of the Baltic Coast and other parts of the former East Germany that were equally undiscovered and therefore something of a holy grail. I said that many young single people as well as young couples were visiting Berlin and enjoying its party scene and cutting-edge culture. So basically we were looking to set up a hotel-cum-bar-nightclub with trendy German cuisine, a hot dance scene, a cool lounge-type bar and by day a spa centre and a base for outdoor activities. It was as simple as that really. And offering guests all this in a converted and renovated *Schloss* was the icing on the cake.

And how about a bit of FKK thrown in, I thought to myself. Saxony's tourist office was plugging its region with the slogan 'Be a Saxist'. Well, I was doing my best. And if the turnover of Pasha was to be believed, it paid. I imagined an episode of *A Place in the Sun*: 'Hello, everybody and welcome to tonight's show, in which we meet the group of London boys who jacked it all in to set up a hip hotel-cum-brothel in Germany!'

I quite impressed myself. It was a good spiel. No! It was more than that: it was a great idea!

Siegfried just nodded as I bolted on each detail. If he thought I was some kind of joker he didn't betray it. It turned out he was an architect and his preoccupations were more practical. Had we considered what size of property we were looking for? Ah, yes, *Grossmannsucht*. Big. Definitely big. Then he rattled off a series of logistical questions about location and budget to which I played a straight bat. It was really just a preliminary reconnaissance trip and I would be discussing everything 'with my associates'. I mentioned a few of the castles that had caught my fancy in the pack Martine had sent me. They were all ones with follies and towers and turrets of some sort. A simple manor house would never do. Maybe my tastes had become those of a Premiership footballer after all!

After a drive of about forty-five minutes we arrived at the first property, which was at the end of the overland commuter line to East Berlin, in a place called Dahlwitz-Hoppegarten. Siegfried hadn't been able to find it at first and we'd taken several wrong turnings. But now we were there.

The town seemed pretty God-forsaken, reeking of the neglect of forty years of East German government. Eighteenth- and nineteenth-century villas stood side by side with ill-judged Communist urban planning projects. Lots of houses seemed boarded up or covered in graffiti and the village-cum-suburb was full of underfunded, dilapidated communal facilities.

Nor was the property we'd come to view exactly a castle. It was set back from the road but without a driveway from which to have a sense of approach and grandeur. It was a fine shell of a building, with two long wings on either side of an entrance complete with columns and pediment. It was on two floors, with an all-important tower, and stood in some hundred acres of land. Yet there was something about the proportions that didn't seem right. It felt as if it should have been much bigger and yet the architectural detail was full of grandiose gestures of *Grossmannsucht* that outgrew the actual building. All the windows were covered with the depressing metal grids of a house that's been repossessed.

A man in blue overalls greeted us and took us inside. He told us something of the history of the building. Originally the manor house for a member of the local aristocracy, the building had been seized by the East German government and turned into a primary school for young pioneers (as the Communists called their red-scarved disciples). As we looked around the peeling, dank walls and tried to imagine the cries and shrieks of joy of rowdy children having fun it all seemed very macabre. It was a spooky place and I didn't have any burning desire to ask the questions that would befit a property developer. I took a few underexposed pictures in the gloomy winter light and we got back in the car.

We were now going to head south-east in the direction of Dresden. It was about one o'clock and with the winter light we would have time to see about five or six other properties before darkness fell.

In silence we passed through a flat landscape of ploughed fields interrupted only by copses of wood and the occasional farm and country house and then joined Germany's newest and most deserted autobahn, which seemed to be a ribbon of tarmac carved through an unending sandy pine forest.

Eventually we found ourselves on the undulating country roads of Saxony, gliding round picturesque bends through mixed woodland, open meadowland and little hamlets of half-timbered houses, model-railway stations, windmills, windfarms and intertwining lakes and rivers. There was hardly a modern building in site, no factories, no ill-judged urban planning. Like the Baltic hinterland, it was an untainted, rural landscape, almost a time warp back to the nineteenth century. Even in winter, with patchy, dirty snow, it was every bit as beautiful as the Loire and I could imagine what all these trees and meadows would look like in spring, summer and autumn. And, like the Loire, it was full of chateaux.

Possessing a grand, curved drive leading up to a stylish, baroque entrance with a columned archway and lots of twiddly decorations, Baruth Castle was a real *Schloss*. From the front, a yellowy sandstone baroque façade fronting three or four floors of large, high-ceilinged reception rooms, ballrooms and bedrooms, the castle went back in three sections that had been added at different times and in different styles. To the left were an orangery, stables and a gardener's outhouse and to the right a tumbling down timber bridge and an elevated walkway leading to the nearby village with its church and town hall. The grounds, which had a lake and plenty of woodland, stretched agreeably into the distance. Detached, grandiose and perfectly proportioned, Schloss Baruth had all the air and style of the local lord's residence. At a pauper's price.

The trouble was, Baruth was officially in the middle of nowhere. We were about an hour and a half from Berlin and the tiny village had absolutely no public transport other than a local bus. I couldn't see a B&B, let alone anything else. The village had a few thousand inhabitants at most, and most of them old. A nightclub or lounge bar disturbing their *Gemütlichkeit* was the last thing they wanted on their doorstep.

It was the same problem in the rest of eastern Germany as I had encountered on the Baltic coast. For all that Berlin, Dresden and Leipzig were touted as dynamic cities, there was still basically no money in the east and not many jobs. And that meant there was a big problem with *Auswanderung*, emigration. I had seen the bored youth in deserted town squares in Mecklenburg-Vorpommern on my summer holiday. Even Berlin was bankrupt and haemorrhaging investors. And now Siegfried confirmed that, despite the tourist board's label of 'Silicon Saxony', this supposed regeneration had as yet not had a noticeable effect on people's disposable income.

Siegfried quoted the example of a project called Tropical Parks, a kind of low-cost Center Parcs for poor easterners who could not afford to join their better-off compatriots in Mallorca. Some bright entrepreneur had attempted to convert a former factory space into a seaside fantasyland slap in the middle of the Saxon forest, with giant hangars full of sand and *Strandkörber* to fight over. It sounded like twenty-first-century *Kraft durch Freude*. But after some initial excitement and novelty value the project was apparently failing. People in this region simply didn't have the money to spend on such frivolity.

Siegfried was a West German, an architect by trade who had recently become interested in German history, and in particular in the history of heritage houses in the east of the country. He had bought and renovated a castle, where we were to spend the night, and which he now ran as a small-scale B&B. In the course of this project, which had taken several years, he had learnt a lot about the process and got to know many important people who could pull this or that string.

Living Space was run by his cousin, an American whose father had emigrated to California, and Siegfried had positioned himself as the company's agent, being the only person who knew what properties were potentially for sale, who all the local dignitaries and officials were, who still controlled most of them, and what subsidies could be arranged.

The East German government had lacked the time, the money and the inclination to keep its *Schlösser* in order. Often these were viewed as a symbol of capitalism, social elitism and an aristocratic past that needed to be stamped out. Many castles and manor houses that had been handed down through generations and generations had been seized by the state and the family owners driven out, only for the properties to be left to fall into disrepair. The government of the reunited Germany initially poured money into the east, often to the resentment of West Germans who were suffering competition for jobs in a faltering economy, to restore the neglected national heritage. The rush of money had now slowed and the business of subsidies had become much more selective. Some mayors and councils didn't want any more hotels, while others did because they attracted jobs and tourism to the area. As far as Siegfried was aware, no council in the east had ever been approached about a castle-brothel.

If only I could raise a million euros, I thought to myself as we visited the other castles. Beate Uhse would have done it in her sleep. By now I had lost all sense of reality and proportion. I wanted to own a piece of German castle, just for the fun of it, but perhaps I'd also see the value appreciate. Sod my associates and the bar-nightclub venture. Maybe I could convince my wife we really ought to move to Saxony and run a quaint, eco-B&B in a castle in some German version of *The Good Life*!

That afternoon I saw six more castles, ranging from former Prussian barracks that were too forbidding and laid out around a parade ground, via a run-down tacky hotel and golf course, to a beautiful, tall manor house with stables and a beautiful lake with lilies and swans. By this time it was dark and impossible to view any more properties. Besides, I was castled out. Each place had its own qualities and it was hard to find fault with any of the buildings for pure elegance and grandiosity. It was simply incredible that there were so many such properties just crying out for care, investment and ownership. I had no idea what to do next, but I was convinced I was on to something.

Before we headed for his own castle retreat, Siegfried suggested a stop in Meissen, home of the famous hand-painted porcelain. He had clicked out of business mode and was keen to tell me more about Saxony. Through his own castle endeavours he had clearly discovered a passion for social history and this part of the world.

Meissen reminded me of Marburg, where I had set off on the Fairytale Route. Rising steeply up from the banks of the River Elbe, it was a town of cobbled streets lined with crooked half-timbered houses whose beams sagged with the strains of the centuries. From a deserted restaurant at the top of the town we looked out over the twinkling lights, which were just being turned on as the late-afternoon light faded. Over a well-deserved glass of local Elbe valley *Grauburgunder* white wine I listened to Siegfried's story.

It was a piece of German history, the other side of the coin, that, as far as I was aware, was not often told.

Siegfried's family were originally from Silesia, a German region that once encompassed land that now belongs variously to Germany, Poland and the Czech Republic. Silesia had become part of Prussia in the eighteenth century and the overwhelming ethnic majority, among Czechs, Poles and a Slavic-German people called the Sorbians who still existed in a twilight ethnic pocket in the Spreewald near Berlin, was always German. After the First World War it became one of the most hotly contested parts of Europe owing to its ethnic mix and the designs all neighbouring countries had on it. There were many uprisings and battles and in the end the region was divided up. In the process Germany had relinquished its rule over a large part of it and Hitler's attempt to reannex it to regain German *Lebensraum* was the opening move of the Second World War. At the end of the war in 1945, as part of a Polish backlash against Germany, over four million of its civilians were forcibly expelled from Silesia, several thousands of them on the ill-fated KdF ship, the *Wilhelm Gustloff*, that I had learnt about on my Baltic holiday, and many thousands were brutally massacred.

Siegfried's family was caught up in this bloody episode. His father was a survivor of Stalingrad and in 1945 his family had been evicted from Silesia. So, shortly after the war, Siegfried was born in West Germany, instead of in his original *Heimat*, which was now Polish. He had grown up always knowing that there was a part of his family history in Poland. But his father had refused to ever go back and Siegfried – were those eyes a little more watery now as he spoke? – told me he didn't think he would ever go. Through so many decades of Soviet isolation it had been an impossibility and he had got used to the idea of never seeing his family seat. But when the Wall came down, there it was all of a sudden, confronting him as a real possibility. Yet still he had not been able to bring himself to go back. Instead he had exorcised this urge by focusing on the land that was still Germany and living his own family heritage vicariously through the similar stories of others. The same fate had befallen the wider Ortlieb family and friends, among them his cousin Herman, who had emigrated and grown up in California and now ran Living Space with his wife, Martine.

The East German government had repossessed aristocratic houses such as theirs and now that the government no longer existed, Living Space undertook the rewarding detective work on behalf of others. In 1990 the government of the newly reunified Germany had decreed that families who had fled the east in the 1950s and early 1960s could stake no claim on any houses or land they or their families had lived in four decades earlier. That was why there was so much property around now, ready to be bought. There were probably hundreds of families whose ancestral manor house or *Schloss* was now up for sale to the likes of me or some Japanese developer who would turn it into a hotel or even a brothel. The only thing families could claim were objects and artefacts. Always assuming they could be found. But trying to trace your family gold, Kandinsky original or crown jewels was almost impossible and instead there was a thriving black market in art and artefacts that the state had declared up for grabs.

I had not been expecting this almost uninterrupted stream. Siegfried had something of the evangelism and urgency of Manny. It was as if he didn't often meet people to tell of his enthusiasm for German history. And sadness. For in his own family's story there was a hint, not of bitterness, but of injustice and real hurt. I also sensed a nostalgia for the mores of an East Germany that was less materialist and less individualistic and had a greater sense of society. I thought about my suit, how I had prepared myself for the day and the person I'd expected to be dealing with, and felt guilty. The salesman I had pictured was quite a contrast with the old man with watery eyes, father of one and more school teacher than businessman, who sat in front of me now.

Siegfried told me how Saxony had once been the cradle of Germany, the real powerhouse of German culture, and the epi-centre of what it meant to be German, engaged in a constant battle of one-upmanship with Prussia. According to him, every-thing that was truly German spread south and west from its origins in Saxony. Not just the traditions of music and the arts, which had their heart in the Leipzig of Bach and Schumann, home of Auerbach's Keller, where the original Faust danced with the devil and where Goethe set his *magnum opus*. But also expertise in finance and industry. The Dresdner Bank and the Deutsche Bank, two global giants of finance, both had their ori-gins in Saxony. Johann Bottger invented the European porcelain industry and perfected it in the hand-painted masterpieces of

Meissen with their famous emblem of crossed blue swords. August Horch had invented the Audi (a Latin translation of his name, meaning 'listen') and made Zwickau the car capital of Europe, outstripping Mercedes. The union symbolised by the four-ring emblem of his firm then went on to produce the iconic Trabant.

Travelling around Saxony I saw that despite the deserted countryside the cities were without doubt rediscovering their creative edge and place at the heart of European culture. The façades of its towns were returning from grey to their shades of yellow and rose pastel, and ruined buildings were being given a facelift and a new lease of life and purpose. There was no greater symbol of this renaissance than the reopening of the Frauenkirche, the Church of Our Lady, in Dresden, the St Peter's of the Protestant world, in the city they once called 'Florence on the Elbe'. The church had been pieced together stone by stone, with the meticulousness of an Audi engineer, and on top of its dome had been placed a golden cross made by a British silver-smith son of one of the bombers who had scorched it and the city in the dying days of the Second World War. The Frauenkirche and its cross were a symbol of reconciliation, of *Selbstwahrnehmung* and the reunification of an extravagant baroque city, second-favourite subject of Canaletto, who was court painter here for twenty years, with its gritty twentieth-century history.

South and east of Dresden lay 'Saxon Switzerland' and the oneiric land of Lusatia, a world of strange, bulbous sandstone formations similar to the limestone stalagmites I had discovered in Franconia east of Bayreuth. It was a hiker's paradise of *Wanderwege* that led through river valleys and rock formations with waterfalls, interspersed with smoking little hamlets with cosy pubs. And of course the narrow-gauge steam-railway with-out which no German landscape would be complete.

It was Siegfried's dream to make this part of the world more widely known and appreciated. Where had I heard that before? His castle B&B was part of an organisation rather like the Landmark Trust, that brought together renovated castles in order to offer tourists the chance to stay in history-laden resting points on a join-the-dots tour of Germany. I recalled how I had scoffed at the idea of a book on *Charming Hotels of Germany* when I'd first found it in Manny's therapy pack. But here was something of an altogether different calibre. It portrayed Germany in a sexy – should that be 'Saxy'? – and seductive light. I didn't see why Germany, and in particular Saxony, couldn't become the next Loire or Dordogne.

It was eight o'clock and dark when we arrived at Siegfried's castle. We had driven into the sunset along the banks of the Elbe, on a road winding through villages that were laid out along the river as if on the coast. They were full of cafés and gardens and I could see that in summer they would have a Mediterranean holiday atmosphere. Above and behind these villages lay vineyards.

Siegfied's Schloss was a seventeenth-century castle in its own grounds on the edge of a tiny village. It was a fine building: a typically solid German country house with huge slabs of wall and small windows. I could see immediately that it had been perfectly, almost too perfectly, restored. The stonework was covered in that smooth white cladding that I had seen all over Germany and which contributed to making the house look slightly fake. Added to this, Siegfried had painted the window frames an odd bright red. But apparently this was how it would originally have looked.

Inside it was no less immaculate. A stairway of beautiful smooth flagstone led up to the main hallway, which was furnished like an antiques shop, with cupboards, sideboards and corner chairs from various periods, oriental carpets, swords, boars' heads and portraits of people who had nothing to do with the castle but looked seventeenth-century. You couldn't fault Siegfried's effort and dedication to history. If you were going to raise 1.5 million euros and spend years of your life renovating a castle, you couldn't fill it with furniture from Ikea.

Siegfried showed me up to my room on the first floor; or rooms as it turned out. An antechamber, kitchenette and huge bedroom, provided with various incongruous period furnishings of dubious comfort and painted in a childish pastel blue as if it were a nursery. I half-expected to find a bedpan instead of a bathroom. The kitchenette was at odds with the rest of the minute restoration work; more like one in a ski chalet set-up. But, according to Siegfried, that was what most of his guests wanted. He didn't normally lay on supper and guests liked to be self-sufficient, especially as there were precious few restaurants or pubs nearby. The area was obviously crying out for a bar-resto run by Brits!

At the top of the red-carpeted stairs was a landing in the corner of which stood two waxwork figures leaning over a desk at which sat a third poised to sign a document. They were dressed as Prussian soldiers in full military regalia. I pointed at them and Siegfried explained proudly that they had been set up there for a festival day in the village, when he had opened up the castle to the public and the local council had put on an exhibition of local Prussian-era history. When was the exhibition? I asked. It had been last summer. Eight months later Siegfried still hadn't dismantled the exhibit. If you were Siegfried's wife you'd really have to love Prussian history, or a bit of uniform. I couldn't help thinking it was a bit weird.

Siegfried's wife had laid on a filling supper of soup, cold meats, cheeses and salad with some fantastic fresh pumpernickel bread. I was tired after so much looking and listening and made it known as politely as I could, then retired to bed with dreams of a *Schloss* in Saxony

It wasn't as if I needed any more *Lebensraum* than I already had but a small entrepreneurial part of my brain told me it made sense. Germany was as untouched in the property market as it was in travel. Saxony had a rich social and cultural history combined with fun-loving and creative cities looking to the future. It had pristine, intriguing and vast landscapes that were every bit as idyllic as those of other countries that were more common currency. It may not have had olive groves or lemon trees but it had vineyards and local breweries aplenty. I had to hurry . . .

The following morning I meandered across a frozen landscape dusted with overnight snow, a dot against a vast, cold blue sky. I felt uplifted, invigorated and moved both by Siegfried and this strange country I had travelled with and befriended over the past few months. Something told me I had unfinished business here and that didn't necessarily mean the purchase of the *Schloss* after which I now hankered. Maybe this was *Sehnsucht* at last: an all-Romantic and all-German longing?

13

Wanderlust

nm, *the joy of travel*

(lit. walking love)

The Germans referred to the reunification of their country as *die Wende*, the turning point. Well, since I had met Manny, my travel doctor, and undertaken his course of travel rehab I had experienced something of a *Wende* of my own in relation to Germany and was no longer willing to be beastly to its folk. And, as a useful side-effect, where until recently I had been a case of wonder lost, I was now a case of *Wanderlust* regained.

I had always considered Germany part of 'old Europe'. And in American terms it was. But now I knew it was actually one of the youngest European nations. What's more I had known almost nothing about these eighty-three million people living almost next door to me at the heart of Europe, and couldn't even have picked out their country's silhouette on a map. And yet somehow Germany had always loomed so large, not just militarily but also in terms of the arts, literature and philosophy, as if it had in fact existed for all the millennia Germans believe and would have others believe. For that reason, like Germans themselves, I had always expected so much of Germany. But I'd always found it wanting. And equally, influenced by the bland, humourless caricature, I had also expected so little of Germany. And still I'd found it wanting, just the same. It was a lose-lose situation.

Now Manny had sent me not so much on a tour of Germany as on a tour of the German soul and through the *Spiegelwand* (mirror wall) of ideas, loves, desires and obsessions of which it was composed. Not only had I found myself reappraising my view of Germany but, in doing so, I had confronted my prejudices and was supposed now to have a renewed, re-enchanted outlook on life itself. I had, after all, discovered the art of being German and now knew that Germany was in fact the best country in the world!

It hadn't been an easy reunion, rather like Germany's two halves making up after decades of estrangement. But supposedly I had relearnt the original wild and boundless meaning of Romance and got back in touch with my Romantic side. I had learnt to fall in love again and should now be as newly inspired with *Sehnsucht* for Germany's beautiful rivers, lakes, mountains and forests as for the rest of the world. I had seen Germany as new again, a country of sun, sand, beach baskets and islands. And I could now appreciate the health and philosophical benefits of nudism and knew better than to give in to the weakness for bikinis and to respect the human body as a philosophical object. I had not had to fight Germans on the beaches. Instead I had joined them in their spas, on their bicycles, walks, exercise routines and even in their brothels in the daily German quest for purity and *Gesundheit*. I owned a pair of *Lederhosen* and was a convert to leather, if not to German fashion.

I had laughed a lot at, but also with, Germans, occasionally tickled by a sense of humour that I now knew lurked somewhere in every German's closet. I had discovered a rolled-back German state of tolerance, and an all-inclusive, inoffensive and slightly witless party spirit they called *Gemütlichkeit*. And in places I had even uncovered a renascent German popular culture finally making up for sixty lost years and at the tipping point of cool. Indeed Germany, I now knew from Manny, had been responsible for everything from musical harmony to film noir to the design that surrounded me. It just wasn't very widely reported. Being a German-style eco-warrior was now cool, as was having an allotment like Germany's *Schrebergarten*.

I could now appreciate the finer points of German bread, sausage and beer – even German wine – and Germany's extensive re-emerging regional and 'delicate' cuisine. For Germany had a regional variety and an enviable sense of local cultures and traditions I had little suspected. I had even learnt to love the German language as powerful and expressive of something other than military orders and porn-movie dialogue (or a combination of the two), and now had an impressive list of German concept words I could deploy at dinner parties to sound cool. And most of all I now understood German technological excellence, not as the dry pursuit of science but as the passionate search for absolute perfection and harmony, the Romantic tantalus of tortured, deep-thinking souls. And because the world so often fell short I had found a country contrived out of fantasy and where the spirit of childish wonder and illusion was alive and well. My wife loved it and even wanted to send our son to the German school in Ham. She just drew the line at facial hair.

I quite fancied myself as an original Romantic. OK, I was rubbish at science and had never set eyes on what lay beneath a car bonnet but I could do the kitsch and the childish idealism very well and willingly. I reckoned there was a bit of Ludwig II in everyone.

The German Ambassador would be pleased too. I had even learnt some German history and discovered a country wrought not by an Iron Chancellor but, among others, by a monk, a nudist, a gardener, a poet, a PE teacher, a *Bademeister*, two sibling fantasists and a porn queen. Luther, Jahn, Kneipp, Schreber, Uhse and the rest of them had combined to create the Froebel building blocks on which the German nation was founded. Germany was not Hitler or the Third Reich. It was Mother Nature, nudism, gardening, sex, exercise, hygiene, spas, beer, bread, sausages and Protestantism.

Best of all there were no other tourists. And in its new light as an undiscovered corner of the globe – though not quite a Shangri-La – that fact alone was possibly enough to make it cool and an unexpected ace at the Condé Nast poker table. Briefly I had delirious visions of a dinner party in a post-*Selbstwahrnehmung* world: the wine has changed from Sancerre to Riesling and the host has served up a trendy potato and apple purée topped with onion and bacon. 'It's a speciality from northern Germany. It means "Heaven and Earth". Rather beautiful, don't you think?' Meanwhile the winner of the iPod war shouts out, 'Listen to this. I was surfing around on iTunes and came across this beautiful German jazz-folk singer.' And of course everyone is naked in accordance with a new German life-coaching trend that is doing the rounds.

When the conversation turns to travel I'm feeling pretty pleased with my hand. Forget the safari in Mozambique and dog-sledding past the Northern Lights; and even the couple who went on a 'walking and wellness' retreat in central Germany: pretty *Zeitgeist* these days. 'Well, we've just bought a rambling old Saxon *Schloss* in a hundred acres outside Leipzig,' I boast. 'It needs a lot of work but we're going to move to Germany, do it up and make our own *Elbwein*.' Nods all round of trumped appreciation. That'll be a full house, then.

OK, it was a little unlikely. But one thing was sure: I had only scratched the surface and, in the closing words of *Cabaret*, it was definitely a case of '*Auf Wiedersehen, à bientôt*'. And that too was surely a victory for the Fatherland.

14

Weltmeister

nm, world champion(s)

(lit. world master)

Before checking out with Manny I found myself in Germany independently of his course of therapy. It was a good opportunity to see what cultural learnings held true without being directed in one way or another by one of his 'modules'.

Leaving aside the largely forgettable football, the 2006 *Weltmeisterschaft* (World Cup) which Germany hosted was a fascinating moment in German history.

Since 1966 football had been the prism through which England saw Germany. Ever since then the salient points of England's international football near-misses were a story of three bouts of extra time and penalties, all against Germany. So it was a good opportunity to test my new-found appreciation of the country.

But it was an issue for Germany too. Ever since 1954, when West Germany (courtesy of the invention of screw-on studs by a certain Adi Dassler, who would go on to found Adidas) won the competition at their first attempt in the so-called 'Miracle of Berne', football had been an expression of Germany's post-war uneasy nationhood. The victory was the first time after the war that Germans had felt a sense of being a nation again. Yet even in victory they did not allow themselves to flag-wave and celebrate.

Now Germany was the host nation and trying to be loved by everyone in a bid to change cultural stereotypes. But Germans would also be wanting to be patriotic in support of their own team. Could this be a watershed? What would happen?

Well, a rare spike in visitor numbers for a start. Plus all the predictable tabloid xenophobia in Britain. The largest invasion of German soil by the English since the Second World War was always going to be a big test of recidivist tendencies and Anglo-German diplomacy.

Sven weighed in early with a plea to fans not to sing their beloved 'Ten German Bombers' to the tune of 'Ten Green Bottles' on the terraces. The BBC ran a competition for alternative songs and lyrics that could be sung without causing offence and was rewarded with 'Jürgen has only got one Ballack' and 'Everybody wants to rule the world'. And Martin Peters, a hero of the '66 squad, sponsored a line of T-shirts that depicted RAF wartime bombing raids on Germany and images of Churchill giving the 'V for Victory' salute. Fans could also download to their phones tabloid-sponsored ringtones of snippets of war songs and Churchill's speeches. And when the German government announced it would deploy a few thousand German soldiers to assist the police if matters got out of hand (as in Stuttgart they inevitably did), for the *Sun* it was like a red rag to, well, a red rag. 'Britskrieg' ran the headline above a scaremongering article suggesting that England fans would be attacked in the streets by Panzer divisions.

In a counter-move the German Tourist Board enlisted the help of Germany's arch football enemy Geoff Hurst (he of the crucial 'of course it crossed the line' goal in the '66 final). 'They thought it was all over . . . but it was just the start of my love affair with Germany,' ran the posters on the London Underground;

'Germany. I had a ball. You will too'; and 'Germany. You can't beat it for a short break.'

In an incredible turn of events it was Hurst versus Peters, all at the service of Germany!

The British Embassy website offered an enterprising lexicon of key football phrases in German to lubricate post-match analysis between English and German fans in the local *Kneipe* (pub). These ranged from the useful and technical, such as *abseits* (offside) and *Querpass* (square ball) to the proverbial and meaningless *der Ball ist rund* (it's a game of two halves), *Beinschuss* (nutmeg) and *ihm war kotübel* (he was sick as a parrot).

And the Goethe Institut tried its luck, offering specialist German lessons aimed at equipping fans for insulting the referee. '*Schiri, bist du blind?*' ('Oi, ref, are you blind?').

Despite all this preparatory work, what would the reality be on the ground?

Well, on the eve of the game against Sweden in Cologne I found a hundred or so England fans, against Sven's orders, jumping up and down, arms round one another's shoulders, singing 'Ten German Bombers' in front of groups of the *Polizei* in the square in front of the cathedral. The police sat around in cool, rather slovenly indifference, probably waiting for some real action.

And here was Claudia Schiffer draped in just a flowing black, red and gold German flag, *à la* Kate Moss, on page three of the *Bildzeitung*. It wasn't so many months before that I'd joked that I wasn't sure if I was ready for such a sight.

Could it be that Germany had finally felt free of the skeletons in its cupboard and able to proudly wave *die Fahne* (the flag) without incurring a barrage of tabloid abuse? Well, yes, apparently so. In Cologne, as all over the country, the German equivalent of 'white van man' (vite wan man) had as many plastic flags fixed to his car as the English did. For Germans, however, this was not merely the latest display of national loutishness, but a philosophical moment in time. Was this a watershed? they asked themselves. When the World Cup circus left town, would they still feel able to fly the flag?

The *Angst*-ridden patriotism showed through in the official anthem. German music had clearly not totally shaken off its cerebral heritage. FIFA had chosen one of Germany's ageing *Schlagermusik* heroes, Herbert Gronemeyer (who played the captain in *Das Boot* and then moved to London for the anonymity guaranteed to any German pop musician). In English it was 'Celebrate the Day', the same in French, '*Fêter la journée*', and, tapping into a bit of *Zeitgeist* West Africana, the tune was backed by the duo Amadou & Mariam. But in German it was called '*Zeit, dass sich was dreht*' ('Time for Something to Happen'). Here was that *Anspruch* again, complete with awkward reflexive verb. For Germans there was a subtext, that extra, more abstract, layer of thought. This was time, not just for kick-off but for Germany to get itself going and see life as a glass half full. In an interview with *Der Spiegel* magazine Gronemeyer drew parallels between the lyrics of his song and a poem, 'Herbsttag' (Autumn Day), by the Austrian lyric poet Rilke. I doubt the England fans saw any Keats in the English version.

Luckily, good things did happen. An unfancied German side had an unexpectedly good run, scored lots of goals with a multiracial side and played with positively Latin abandon and Brazilian expansiveness. I, like many England fans, even found myself supporting Germany later on in the competition, albeit because they were playing Argentina.

As I'd seen at the Oktoberfest, Germany showed it knew how to organise a good time on a grand scale and for a month the country became the party residence of the planet.

I went out to Cologne without a ticket for the match and, having watched the Germany–Ecuador afternoon game in one of the outdoor Fan Fest areas, declined the offer of an overpriced ticket from a Scouser tout for England's evening match against Sweden. The city's Fan Fest park lay on the bank of the Rhine looking back at the towers of the cathedral. It was a cordoned-off area the length of two football pitches to which entry was free. Inside were two swimming pool-sized screens, one at the end and one in the middle, and the usual convivial German mix of sausage stalls and beer tents. During the day, before and between matches there was a sound stage blasting out dance anthems as if it were some kind of carnival and relaying messages from the public on the tannoy. There was also plenty of space to chill out on the grass or play football, going through the motions of some unlikely England goal. And, naturally, a German large-scale approach to sanitation and recycling.

I watched the Germany–Ecuador game and was moved by the emotional rendition that thousands of Germany fans gave their national anthem. They were surrounded by England fans waiting for the evening game but everybody seemed to join in. Maybe by now I had black, red and gold-tinted glasses (and three eagles instead of lions on my shirt) but for a moment the whole Fan Fest area, England fans included, high on the fun the host country had laid on, joined the Germans in singing *'Deutschland, Deutschland über alles'*!

But the newspapers, as ever, sounded a note of caution and German introspection, taken by surprise at such guiltless patriotism. Perplexed, and as if denuded of the mantra of neurotic pessimism that had for so long given their life a purpose, they seemed to say, 'Surely it can't be?'

But perhaps the most eloquent example in all I had learnt about modern Germany was offered by the young German who had put me and my two friends up for two nights in his apartment. Booking at the last minute, I came across a website called host-a-fan.de, through which Germans in each of the host cities were offering rooms in their houses to visiting fans. An idea full of German pragmatism, plus a touch of ecology and the WG (*Wohngemeinschaft*) communal-living movement. Germany's World Cup slogan was '*Zu Gast bei Freunden*' (which conveyed the idea that visitors were among friends even if not on the same side) and Germany was taking it the whole way. As usual.

When I put out a request asking if anyone had room for three nice English fans (honest) my inbox was flooded with offers to the point that we could actually be picky about which German's *Lebensraum* we liked the look of from the webcam. Eventually we plumped for the apartment of one Oliver Dienhoff.

We turned up around nine o'clock in the evening, fully expecting to just drop our bags and head out on our own. We didn't want to be an encumbrance but, to be honest, that probably masked a typically English desire not to have any extra company tagging on. But oh no! Oliver had prepared a feast and we were welcomed to an amazing spread of beers, sausages and meats, over which we then proceeded to get to know each other. This was how a *Wohngemeinschaft* would work. Share your space and give to others. It was also exactly how 'ze host a fan' system was supposed to work! Oliver was an English teacher with typically *über*-impeccable English. He had recently split up with his boyfriend – hey, Germany, as I knew from Berlin and the Love Parade, was a *Zeitgeist* place – and was finding it hard to make ends meet and to pay the rent on his large flat. To be unkind, we were in effect his 'rent boys', albeit for a paltry twenty euros per person.

Oliver was a fantastic host. We stayed up chatting until the early hours and then the next morning we awoke to find he had left for work but laid out for *Frühstück* another huge spread of breads, meats and cheeses. We enjoyed this on his sun-drenched balcony and took full advantage of his apartment. He had a serious piece of German hi-fi equipment and, raiding his CD collection, soon had Kraftwerk waking up his neighbours. By now we felt like locals.

Oliver had said he would like to come and join us later. And so he duly turned up that evening in the Fan Fest area wrapped in the flag of St George that I had felt too embarrassed to wear and left on his sofa.

During World Cup 2006 Germany showed its true colours to the world, in many ways, for the first time. Never mind Italy, it was Germany as a nation that won the World Cup. As the German fans sang (in perfect English) football did come home. And Oliver was a microcosm and superb ambassador of his nation's rebirth as a sunny, fun-loving party land, yet one doggedly and sometimes ingenuously following the idea through to its absolute conclusion. Oliver would have wrapped himself in the Iranian flag had we been from Tehran.

15

Auf Wiedersehen

'And so that was how I grew to stop worrying and learn to love Germany.'

Mesmerised silence around the dinner table. The joker had become an ace – although in theory I was now above Condé Nast poker and my *Weltschmerz* was cured.

The eagle had landed. And derision had changed to the curiosity of one who does not want to be seen missing out on some new travel trend.

'Wow. *Vorsprung durch Deutschland*. Well I never!'

'*Deutschland über alles?* I want a travel makeover too!'

'Who was this guy again?'

'Where can I find one?'

Manny had started a whole new trend. But the truth was I didn't yet know who Manny was.

It was time to discharge myself. And pay the bill.

I went back to the offices of Infinity. But this time found no Renate and no symbolic pretzel and Villeroy & Boch cup of coffee to greet me. Instead there was just Manny in his office;

except this too had been packed up and stripped bare like a theatre denuded of its set. Gone were the water feature, the cinnamon scents and the Beethoven, as well as the leather padding, the desk and the pictures and framed quotations. The room was now white, echoey and bare. Manny sat there on a plastic chair under a lone, unshaded lightbulb.

He looked up and, ignoring my surprise, greeted me as an old friend proven right, quoting again from *Cabaret*.

'*Ver are your trubbelz now? Forgotten!*'

'But Manny. Where is . . .?'

'Herman. Please call me Herman.'

'What do you mean . . .?'

He paused, waiting for the penny to drop.

'Herman? Your name is Herman Heimway?'

He nodded and smiled, coolly.

Images and thoughts suddenly raced through my brain as I computed this revelation: the ageing-copper statue of Arminius, the original Herman and founder of the German people in the Teutoburger forest. It was quite common for Americans, who after all were like Germans and a nation made from disparate immigrant tribes, to change their names; in Manny's case to make it sound less German. Then there were the suspicious connections with the German Embassy. And as for the supposed syndrome? Well, wasn't Heimway just an American way of saying '*Heimweh*': homesickness? Had Manny suppressed his own German-ness while all the time he secretly pined for his *Heimat*? How suitably Freudian and German.

'You're German?'

Herman nodded.

'I was born in Germany.'

That explained the occasionally wayward grammar – those recurring present participles – to say nothing of the impeccable German accent and knowledge of fancy German words and quotes.

'Actually I believe you met a cousin of mine, Siegfried, in Saxony.'

Of course. Siegfried, who also seemed to pine for a lost homeland. Siegfried Ortlieb, which meant 'love of the place'! And hadn't he said that web-based real estate company, Living Space, was run by his cousin, Herman? Of course! 'Living Space' meant '*Lebensraum*'! And Martine?

'Martine is my wife.'

Herman was little more than a travel agent! But no, he was worse than that. Germany wasn't a cure. Otherwise it would have been Norway or something. There had been a hidden agenda all along.

'So the travel therapy, the *Weltschmerz*, your so-called Heimway Syndrome and the values of tourism: the whole thing was an illusion the whole time?'

For all I knew, the Infinity offices were normally some IVF clinic. Herman wasn't so much Freud as fraud.

'Not entirely. But I thought it was time to come clean.'

Typical German. Just like Günther Grass. And incapable of lying.

'And all the time you were duping me, all you wanted was some "Springtime for Germany"? "*Deutschland is on the rise again? Deutschland is happy and gay*"?' I shouted the lyrics from *The Producers* at him. 'I know. You're angry at the low esteem in which Germany, the homeland you secretly love and belong to, is held! And the constant *Cabaret* songs. "Tomorrow Belongs to Germany". Is that what you want to say, really?'

Manny composed himself, as I had seen him do so many times.

'Remember. Travel is the entertainment industry.'

I wasn't sure I had time for any more of his Californication.

'The dictatorship of the brand. Creating loyalty beyond reason. That is the aim of all countries in the propaganda war that is global tourism. Except Germany has been unable to brand itself. And so people have been tricked into not wanting to go to Germany. Yet, as you have seen, it has all the USPs and delivers all the customer benefits you could want! Health, humour, sun, fun, sex, food, fantasy, you name it!'

Herman had worked himself up into a lather again. The personality swings between clinical and impassioned, they were German too.

'On the basis of ridiculous pyramid theories, graphs and webs of jargon the American consultancy world has put together whole league tables of countries, like a FTSE-100 of nations or Nation-daq Index.'

Well, you've only got your ancestors to blame for that, I thought.

'I used to be one of these overpaid masturbation artists. But I was determined to prove them wrong, tear up all their theories. Heimway Syndrome may not be officially recognised yet, but I'll show them!'

I had been a pawn in a battle in the exciting world of bickering academics and psycho-consultants!

'To hell with the cool-hunters. I believe in Romance. Nothing more! I wanted you to see that the holy grail of travel *can* be applied to Germany.'

Herman's voice had crescendoed as if he'd long had all this pent up inside. And now he paused. My anger, too, diffused somewhat as I considered his words in the light of my German experiences and took some pity on his plight.

'If nothing else, I hope you have learnt about your own prejudices. For travel should be a mirror of yourself and your own culture. And, contrary to what most people think, travel is about seeing similarities and human links around the world, not differences. Surely by now the enemy is elsewhere! How many wars with other countries have there been since 1945? And now you even have your own British *Selbstwahrnehmung* about "cricket tests" among your immigrant communities, and "what is Britishness?" How ironic that the British should have taken up self-examination as a national cause. Welcome to being German!'

Then Herman got up and started quoting from *Cabaret* again as he wandered pensively about the room.

'"*Is it a crime to fall in love?! All I am asking is 'ein bisschen Verständnis . . .!' For a liddle understanding.*" Germany is a misunderstood genius of a country,' he continued wistfully, beginning to half-sing '"*She's clever, she's smart, she reads music. She doesn't smoke or drink gin like I do . . .*"'

Then he turned and looked me straight in the eye.

'You know, I am inclined to judge the depth of a man's civilisation by his opinion of Germany and her culture. She is not so easily attractive as Latin countries. But as someone once said, Europe without Germany would be "like Hamlet without the Dane".'

I had often heard how Germans claimed Shakespeare as their own.

'So Germany is the ultimate test of the true Traveller. And if you have learnt something about Romance for yourself, then I am also glad. Until a few months ago Germany seemed commonplace to you. But now, you exalt it!'

Well, I wasn't wearing an 'I Love Germany' T-shirt just yet. But I had to admit it had been a while since I'd had any *Weltschmerz*.

'Maybe you have been cured of something, even had your curiosity sparked and regained a little *Wanderlust*?'

If I was Faust, then Herman had been both my guardian angel and my Mephistopheles.

He sat down in front of me again.

'Now perhaps you are a Traveller again, with a capital "T" like a German noun: a pure and absolute concept.'

He closed his eyes in that priest-like ecstasy I remembered from our first meeting.

'*By giving what is commonplace an exalted meaning, to what is ordinary a mysterious aspect, to what is familiar the impressiveness of the unfamiliar, to the finite an appearance of infinity; thus I romanticise it.*'

Manny came out of his trance, his eyes opening wide as he leant towards me on his way up.

'But don't stop at Germany. Now try Taiwan!'

Then, in one last clinical mood change, as Herman he stopped and held out his hand.

'It's been nice knowing you, Ben,' he said. 'But now it's time for me to go.'

And with that, whoever this man was, Herman walked out of my life, leaving me surrounded by four naked white walls.

The last words I ever heard him say were the closing lines of a familiar song he sang down the corridor as he left.

'"*I understand your objection. Granted the problem's not small . . .*"'

But the rest didn't come. The words hung in the air, waiting for a response. I smiled. Herman wanted me to finish off.

'"*But if you could see her through my eyes,*"' I paused, just as Joel Grey might have done, then whispered the words Herman had put in my mouth: '"*She wouldn't look* German *at all*!"'

16

Wortschatz

nm, *vocabulary, stock of words*
(lit. word treasure)

When Mark Twain wrote up his experiences of Germany in *A Tramp Abroad* he evidently became so exercised by the complexity of the German language he devoted a whole appendix to it entitled 'The Awful German Language'.

Was it time for a reappraisal?

Foreign languages have always been the greatest failing of the British. Only 22 per cent of Britons have basic German, while 97 per cent of Germans speak English, over a quarter of whom consider themselves fluent. And things aren't going to get any better quickly. In 2006 the lowest number of pupils in Britain ever, around ninety thousand, sat GCSE German, thereby reducing it to a minority subject. Mark Twain reckoned it would take a gifted person thirty-three years to learn German and that it ought to be set aside with Latin 'for only the dead have time to learn it'. It is well on the way, it seems.

'But language is crucial to the understanding of any culture, for language shapes our thoughts,' Herman had said. 'You must conquer the language barrier if you are to regain *Wanderlust*.'

As you'd expect for a land of thinkers, the German language

is a language of nouns not verbs; of concepts not actions. A common expression is '*Ist das für Sie ein Begriff?*' – 'Is that a concept for you?' Instead of just 'Know what I mean?' All talk and no action, you might say. And as Twain wrote, 'whenever the literary German dives into a sentence, that is the last you are going to see of him till he emerges on the other side of the Atlantic with his verb in his mouth'. He also quipped that German newspapers 'have to go to press without getting to the verb at all'.

In German it is the nouns, and in particular the compound nouns, that are German's strength and render it of itself a powerful expressive tool. Sometimes, according to Twain, they are so long they are like 'grand mountain ranges stretching across the printed page . . . so long that they have a perspective'. I had come across some bloody long ones, the sort that Twain suggested might be delivered in sections 'with intermissions for refreshments'. And I had discovered that German was the master language, the Übersprache for the concept-noun. Goethe said that 'When an idea is wanting, a word can always be found to take its place,' and the Germans have certainly made an artform of this. Flexibility is not a word I would normally put in the same sentence as 'German', but seemingly any two nouns can be stuck together at will, like children's sticklebricks. This is especially useful when you are in a tight spot with a subordinate clause and verbs are piling up at the end of your sentence. It is often reported that English is the richest language in terms of the sheer number and range of words, nuances and registers, but German surely has an unparalleled infinite capacity for coining new words. Just as the Eskimos have tens of different words for the types of snow that dominates their world, so the Germans have infinite words for the concepts, ideas and complexes that dominate theirs.

It is therefore no surprise that psychotherapy, with its love of concepts, was a German science. But I am also now convinced that it appeals to the German in the American. Hence not only is it standard practice for Americans – and now me – to have therapists, but also psychotherapy seems to be uniquely adapted to the world of business. Business consultants and futurists – and now travel therapists – with all their dogma are shrinks. But all that psychobabble Herman and his colleagues would masturbate over is not American in origin at all but German: verbal nouns like disintermediation, servitisation, commoditisation, interiorisation were all a sort of non-English Mark Twain would have hated. As were nouns made from verbs like 'a learn' and 'a build'. It was as if Americans were trying to translate into English not just the sense but the structure of the German language to create new concept-nouns, which consequently sounded all wrong.

Surely Twain of all people would have enjoyed the verbosity of the German language. Perhaps his appendix was in fact a mark of affection. After all, German is probably the closest European relation to the modern-day English language. Without the Saxons, who came over from Germany and settled in Sussex (south-Sachs) Essex (east-Sachs) and Middlesex, there would have been no Anglo-Saxons and no modern English. Chaucer's Middle English, like Yiddish, Dutch and Danish, were just low, 'corrupted' versions of high German. There are still times in English when we like to put the verb at the end. Most often, ironically, when we're trying to be poetic and dramatic, such as in the wedding vow, 'Til death do us part'.

Twain was aware of the origins of this own language and its obvious debt to German. He almost ended up speaking German, at least according to a popular but unproven legend. In 1776, so the story goes, Americans came within one vote of making German the official language of the newly independent United States. The vote is said to have taken place in Independence Hall in Philadelphia, Pennsylvania, the heart of the German-speaking immigrant community. An extra piece of colour to the myth adds that the vote was passed in favour of English only because a key voter was on the loo.

Twain might have found German an awful language, but it was the language that begat a particular type of American. As a true Brit, brought up in the tradition of Twain's (admittedly Anglo-Irish) counterpart in wit, Oscar Wilde, I could say the same about his own language.

Here is a short glossary of German word-mountains:

Anspruch message
Erbfeind the enemy you inherit
Fernweh pain or longing for what is far off
Frühlingszauber the magic of spring
Futterneid food-envy
Gemütlichkeit cosy nostalgia, pleasantness and tradition
Gesundheit health
Geschwindigkeitsbeschräunkung seven syllables to say 'speed limit'
Heimweh homesickness
Kneipendunst (pub mist) to evoke the fuggy atmosphere of a smoky pub
Sehnsucht longing
Selbstwahrnehmung self-awareness, taking stock of oneself
Sinnbild epitome, the picture that captures the essential sense of something
Sorgenplatz (worry place) the residence of someone's woes
Spiegelwand (mirror wall) the imaginary place where you can find all things that reflect a person's personality and interests
Teufelszauber (*invented), the magic of evil
Torschlusspanik literally 'panic at the closing of a gate' – the fear of diminishing opportunities
Umweltfreundlich environmentally friendly
Vergangenheitsbewältigung conquering of the past

Vorsprung progress
Waldespracht forest splendour
Wanderlust love of travel
Weltschmerz world-weariness

Lyric Credits